Campaigns against Hunger

Campaigns against Hunger

E. C. STAKMAN

RICHARD BRADFIELD

PAUL C. MANGELSDORF

THE BELKNAP PRESS OF
HARVARD UNIVERSITY PRESS

Cambridge, Massachusetts

1 9 6 7

To
all those pioneers
who with faith and skill served
in the campaigns against hunger

Foreword

It may or may not be true that certain timely conjunctions of the stars and planets presage favorable events, but there is no doubt that The Rockefeller Foundation in 1941 found a happy combination of stellar scientists. Requested by the political and scientific leadership of Mexico to help improve the production and quality of its basic food crops, which were in distressingly short supply, the Foundation decided to invite three eminent agricultural scientists, tempered by experience and distinguished by achievement, but not previously associated with the Foundation, to examine the condition of Mexican agriculture at first-hand and to give the Foundation their best counsel and advice.

This was to be no simple or hurried inspection but a complex and sober search, because their verdict would be the basis for the Foundation's decision either to decide against entering the field of agriculture in a developing country on a cooperating basis, or to commit staff and substantial funds over a long period of time. Implied in the commitment was their judgment whether the Foundation could, in association with Mexican colleagues, reverse unfavorable food production trends in that country.

Experienced Foundation officers, at my request, began the search for a small team of men who might undertake this critical assignment. Through a rare blend of judgment and luck, the Foundation decided upon the combination of Richard Bradfield, professor of agronomy and head of department, New York State College of Agriculture, Cornell University, Paul C. Mangelsdorf, professor of plant genetics and economic botany, Harvard University, and Elvin C. Stakman, professor of plant pathology and head of department, University of Minnesota. All three of these distinguished scientists had already achieved international reputation in terms of both their research activities and the numbers of foreign students who received training in this country under their supervision. All had traveled widely and had a strong interest in the developing nations of the world. They were therefore excited by the possibility that the Foundation might embark in Mexico on what might be called an entirely new career—cooperative agricultural development.

The results of the original survey in Mexico by the three Foundation consultants are now part of history. They traveled the country from Coahuila to Chiapas and from Veracruz to Guadalajara. They looked, listened, and conversed and gradually built up a body of knowledge and understanding that enabled them to prepare their report to the Foundation. It was favorable—indeed, enthusiastic. The Foundation responded with equal enthusiasm in the belief that the combined judgment of these eminent scientists was sound and convincing.

The Agricultural Program of The Rockefeller Foundation, begun in Mexico early in 1943, has now been extended, either formally or informally, to many countries throughout the world. During the entire evolution of this effort, the three original consultants have had a continuing association with it, first as a three-man board of consultants, later as members of an enlarged board that included other specialists in related disciplines. Over the years, Dr. Stakman has served as a wide-ranging consultant for the expanding interests of The Rockefeller Foundation. Like Dr. Stakman, Dr. Bradfield was a consultant, but he interrupted his work to serve on the Board of Trustees of The Rockefeller Foundation for four years. Today he is again deeply involved in carrying on professional research on tropical soils at the International Rice Research Institute in the Philippines. Dr. Mangelsdorf also has been called upon over the years and has always responded, as consultant and adviser. Now all three have joined forces to record in this book their description of the aims, objectives, and accomplishments of the total program, from its inception at their favorable recommendation to the present time. Friends, colleagues, and former students throughout the world, within and outside The Rockefeller Foundation, salute these men, affectionately known as "The Three Musketeers of Agriculture."

RAYMOND B. FOSDICK

November, 1966

Preface

This book was written because The Rockefeller Foundation invited us to write it. When asked what kind of book they had in mind, President Harrar replied, "The kind the three of you want to write." So the "Three Ancients" wrote what they knew about the Foundation's campaigns that are called "Toward the Conquest of Hunger," naturally hoping that the writing might be worth reading.

Our primary aim has been to tell how the Foundation conceived, organized, and operated its various programs for increasing food production. We hoped, of course, that this story might contribute to a wider realization that science, education, and common sense are essential in producing more food to alleviate hunger and to avert the continual threat of famine among at least half the people in the present world. Although we have tried to stress the fact that there are no easy solutions to the complex problems of human subsistence, experience has strengthened our conviction that the food problems in most of the needy countries can be solved—but only if intelligent and persistent attempts are made to solve them.

We have adopted as our theme "campaigns against hunger" because we wanted to emphasize the importance of coordination and continuity of effort. A dictionary tells us that a campaign is: "1. A connected series of military operations forming a distinct stage in a war. 2. A connected series of operations to bring about some desired result; as, an advertising campaign." It has not been our purpose to advertise any institutions or individuals nor to overwork military analogies and terminologies. It does seem appropriate, however, to think in terms of a worldwide war against hunger. However intelligently and vigorously this war is prosecuted, it will take a long time to win it. It may never be won completely, but hunger can be reduced to a minimum if the attacks against it are integrated into wisely conceived and skillfully executed campaigns. Sporadic and disjointed attacks may yield partial and passing successes but will never win the war; the obstacles are too strong and varied to be overcome by separate bands of temporary skirmishers directed by a succession of armchair strategists and field tacticians. Concentration and continuity of effort by competent, long-term personnel are essential.

Although we have described only a few of the many organized efforts to alleviate hunger, those that we have described were campaigns in the true sense. Objectives were definite and realistic; operations were purposeful, efficient, coordinated, and continuous. The basic objective of increasing food supplies as quickly and directly as possible by means of the genetic and cultural improvement of the most important food and feed crops was always paramount. Intellectual and financial resources were not frittered away in distracting side operations, however alluring they might have been. Attempt was made to enable every man and every dollar to contribute their maximum to the attainment of the final goal of helping each cooperating country onto the road of independent progress in agricultural production, research, and education.

To help the "less developed" countries to the road of independent progress is feasible but not easy. Given adequate help, many countries should be well on their way within a decade; others will require more help and much more time. Zooming populations, ignorance, poverty, venality, sociologic naiveté, and political instability are formidable barriers to rapid progress in some countries. To convert an unsophisticated society into a sophisticated one, to substitute social cooperation for social contention will require more than the services of agricultural sciences. We not only admit this; we insist on it. Even though we have not expatiated extensively in this book on the complexities of social evolution, we are aware of them and concerned about them. But we did set limits to our objectives and, in general, have restricted our discussions to subjects that we have studied intensively for many years.

Although we planned the general outline of the book together and agreed on general objectives, each author has written certain chapters according to his own lights—and in his own way. We have always agreed on basic principles during the quarter century of our association, but we have sometimes agreed to disagree on subordinate issues. Consequently there may appear in the book some discrepancies in matters of opinion, emphasis, or style, but we hope not in matters of policy or principle.

We did not set out to write a documentary history of The Rockefeller Foundation's activities in the campaigns against hunger. We have tried to describe the most significant procedures and results of its "operating programs" and have not included details of its grants in aid to individuals and institutions. We have tried to tell of the Foundation's accomplishments as simply and nontechnically as is compatible with scientific accuracy. We hope we have succeeded.

Acknowledgments

We are grateful to the Foundation and to President Harrar for giving us the privilege of writing this book and particularly for letting us write it the way we wanted to write it. To the "Persistent Pioneers" we are indebted for various kinds of help. Numerous others, in the Foundation and outside of it, generously gave us valuable criticisms and suggestions. We have tried to thank them personally but refrain from listing their names here for fear of not doing complete justice to all of them. Anne Newbery, however, editor in the Foundation's Office of Information Service, has contributed far beyond the call of duty.

Most of the pictures were obtained from the files of The Rockefeller Foundation; those that illustrate Chapter 17 were furnished by the International Rice Research Institute, and we appreciate the generosity of both organizations. We thank the individuals who supplied portraits and all others who helped us in assembling the illustrations.

Contents

10 The Livestock Story: *More and Better Feed to*
   Produce Milk, Eggs, and Meat 160

11 Education: *The Evolution of Agricultural Scientists*
   and Educators 177

12 Extension: *Getting Farmers to Use the Results*
   of Research 197

13 Extending the Mexican Pattern: *Action Programs in*
   Colombia, Ecuador, and Chile 216

14 India: *Modifying a Pattern to Suit Special Conditions* 235

Campaigns
against
Hunger

Chapter 1

Then and Now in Mexico

A Preview of the Agricultural Revolution

Then was 1943; Now is 1963. The place is Mexico, both then and now; but it is not the same Mexico now as it was then, for there has been a revolution between then and now. True, it was not the kind of revolution that is usually glamorized, for it was a bloodless one. Yet it was a heart-warming revolution, because it helped make the land more bountiful for the land-loving Mexican people. And it is a continuing revolution, with constantly accelerating momentum and continually increasing benefits to Mexico, to her Latin American neighbors, and to other countries of the world.

Agrarian Reform and Its Limitations

Agrarian reform had long been one of the principal aspirations in Mexican revolutions, and it became one of the explicit goals of "The Revolution," which began in 1910. The Mexican Constitution of 1917 legalized the redistribution of lands, and by 1943 allotments had been made to more than 1.7 million landless individuals, in parcels averaging about 11.5 acres of "cropland" per person. Mexico was being transformed largely from a country of *latifundia* to one of *minifundia;* whereas a few people had owned much of the land, each of many people now farmed a little land. The history of the agrarian revolution and its consequences is a fascinating and signifi-cant story, but it is pertinent here only as it affects the revolution in agriculture. Land redistribution was satisfying the hunger of the landless for land, but was it satisfying their hunger for food?

It soon became apparent that land redistribution alone did not guarantee freedom from hunger, for well over 50 percent of the new *ejidal* farmers were unlettered and had neither the experience nor financial means to become immediately successful as independent operators. The tendency for food production to decline, which accompanied the violent phases of The Revolution, was continuing during the postwar period of reconstruction and readjustment to changed conditions. But the rate of population increase was rising rapidly, from 19 percent during the 1930–1940 decade to what finally amounted to 31 percent during the next decade.

Mexico needed more food; how could she get it? Perhaps the answer is epitomized in a little-known mural by Diego Rivera in the administration building of the National School of Agriculture at Chapingo. "Aquí se enseña a explotar la tierra, no a los hombres." These words appear on one of the panels of Rivera's mural; their essential meaning is "Here we teach how to husband our lands, not how to exploit our fellow men." Once, land had seemed abundant and farm labor had really been dirt cheap, but the growing population and the changes wrought by the agrarian revolution were forcing a reappraisal of the relations between land and people. It was time to take inventory of Mexico's land resources and of their actual and potential productivity.

As early as 1924, Cosío Villegas had written: ". . . The industry of agriculture in our country is deficient not only because our methods of cultivation are backward . . . but because the soil itself is poor. In order that our agriculture shall be able to satisfy our necessities . . . costly engineering works, especially of irrigation, will be necessary throughout the whole nation. We cannot expect anything as a gift of Nature; everything in Mexico depends upon the activity and ingenuity of man. It is for this reason I say 'economically we are poor'; but more than this, the origin of our economic poverty is our natural poverty."[1]

Evidently, however, some individuals had abounding faith in "the activity and ingenuity of man," for President Obregón stated in the preamble to an agrarian law that Mexico "has sufficient capacity to provide the necessities for more than a hundred million inhabitants."

Although the vision of both optimists and pessimists had some truth, Mexico in 1940 was confronted with two inexorable facts: the population was almost 20 million, and crops were being har-

[1] Daniel Cosío Villegas, *Sociología Mexicana: I. El Territorio* (Mexico: Editorial Juris, 1924), pp. 26–27.

vested from a scant 17 million acres of cultivated land. In combination, these facts meant less than an acre per capita, and it is commonly estimated that it takes two acres or more of reasonably good land to feed and clothe one person reasonably well if the land is reasonably good and if it is reasonably well tilled. But much of the Mexican land was not reasonably good and much of it was not reasonably well tilled; consequently the efficiency of food production was low.

Acre yields of basic food crops were low. Corn, the Mexican staff of life, yielded only about eight bushels an acre, as compared with 28 in the United States; wheat averaged four bushels less than in the United States despite the fact that Mexican wheat was mostly irrigated; and the average yield of beans, the meat of the poorer Mexican, was only a third of that in the United States.

Although the efficiency of food production was low, the efficiency of human reproduction was high and going higher. During 1930–1940, the population of the United States had increased 7.2 percent but the Mexican population had increased 18.7 percent, from 16.6 million to 19.7 million; there were three million more people to feed. And the rate of increase was still rising in Mexico, with prospects that there would be five million additional people within the next decade. Looking backward, the number actually exceeded six million.

Although Mexico had expanded her cultivated acreage considerably by means of new irrigation projects and the conversion of grasslands into croplands, it was increasingly evident that each acre would also have to produce more.

The Agricultural Revolution: Making the Land More Bountiful

NEEDS AND BEGINNINGS

By 1941 some of the wiser Mexicans realized that a revolution in agriculture was needed to supplement the agrarian revolution if Mexico was to feed her rapidly growing population. Conspicuous among them was Ing. Marte R. Gómez, Minister of Agriculture, who recently spoke essentially as follows, in the film *Harvest*: ". . . We were obligated to provide our countrymen with corn, wheat, and other essentials badly needed in Mexico. At that time, we had organized the production of Mexican agriculture as best we could. For years we had been engaged in our program of land reform, but we needed to complement it with an agricultural revolution. To initiate a revolution in agriculture properly, we urgently needed technical assistance."

Fortunate it was for Mexico that Minister of Agriculture Gómez was deeply conscious of the urgent need to produce more food, envisioned a revolution in the art of agriculture to help provide it, and had the enterprise to ask for help where help was needed. And it was fortunate, too, that the Subsecretary of Agriculture, Ing. Alfonso González Gallardo, also was a man of vision with a realistic approach to practical problems. The implication of "technical assistance" was that some help must come from outside of Mexico; the scientific potential was within the country, but help would be needed to make it functionally effective as quickly as possible. But whence was to come the help?

The Rockefeller Foundation was called, and it was chosen. Indeed, there was not much choice at that time, because it was before the day of the numerous national and international agencies for aid to the "less developed countries." The United Nations and its offspring, the Food and Agriculture Organization, had not yet been born, and technical assistance had not yet been conceived. Nor had The Rockefeller Foundation, established in 1913 "to promote the well-being of mankind throughout the world," started its efforts to help provide more food for the hungry peoples of the world. Thanks, however, to its president, Raymond B. Fosdick, the Foundation was willing to try. It had learned from its worldwide public health programs that agriculture is a necessary ally of medicine in the hungry areas of the world. And so the Foundation responded to the call of Mexico.

How could the Foundation help most effectively? It appointed a commission of three—a distinguished plant geneticist and breeder, an eminent specialist in agronomy and soils, and a plant pathologist —to help answer the question by studying Mexican needs and possibilities on Mexican ground.

The Survey Commission went to Mexico in July, 1941, consulted with officials of the Mexican Ministry of Agriculture and many others, studied many agricultural areas, visited agricultural schools and colleges, tried to get as much information as possible from other sources, and finally wrote a report containing many conclusions and a few recommendations.

The essence of the recommendations was that, as a first step, the Foundation send to Mexico a carefully selected group of four competent and dedicated scientists to cooperate with the Mexican Ministry in breeding better varieties of the principal food plants, in improving methods of soil management and measures for crop protection, and in increasing the productivity of domestic animals. It was clearly recognized that the proposed program should be flexible and expansible. Minister Gómez, Subsecretary González Gallardo, and other clear-sighted Mexicans obviously hoped for deeds, not words; they wanted to produce more food as quickly and economically as possible. Because corn, wheat, and beans were the basic foods of the country, it was logical to start with the immediate objective of improving them by the simplest and most practicable means, in the expectation that the direct benefits would be accompanied by many valuable indirect benefits.

The success of any undertaking depends upon the men who undertake it and the environment in which they work. The Foundation chose Dr. J. George Harrar as its leader in Mexico, and he started operations there in February, 1943. The choice was wise and the Foundation wisely gave Harrar the degree of freedom that is essential to the success of a creative man in a creative task. For this, President Fosdick deserves much of the credit. The Mexican Ministry of Agriculture strove to provide a favorable environment for the free exercise of Harrar's talents; for this, Gómez and González Gallardo deserve major credit. Harrar availed himself of his opportunities and functioned in extraordinarily effective ways; for this, he himself deserves credit. These were the far-sighted pioneers who initiated the agricultural revolution in Mexico. To help implement it, Dr. Edwin J. Wellhausen, a corn breeder, started work in the fall of 1943, and in 1944 plant pathologist Dr. Norman E. Borlaug and soils expert Dr. William E. Colwell joined the ranks and went to work. Subsequently many other men, from Mexico and from the United States, contributed significantly to the program, but its general course was set during those first two eventful years.

The cooperative campaign quickly got under way. Based initially on a realistic appraisal of needs and feasibilities, it expanded as results created new opportunities and revealed new possibilities. To provide for freedom of action, the Mexican Ministry, in 1943, created within itself the autonomous Oficina de Estudios Especiales—Office of Special Studies—with Harrar in charge. The Office grew steadily and at the maximum comprised 21 U.S. scientists and 100 young Mexican associates. Unhampered by unnecessary red tape and push-button direction, its operations were extraordinarily free and fruitful. Rapid progress was made in the improvement of agricultural materials and methods. Possibly even more gratifying was the rapid development of young Mexican scientists, for the Office of Special Studies combined exceptional productivity in research with remarkable effectiveness in informal education.

MORE FOOD FOR MORE PEOPLE

"Then and Now in Mexico." What are the differences between then and now? What has the agricultural revolution accomplished?[2]

Then there were 20 million people to feed, and certain prophets of gloom said that no more could be fed; now there are 35 million people, 15 million more, and they are fed. Then it was necessary to import corn and wheat; now Mexico produces enough of both and has even exported some. Then the total production of corn was about two million tons; now it is six million tons. Then wheat production was a third of a million tons; now it is a million and a half tons or more. Then the production of beans was 150,000 tons; now it is close to half a million tons. The population increased 70 percent between then and now; but the production of the three basic foods increased 300 percent.

This increase in food production is a noteworthy and significant accomplishment. Even more noteworthy, however, is the way in which it was accomplished, for it was done not so much by using more acres as by helping each acre produce more.

The average acre yield of corn is now 14 bushels instead of the eight it was when the campaign began. As 12 million acres are planted to corn, this means 72 million bushels more each year. About 70 percent is used for human food, so there is almost a bushel and a half additional for each of Mexico's 35 million people. Moreover, Mexico can now spare close to 20 percent of her total production for animal food and 10 percent for industrial purposes.

Acre yields of wheat, increasing in each of the 11 successive years since 1952, averaged close to 34 bushels an acre in 1963, as con-

[2] "Then and Now" means 1940–43 and 1960–63 as concerns certain conclusions derived from official statistics.

trasted with the 11.5 bushels of 20 years ago. In the best wheat areas good farmers harvested between 50 and 88 bushels an acre in 1963, and in the less-favored areas the best farmers obtained yields of about 50 bushels on soils that were considered "worn out" a few years ago. If the population continues to increase at the present rate Mexico will soon need 75 million bushels a year, 15 million more than the record-breaking 60 million in 1963; and it now appears that the need can be supplied by raising acre yields still higher, without adding more acres to the 1.8 million now being used for wheat.

The average yield of beans has increased from 3.6 bushels an acre in 1950 to almost seven in 1962, largely because of the use of several improved varieties, all with more disease resistance and each especially suited to particular climatic zones, from the high and dry plateaus to the low and humid tropics.

Corn and beans have not matched the three-fold increase in acre yields of wheat, but they are handicapped. Wheat is grown mostly by skilled farmers and almost entirely under irrigation. Corn and beans, on the other hand, are grown by all kinds of farmers, on all kinds of land, mostly without irrigation, and are therefore often victimized by the vagaries of Mexican rainfall. Nevertheless, acre yields are approaching twice those of 20 years ago; and surely that is progress, even if not so revolutionary as some revolutionaries might wish.

The story of how Mexico got more corn, wheat, and beans, the Big Three of her basic foods, would alone justify the title "revolution in agriculture," but additional concrete accomplishments help validate and broaden the meaning of that title.

Mexico now produces three to four times as many potatoes as then, and acre yields are at least three times as high. Then, late blight often destroyed the crop in some of the best potato areas unless the fields were sprayed, and spraying cost 15 to 30 U.S. dollars an acre; now, blight-resistant varieties developed in Mexico can be grown safely without spraying. Then, Mexico imported expensive seed potatoes from Europe; now, she produces her own certified seed. Thus she has reduced the cost of production and has insured the crop against its most dangerous menace. Not only is there a thriving commercial industry, but many small farmers are growing potatoes for local consumption, thus adding another staple food to vary the diet.

New kinds of plants, like sorghums, soybeans, and many forage grasses, have been introduced, and some have proved their value as immigrants. Certain imported grasses, such as pangola and merkeron, have doubled forage production for animals in some tropical areas, and sorghums are helping to insure feed production in the drier areas of Mexico as they have done in the United States.

That there has been a revolution in the understanding and management of Mexican soils is apparent for all to see. Twenty years ago it was considered obvious that Mexico could not afford to use commercial fertilizers; now it is considered axiomatic that she cannot afford not to use them. The demand already exceeds the supply, but Mexico is striving to produce enough within the country so that they may be available to all who need them.

Happily, there are indications of incipient revolution in animal production also, even though the animal program started 13 years later than the plant program. "All flesh is grass," and a basic requisite for improving animal production is to increase the quantity and improve the quality of feeds and forages. The more corn Mexico produces, the more she can afford to feed to animals; the more alfalfa and other forages she produces, the more animals she can produce; and the better the range plants, the greater the meat production on range lands. The improvement already made in alfalfa and grasses is having an impact on meat and milk production, although it would be difficult at present to weigh that impact.

Important advances have been made in poultry husbandry. Then, chickens were so busy picking up what food they could that they laid few eggs and made poor pickings at the table. Now there is a modern poultry industry. True, this industry antedates the cooperative program, but it has been improved and insured by applying the results of researches on nutrition and on disease control. Small animals first, bigger ones next.

That Mexico is intelligently conscious of her agricultural revolution is shown by an editorial in the monthly magazine *Tierra*:

"We have before us the report published by the Office of Special Studies entitled 'Advances in Investigation,' which gives the results obtained by this official organization in Ciano, La Campana, El Horno, and Cotaxtla [Experiment Stations] during the period September 1959 to August 1960. The results are really noteworthy, not only because of their diversity, but also because of their scope; and they serve to refute the unfounded charge made by malicious people that *agrónomos* engage in everything except the practice of their own profession.

"It is because of their efforts that the production of basic foods has reached a stage never previously attained in Mexico, maize production amounting to some 6 million tons, thanks largely to the more extensive use of improved varieties and hybrids and the continually increasing use of fertilizers, in accordance with the recommendations of agronomists. Another similar advance is with wheat, the production of which in recent years has been a million tons, thus avoiding resort to onerous importation and yet assuring food for the people, including the detractors of agricultural scientists.

"Sorghum is continually assuming greater importance in those areas in which corn is a risky crop, and there are malting barleys which are highly prized by the malting industry. . . . Many other aspects of experimentation demonstrate that Mexican agriculture is clearly on the road of tremendous progress, and for this reason the country can proceed with its industrialization program on a much sounder foundation and with much more confidence."[3]

"Agricultural revolution" is no mere figure of speech, for Mexico is indeed "on the road of tremendous progress." In 1941 agriculture was traditional; now it is progressive. And it will continue to progress because it is continually becoming more scientific, thanks to a new generation of Mexican scientists. The concrete contributions of the revolution can be measured in bushels and pesos—more corn, wheat, beans, and potatoes. And that value is great. But the value of the scientists and the scientific attitude developed in the revolution cannot be measured in bushels and pesos. And yet, in the long run, that is the greatest value of all.

The Intellectual Revolution: More Scientists and Science

EDUCATING A NEW GENERATION OF SCIENTISTS

"The Office of Special Studies has carried on one of the best educational programs within the purview of my experience." This quotation could be attributed to several qualified observers; be that as it may, however, the Mexican revolution in agriculture could not have

[3] In *Tierra*, Vol. 17, No. 6, June, 1962, p. 411. (Translated from the Spanish.)

progressed so rapidly or yielded such permanent results if education had not been combined so intimately with investigation. The educational principle of learning to do by doing is old, but rarely has it been applied with greater success. True, the education was largely extramural, mostly informal, and without academic credit. But it was remarkably effective.

Some 550 young graduates of Mexican agricultural colleges participated as paid apprentices or interns in the work of the Office of Special Studies. This was exactly the kind of education that they and Mexico needed at the time. Previously their education had been largely theoretical; from lectures and books they had learned words about things, but they did not know the things themselves. They had not developed the experimental attitude, nor had they learned how to make experiments. Like a theoretical surgeon who could talk about operations but could not do one, they could talk about crossing corn or wheat but most of them did not know how to make a cross. It was not their fault; their education had not emphasized the development of powers of independent learning from the things to be learned and the development of skills by doing the things that needed to be done. But they wanted to learn, and many of them learned fast.

Between 1943 and 1963 about 250 of the best interns were rewarded with fellowships for study in universities in the United States or elsewhere, and 90 percent made good academic records. From 1947 to 1957 The Rockefeller Foundation alone granted 76 such fellowships, and at least one third of the fellows are now in important positions of leadership in science and education.

In 1941–1943, there was not a single Mexican in the field of agricultural sciences with a doctoral degree; now there are close to 30. Even the master of science degree was a rarity then; now close to 200 individuals have it. On the staffs of the National Institute of Agricultural Research and the National School of Agriculture there now are 20 specialists with the Ph.D. degree and some 70 with the M.S. degree. In 1943 there was not a single experienced plant pathologist in Mexico; now there are six with the Ph.D. degree and more than a dozen with the M.S. in these two institutions alone. The numbers of specialists in plant genetics and breeding, soil science, and entomology are of the same general order. Total numbers are indicated by the fact that the Mexican Entomological Society comprises 120 members, and the Mexican Society of Plant Pathologists, between 30 and 40—not enough, but a good beginning for an infant of three years. The recently formed Society of Soil Scientists has a hundred or more members.

What a contrast between then and now! Then, there were relatively few *ingenieros agrónomos*,[4] fewer with specialized knowledge and skills, and almost none who were engaged in productive research. They were poorly paid, often had to supplement their income with nonprofessional jobs, were often dissatisfied and discouraged, tended to be politically minded, disdained the manual work that is necessary in field experimentation, and, very understandably, could not and did not contribute significantly to the advancement of agriculture. Their preparation had been inadequate to the larger tasks, and they were so preoccupied with personal problems that they seldom came to grips with agricultural problems.

Now, as contrasted with then, *agrónomos* are far more numerous, many have acquired basic knowledge and specialized skills, and a constantly increasing number are productive scholars in research and education. Now, they are much better paid, do not have to do nonprofessional work in order to live decently, can concentrate more on science than on politics, have learned the dignity of work, and are pushing along the "road of tremendous progress" with intelligence, determination, and moral purpose. And this is not mere eulogy; it is fact.

Invidious comparisons are odious, and an honest comparison should be free from the taint of odiousness. Then, the able and ambitious lacked the favoring environment and the educational and professional opportunities of the present. Those of the old-timers who rose to eminence in their profession did so largely despite their environment, not by virtue of it; those of the present generation who are rising to eminence are doing so because they did have a favorable environment and the wit to take advantage of it.

LANDMARKS ON THE ROAD TO SCIENTIFIC MATURITY

The education of productive scientists was a first step in the educational phase of the agricultural revolution. But how would these scientists use their education? Would they use it to satisfy their

---

[4] *Ingeniero agrónomo* (agronomic engineer) is a professional degree granted by agricultural colleges to *pasantes* (graduates) who have had the requisite professional experience, have written a thesis, and have passed an oral examination.

personal ambitions; would they use it to contribute only to science; or would they use it to contribute also to Mexican society? They had become independent scientists; would they help Mexico to become independent scientifically? Most of them did help, each in his own way.

Five outstanding events mark the progress of science in agriculture in Mexico:

Landmark one. "For the first time in my quarter century of service in the Ministry of Agriculture, I have heard Mexican investigators give Mexican extension men useful information derived from their own experiments. At last I have seen a group who had something of their own to tell and who knew how to tell it." Thus spoke Ing. Emilio Gutiérrez Roldán, now in charge of the federal seed production agency, at the end of the first conference of investigators and extension men, held April 30 to May 2, 1954, at the Planta Gabriel Ramos Millán at Cortazar, Guanajuato.

This meeting was an epochal event; it marked the beginning of a new era. The meeting place was a modern drying and storage plant for seed of improved corn varieties, constructed and managed by the National Corn Commission under the chairmanship of Lic. Gabriel Ramos Millán, a senator who became the "apostle of corn" and lost his life in 1950 when an airplane crashed against snow-capped Popocatépetl during a heavy fog. Thus it was fitting that this meeting be held in a building dedicated to him. But the meeting itself was even more significant than the place in which it was held.

Of the 30 people listed on the program, 21 were Mexicans. True, many of the investigators were still junior partners in the Office of Special Studies, but it was largely a meeting of Mexicans talking to Mexicans. And they talked well, for many were young men of exceptional ability who later attained distinction in their chosen fields; seven of them now have the doctorate and 11 hold distinguished positions in agricultural administration, investigation, or teaching. This meeting was indeed a landmark in the progress of the agricultural revolution.

Landmark two was the field day in 1957 at the Cotaxtla Experiment Station, near the city of Veracruz. This was a pioneer all-Mexican demonstration of the results of extensive experimentation. Under the general supervision of Dr. José Guevara, director of the station, more than a thousand farmers and other visitors were taken in squads to see the various experiments on the 360-acre station, most of which had been tropical jungle two years previously. As each squad arrived at each experiment, young Mexican specialists explained the purpose, the procedures, and the significance of the results. Every specialist knew what he was talking about, and he spoke in terms that the farmer could understand. And the farmers did understand, because they saw with their own eyes that some forage grasses were far better than others, that the piles of corn from good varieties were twice as big as those from poor varieties, that the yields from fertilized plots were much higher than the ones from nonfertilized plots; they could see the difference between plots of vegetable crops badly damaged by insects and diseases and those protected by spraying, and they could see the difference between weedy plots and those in which weeds had been controlled. It was not necessary to say, "Go thou and do likewise"; the farmers wanted to do likewise, and, if they did not understand how to do it, they asked questions and usually received useful answers based on the experience of the respondent. Each farmer had been given a little notebook and a pencil to record specific information. There were indications that some of the older ones were better acquainted with a plow than a pencil, but at least they deserved an A for effort.

When the last farmers left as the sun was going down, the thought surged up: "An all-Mexican day it was, and what a great day it was for Mexico!" Indeed, it was the beginning of a new day; the agricultural revolution was on its way to the farms of Mexico.

Landmark three was an "office seminar" of the Office of Special Studies held in February, 1960, to report results of the previous year and to project plans for the ensuing year. Sixty-five excellent scientific papers, of which young Mexicans were sole or joint authors, were presented during the three-day session to an audience of as many as 125 listeners. The speakers spoke well, the listeners listened well; and all discussed progress, plans, and problems well. At the end, one critical listener said: "I have seen a revolution in agriculture. There is light over the fields of Mexico, for some of these young scientists already are stars, possibly of minor magnitude now, but some will soon be stars of greater magnitude, and the light that they shed will keep Mexican agriculture from lapsing again into darkness." So far, this has been both conclusion and prophecy.

Landmark four was the inauguration of the Postgraduate College of the National School of Agriculture on February 22, 1959, when Minister of Agriculture Rodríguez Adame said: "Today this national institute of higher learning in agriculture is completing 105 years of academic life. . . . The scientific and technologic progress of the world during the past 100 years has necessitated the transformation of agriculture. . . . The days in which routine and empirical agriculture could be successful are definitely past. It is now a highly technical and complicated activity which requires the wise use of very extensive knowledge. Consequently, the technically trained man is a determining factor in the prosperity of all agricultural countries, and to discharge his obligation effectively it is essential that he be a professional with sound preparation and that he keep abreast of the very rapid progress in the various fields of agricultural sciences." Wise words these; simple but wise.

The educational statesmanship of Rodríguez Adame was prerequisite to the establishment of a postgraduate school in the tradition-steeped National School at Chapingo. And the actual establishment needed the services of a bold and skillful young director of the institution, Ing. Jesús Muñóz Vázquez, a man with a mission to modernize the school and make it more scientific, regardless of opposition and personal consequences. Despite a precarious infancy, the Postgraduate College has grown in numbers and in strength, first under the directorship of Dr. Gabriel Baldovinos and now under Dr. Basilio Rojas. In 1959 there were 10 professors, five on full time; in the fall of 1962 there were 30, with 15 on full time. The number of students has trebled, from about 20 to 60, and students from a dozen countries other than Mexico have been enrolled.

Landmark five occurred on May 14, 1963, when advanced degrees in agriculture were conferred for the first time in Mexico. In an impressive ceremony at Chapingo the Minister of Agriculture handed diplomas to 16 young Mexicans, 15 men and one woman. Twelve received the degree of Master of Agricultural Sciences and four the Master of Science degree from the National School. The School of Agriculture of the Technological Institute of Monterrey also has provision for postgraduate work to the Master of Science level in some fields. For the doctorate it still is necessary to go abroad, but Mexico is well on the way to developing her own agricultural scientists.

LINKING RESEARCH AND EDUCATION

There is a growing realization in Mexico that investigation and education are mutually complementary and supplementary. Twenty years ago they were far apart, in distance, in attitudes, and in operation; now, unity has already been attained in some places, and the principle of contiguity and cooperation between research and education is being implemented in several other places where it is feasible.

The School of Agriculture of the Technological Institute of Monterrey has operated an experiment station from its establishment in 1948, and with cónspicuous success; there, research and education are joint partners in improving agriculture and agriculturists. This school is living evidence that the educational objectives of the cooperative program are being realized, for the first and only director, Ing. Leonel Robles, M.S., and 10 of his 13 early colleagues formerly were interns in the Office of Special Studies; they could not have implemented the educational objectives more completely if they had written them themselves. The agricultural department of the University of Nuevo León, also in Monterrey; the Antonio Narro agricultural college in Saltillo, now a part of the University of Coahuila; the University of Sonora at Hermosillo; and the National School of Agriculture at Chapingo, all have some provision for field experimentation and for laboratory research.

Research and education are growing together.

SCIENTIFIC INDEPENDENCE AND ITS PROBLEMS

Mexico has reached its majority. The official responsibilities for research in the federal Ministry of Agriculture have been concentrated in the National Institute of Agricultural Research (INIA). The Office of Special Studies is no more; its functions were transferred officially to INIA on January 1, 1961, and it now lives only in memory. But may that memory be kept alive as a symbol of realistic idealism and of cooperative work well done; the Office was a powerful instrument in enabling Mexico to become independent in respect of basic food supplies, and in respect of the basic need for scientists to assure future food supplies.

How will Mexico use her scientific independence? She now has a relatively small but competent and dedicated corps of agricultural scientists who understand the meaning of "Science in the Service of Society." They will contribute much to Society if Society will give them the necessary working facilities and the freedom to use them. The dead weight of a smothering bureaucracy and the strangulating effect of red tape are the ball and chain which hobble scientists and hamper scientific progress in many countries. May the chains never be forged in Mexico!

The Revolution in Outlook: Expanding the Horizons

In 1943 Mexico was national in scientific outlook; the exigencies of the time demanded it. Now she is both national and international in outlook. Mexico has received much from other countries; she is now giving much to other countries; and she is receiving much in return for what she is giving. From the outset it was hoped that some benefits from the Mexican program would overflow national boundaries into neighboring countries of Latin America. As benefits began to accrue, plans were made to help channel the flow, and now there is an ever-increasing number of streams of ever-increasing volume.

The first planned step was to invite a number of Latin American corn breeders to come to Mexico, in 1949, to see what was being done there and to tell what they themselves were doing back home. Because of the conspicuous success of this meeting, a second one was held in Mexico in 1950, this time for plant pathologists and entomologists. The results of these meetings generated faith in the feasibility of cooperation among Latin American countries for the solution of common problems. The Rockefeller Foundation therefore encouraged Latin American scientists to take the initiative in creating a self-perpetuating organization to arrange for future meetings, and a regular system of plant science congresses has evolved.

There have now been five congresses. The 1949 meeting is counted as the first, and subsequent ones have been held at three-year intervals in Brazil, Colombia, Chile, and Argentina.[5] At the fifth was created a formal and independent association, the Asociación Latinoamericana de Fitotecnia, born November 11, 1961. There were 271 charter members at the birth rites of the Association; of these, 265 came from 17 Latin American countries and six from the United

[5] After this chapter was written, the sixth congress met at Lima, Peru, in November, 1964.

States. Mexican scientists had helped write the constitution and formulate the objectives, and Mexican entomologist Dr. Marcos Ramírez Genel became a member of the first Board of Governors.

The Mexican program has grown in concrete ways also. The corn and wheat programs have grown gradually to worldwide and sky-high scope, and the potato program has become inter-American. Thus the germs sown so hopefully and the sprouts nurtured so carefully in Mexico are now bearing fruits far beyond Mexico, but they are still at home in Mexico and Mexico is still their basic home. Here they were born, and from here they are still being guided.

The Agricultural Revolution: Retrospect and Prospect

Twenty years have intervened between then and now; and much has been accomplished during those years. In retrospect it may seem that the accomplishment was easy and foreordained. But it was not; there were many difficulties, discouragements, and frustrations. That the agricultural revolution has been successful is due not to predestination, but to the intelligence, resourcefulness, and tenacious persistence of those who fought it.

Perhaps this revolution would have occurred eventually in the normal course of evolution. But it would not have started so soon, nor could it have progressed so rapidly if Don Marte Gómez had not had the wisdom to ask for help and Dr. Fosdick had not had the vision to give it. These men made it possible to initiate the revolution, and they supported it during the early years when the going was rough. Nor would the gains of the revolution have been capitalized so fully under lesser men than Rodríguez Adame and Harrar. Nor could Harrar, Wellhausen, and Borlaug have accomplished as much as they did in the early years without the wise counsel and effective help of González Gallardo, who understood the meanings and the mechanisms of true cooperation. Many others, rank and file, from both sides of the Río Grande deserve full measure of credit; and may they receive as they deserve. Unfortunately, however, not in this chapter.

According to Fabre, "History records the battlefields on which we lose our lives, but it disdains to tell us of the cultivated fields by which we live; it can tell us the names of the kings' bastards, but it cannot tell us the origin of wheat. Such is human folly." Is not learning how to produce more wheat just as important to hungry people as knowing its origin? May the time come when history will record more fully the names of those who made it possible to produce more corn and wheat and rice and beans and the other things by which we live!

"Then and Now in Mexico." The detailed accounts of what transpired to win the revolution in agriculture between then and now lie ahead in subsequent chapters.

We have looked backward, but may we look forward also!

Chapter 2

The Genesis of the Mexican Program

*The Events That Produced It
and Determined Its Pattern*

That the Mexican agricultural revolution was successful is evident in the facts and figures of Chapter 1. Mexico has shown many retarded countries a road to progress if they have the will to follow it. The reasons for her own success are simple and clear for all to see and follow. The original concepts and plans were sensible and flexible, and they were carried out by intelligent men who adapted them sensibly to special needs and opportunities. Common sense, the application of simple but sound scientific and educational principles, dedication to society rather than to self, and persistent resourcefulness in surmounting difficulties formed the foundation on which success was built. But why was the program started in the first place and why did it take the shape that it did?

Naturally, the establishment of a cooperative program had to be based on Mexico's desire for help and on The Rockefeller Foundation's willingness to give it. As we have seen, the men who expressed Mexico's desire most explicitly were Ing. Marte R. Gómez, Minister of Agriculture, and his Subsecretary, Ing. Alfonso González Gallardo. The man who played the decisive role in actually providing the help was Raymond B. Fosdick, president of the Foundation. And the man who did the most to make the help effective was J. George Harrar.

The establishment of the Mexican Agricultural Program took its "immediate rise" from an interview in Washington on February 3, 1941.[1] On that day, President Fosdick and Dr. John A. Ferrell, of the

---

[1] Much of the information about the "prehistory" was obtained from an unpublished report, "The Beginnings of the Mexican Agricultural Program," by William C. Cobb of the Rockefeller Foundation staff.

Foundation's International Health Division, visited Henry A. Wallace, Vice-President of the United States, to learn his views on health and food in Mexico. And the visit was decisive.

The Foundation had been officially interested in Mexico since 1919, when it had entered into a cooperative public health program that made substantial progress in controlling infectious diseases. It had become apparent, however, that better nutrition was also needed to help raise the standard of health among the poorer Mexicans. As better nutrition obviously required a more productive agriculture, some members of the International Health Division realized the desirability of supplementing the medical help with help in food production, and Dr. Ferrell, regional director for Canada, the United States, and Mexico, had mentioned the subject in several of his reports.

In considering the possibility of helping Mexico to produce more food it was natural that Fosdick should solicit the advice of Wallace, who had been United States Secretary of Agriculture from 1933 to 1940 and was known to be deeply and intelligently interested in Mexico. As Vice-President-elect, Wallace had represented the United States officially at the inauguration of Manuel Avila Camacho as President of Mexico on December 1, 1940, and had stayed for about a month as a guest of United States Ambassador Daniels. Wallace's genuine interest in Mexican agriculture and other things Mexican made him very popular in that country. To many Mexicans he symbolized scientific agriculture because of his comprehensive knowledge of the field and his special knowledge of corn, which then was and still is the basic food of most people in Mexico. Wallace was such an enthusiastic missionary for corn that Mexico soon established a corn breeding program at León, as described in Chapter 4. And he was such a convincing exponent of better agriculture generally as to stimulate the thinking of many influential Mexicans and inspire them with hope for the future. They wanted the kind of help that he typified, and Wallace wanted them to have it. So also did Ambassador Daniels.

Josephus Daniels, United States ambassador to Mexico from 1933 to 1942, was a devout man and had good reason to understand the plight of people in underdeveloped areas. Born in North Carolina in 1862, he lived in the South during the dark days following the Civil War, when farming was poor, sanitation was poor, education was poor, people were poor, and the entire South was poor. During his early life the American South was in reality a very backward region. But Daniels was a very progressive man. He became a newspaper editor in Raleigh, North Carolina, in 1885 and established his own paper in 1894, and as a newspaper man in the rural South and as a trustee of North Carolina State College of Agriculture and Mechanic Arts, he developed a deep human interest in problems of agriculture and rural life. In later years he could sympathize with the struggle of the Mexican people to build a new life after the devastation of their Revolution, having seen the people of his own Southland struggle to build a new life after the wreckage of the American Civil War. He had seen how the General Education Board, supported by Rockefeller funds before the days of the Foundation, and the Rockefeller Sanitary Commission had helped to increase the wealth and improve the health of the American South, and he thought the same methods could produce similar benefits for Mexico.

Daniels had been deeply impressed by the success of two pioneer "technical assistance" programs in the southern United States: the Seaman A. Knapp cooperative farm demonstration campaign, operated by the United States Department of Agriculture and the Southern states, and supported partly by General Education Board funds to facilitate its interstate activities; and the antihookworm campaign of the Rockefeller Sanitary Commission. The so-called Knapp program was an extension-demonstration campaign of regional scope that started Southern agriculture on the road to progress and had a strong influence on the enactment of the Smith-Lever Act in 1914, providing for the establishment of the present federal-state-county agricultural extension system. Daniels envisaged and persistently advocated an extension campaign of the Knapp type for Mexico, apparently without realizing that research had not yet provided the facts and materials for an effective extension campaign in that country as it had in the United States. Whatever direct or indirect influence Daniels may have had in obtaining help for Mexico, he and Wallace had helped to create a desire for it in some of the Mexicans.

Dr. Fosdick was a man of vision but not a visionary. As he did not know intimately the problems and prospects in agricultural improvement, he wanted the opinion of someone who did. Wallace did know the problems and had sound concepts regarding their solution; he thought that it would be desirable to expand the Rockefeller Foundation health program in Mexico to include sanitary engineering and nutrition. And better nutrition would obviously require better agriculture. Raising the acre yields of corn and beans, Wallace thought, would have an effect on the national life of Mexico greater than almost anything else that could be done.

Fortified with this opinion from a man of Wallace's prestige, President Fosdick proceeded to consider further what the Foundation could do and how best it could do it. After describing the Mexican situation to Dr. Warren Weaver, director of the Division of Natural Sciences, he asked whether the Foundation could do anything to alleviate it. Weaver said that he did not know but knew how to find out: get a few competent and experienced agricultural scientists and send them to Mexico to study the situation. And that is what the Foundation did.

A Survey Commission Is Appointed and Goes to Mexico

President Fosdick called a general staff meeting for February 18, 1941, at which it was decided: (1) that the agricultural program, if undertaken, would be administered by the Division of Natural Sciences, whose acting head during the absence of Warren Weaver for war work was Dr. Frank B. Hanson; (2) that a committee be appointed to investigate and report. President Fosdick appointed Dr. Hanson, Dr. Harry M. Miller, Jr., also of the Division of Natural Sciences, and Dr. A. R. Mann, vice president of the General Education Board. Dr. Mann was an agricultural scholar who had been dean of agriculture at Cornell University, director for agriculture in the International Education Board for two years while on leave from Cornell, and an officer of the General Education Board after his retirement from the university in 1936. According to him, "Experience has shown that the greatest practical contributions to agriculture come through the fields of genetics and plant breeding, plant protection, soil science, livestock management, and general farm management." The committee therefore decided to select men from the first three fields to constitute the Survey Commission.

The Foundation invited Dr. Richard Bradfield of Cornell, Dr. Paul C. Mangelsdorf of Harvard, and Dr. E. C. Stakman of the University of Minnesota, representing soils and agronomy, plant genetics and breeding, and plant protection, respectively, to serve as members of the Survey Commission. All of them accepted with alacrity.[2]

The combined professional experience of the three men on the Commission amounted to about 75 man-years, mostly in land-grant colleges of the United States, where they had participated in research, teaching, extension, and administration. Among them there also had been first-hand experience of agriculture, agricultural institutions, and agricultural problems in most of North America, including Mexico, in northwestern South America, Europe, parts of Africa, parts of Asia, and Australia.

All three had seen the contributions of science, technology, and education to the phenomenal progress of agriculture in the United States during the quarter of a century prior to 1941. They had seen the introduction of many kinds of crop plants and the genetic improvement of old kinds. They had seen early-ripening, frost-escaping varieties of corn extend the corn belt 500 miles northward and had seen the spring-wheat area extended even farther northward and westward. They had seen the winter-wheat belt extended half a thousand miles westward in the Great Plains region by the development of hardier varieties. They had seen the sorghums convert 10 million acres of range lands into productive plowlands in the semi-arid Southwest. They had seen immigrant soybeans become one of our most profitable crops. They had seen, and indeed one of them had helped, the increase of the acre yields of corn by upwards of 25 percent through the development of hybrid lines. They had seen how a succession of improved varieties of cotton, wheat, barley, oats, flax, alfalfa, and other crops had helped to increase and insure production.

And they had seen the yields of many crops increased by 15 to 100 percent through the use of chemical fertilizers on lands whose native fertility had previously been considered inexhaustible. They had seen the cotton boll weevil, which had threatened to topple King Cotton from his throne in the South, brought under control by means of clean farming, better varieties, and better insecticides. They had

---

[2] At the suggestion of Mangelsdorf, Richard Schultes, who had recently completed work for his doctorate in botany at Harvard, was invited to accompany the Commission because of his first-hand knowledge of Mexican flora, Mexican botanists, and the Spanish language.

seen years in which stem rust destroyed 300 million bushels of wheat in the United States and Canada and subsequent years in which newly created varieties of wheat had almost completely resisted the onslaughts of this scourge of the grain fields. They had seen, too, how scrub cattle had been replaced by better beef and dairy breeds that had increased the efficiency of meat and milk production 25 percent within 25 years. They had lived from the days when cholera alone killed one pig in seven to the day when the disease was no longer a menace.

From the ox to the tractor, from back-breaking peasant farming to the intelligent business of farming is a long and happy step; but the Survey Commission had witnessed that step in various areas of the United States. And they had faith that Mexico could take the same kind of step in an even shorter time because the general guidelines to progress had already been developed in certain other countries. The members of the Commission therefore got ready to go to Mexico, armed with considerable experience, much zeal, few presuppositions, and no prejudices.

That the Commission went to Mexico without preconceptions was due not to ignorance of previous agricultural improvement programs but rather to the realization that the effectiveness of any kind of program must depend on the particular time, place, and circumstances of its operation. They knew of the work of Knapp and the General Education Board in the South as a matter of course in their profession. They knew, as did every intelligent American, about the antihookworm campaign and the accomplishments of the International Health Board. As agricultural scientists they knew in general about the agricultural and health projects in China and about the scientific activities of the Foundation in Europe. But they knew also the limitations of research, of formal education, and of extension when operated as separate and uncoordinated activities and their tremendous potential when well coordinated. In any case, as scientists they tried to approach all problems objectively.

The officers of the Foundation were as objective as the members of the Commission. On June 5, 1941, President Fosdick, Dr. Hanson and Dr. Miller of the Division of Natural Sciences, Dr. George C. Payne, resident representative in Mexico of the Foundation's International Health Division, and several others discussed plans with the Commission in New York. The mandate was simple: "Go to Mexico and find out whether you think the Foundation could make a substantial contribution to the improvement of agriculture, and if so, how?" There was no attempt to indoctrinate the Commission but every attempt to facilitate its work.

Dr. Payne, who knew Mexico well, assumed the immediate responsibility of acting as advance agent and counselor in Mexico; he also made available the facilities of his office in Mexico City. Dr. Miller, who traveled extensively in Latin America in the Foundation's program for improving the natural sciences by means of financial grants to individuals and institutions, had spent about three weeks in Mexico during the spring and had become acquainted with Minister of Agriculture Gómez, Subsecretary González Gallardo, and other prominent men in the Ministry and at the National School of Agriculture at Chapingo. Both he and Dr. Payne provided orientation without attempting to predispose the Commission toward particular viewpoints; they prepared and eased the way very pleasantly and effectively.

As agriculture is found out in the country, the Commission wanted to see the Mexican countryside. To enable it to do so, the Foundation provided a G.M.C. Suburban Carryall, originally red in color but repainted green, possibly more in keeping with its mission. Bradfield broke it in at Ithaca, and on July 1 he, Mangelsdorf, and Schultes started from there for Laredo, Texas, where Dr. Payne met them on July 7 and guided them across the border. They then started their study of northern Mexico, from which Stakman was excused because he had taken that course many times previously.

On July 20 the entire group met in Mexico City; there they remained for a week, absorbing information and ideas from the Minister of Agriculture and his principal aides, from various professors, from the Irrigation Commission, and from many other sources. But they wanted to see more for themselves, so they went back to the country to see what they could see; and they traveled far, saw much, and seldom stopped discussing what they saw.

On the Mexican Highways and Byways—
Reading and Misreading the Land and the People

The members of the Commission were under no illusion that they were discovering Mexico in 1941; Cortez had already "discovered" it and its civilizations in 1519. Being somewhat myopic about civilizations other than his own, however, he considered those in Mexico exotic and therefore tried to modify them considerably or annihilate them completely. And thereby hangs a painful tale, too long to tell here.

In 1941 many American tourists were "discovering" Mexico, each in his own peculiar way. These discoveries were made mostly along the main-traveled roads, which were dressed up for tourists, but what was it like along the byways and on the backways? As it was hard to travel on any ways except the highways, many people discovered Mexico without understanding it; they saw its face but never felt its pulse.

To some it was a land of deserts and volcanoes, of oxen and burros, of goats and beggars, and of charming but lazy people. To others it was a vast panorama of scenic and architectural beauties. To still others it was a land of infinite resource and promise, provided only that American "know-how" be imported to make the deserts bloom and the tropics gush.

As one apparently intelligent tourist asked while flying across a northern desert, "Why don't the Mexicans farm this land? There's a lot of it." The reply was, "Yes, there is lots of land, but this land needs lots of water." "They could get water easy enough." "From where?" "From anywhere." "Well, do you see any rivers flowing over the land or geysers spouting water out of it?" After a quick glance out of the window there came the honest answer, "No," and then the almost automatic assertion, "Just the same, if we had this land in the United States we would have had it all in farms long ago." That seemed to settle the matter until a man across the aisle drawled, to no one in particular, "Maybe so, but I'm from Arizona." Which provoked the reflection that much of nature still defies man's conquest. And there is much defiant nature in Mexico.

Other tourists pontificated no more wisely but somewhat more eloquently. From an American schoolmistress riding through a grain-growing area at harvest time came this bit of profundity: "There may be hunger in Mexico, but there would be plenty of food if the Mexicans spent more time gathering in the sheaves and less time lying in the shade of the trees." The country people did like their siestas when the sun was high, but they also knew that they could accomplish more by working in the cool of the morning and evening than in the heat of the noonday sun. The tragedy was not that they did not work hard enough but that they had to work so hard for what they got. They could readily explain their alleged indolence. On one occasion, when a Mexican agrónomo accused two laborers on an experiment station of being "lazy loafers" because they were sitting under a tree instead of working in the experimental plots, they replied politely but in a sad tone of injured innocence: "No, *patrón,* excuse us, but we are not lazy; we got a little tired in the sun so we walked to the nearest shade, not the farthest, to rest a little so that we could work that much harder. And we were not really loafing while we were resting; we were philosophizing about the agricultural problems of Mexico." Under the circumstances this seemed to be a very pertinent remark.

The Survey Commission, too, had to develop a philosophy, derived insofar as possible from adequate knowledge of the country and understanding of its people; the validity of their recommendations would depend on the soundness of their concepts. And so the Commission set out to see the country. They traveled in 16 of the 35 Mexican states in various climatic zones and studied the various types of agriculture, both at their best and at their worst. The rugged station wagon carried them over about 5,000 miles of passable and semipassable roads; when necessary, trucks, horses, and more or less cooperative mules were impressed into service on trips to see how people farmed and how they lived in remoter rural districts.

The Commission tried to talk with an adequate sample of these back-country people but found that discourse without communication was of limited profit. Apparently there was considerable truth in the official estimate that two or three million Mexicans habitually spoke one or more of 54 Indian dialects, and, although a million of them reputedly spoke some Spanish also; the Commission often consoled themselves with the statements of more experienced observers that "some Spanish" usually was "very bad Spanish."

Despite this handicap of mutually bad Spanish, the Commission learned to appreciate some of the problems and the hopes of the humbler peoples who lived near the end of the trail, close to the land but far from water in the drier areas and close to the water but too far from dry land in the wetter areas. And the horizon was too close to the earth for many people in all areas, because their land was poor, tillage was poor, and they were poor. There was little evidence that the Mexican peasant was "happy because his wants were few"; on the contrary, he seemed more resigned than happy, but not so resigned that he did not want a better life for himself and for his children. It was obvious that a better life would depend on a better agriculture and that a better agriculture must depend on a better education. Therefore the Commission studied the schools.

Mexico's Early Efforts in Agricultural Education and Experimentation

An educational revolution was under way in Mexico, and it was badly needed, for more than 50 percent of the people were still illiterate and in some rural areas the percentage was 80 percent or higher. As expressed by Sanchez, "It required no meticulous researches to point out the needs of the people. Illiteracy had reached staggering proportions. Disease was rampant. The people were hungry—for food and for the land that produced it. They lacked the training and the tools to perform the common and technical tasks of production." But "the school program seeks to become an integral part of community life—of farming and marketing, of health and sanitation, of homemaking and social organization."[3]

Clearly, however, zeal for education was still far ahead of skill in educating. In 1941, 93 percent of the rural schools did not teach beyond the fourth grade and only three percent of them gave six years of schooling. They had helped reduce illiteracy from 66 percent in 1921 to 52 percent in 1940, but they were expected to help improve agriculture and rural life as well. Each school was supposed to have a plot of land, simple but modern tools, and a teacher trained in methods of farming. But there were too few teachers who knew agriculture. Because traveling teachers' institutes and other quick methods for improving teachers had not produced the desired results, rural normal schools had been established "to train teachers properly."

The rural normal schools were pathetically poor in 1941, according to the Survey Commission. More authoritatively, Dr. Jaime Torres Bodet, eminent Mexican educational statesman, wrote in 1944: "Their condition is pitiful. The students have no clothing. The bookshelves do not contain any books. And why speak of laboratories or workshops, when in many instances we have not even been able to

[3] George I. Sanchez, "Education: Mexico Today," *The Annals of the American Academy of Political and Social Science,* March, 1940, pp. 148, 149.

provide farm implements or even farm animals with which the students might work. . . . If we want the rural teacher to play a decisive role in the emancipation of Mexico, we must carefully supervise the institutions which are designed to prepare him for the task."[4] These normal schools could not have a quick impact; at best, theirs would have to be an evolutionary role.

Two other types of schools had been established to improve agriculture and rural life: schools for Indians, and practical schools of agriculture. All have now been disestablished, but they helped educate the Commission. In 1941 there were 32 special schools for Indians, some probably on paper only, and nine practical schools of agriculture. The Indian schools were designed to educate boys and girls for their environment by means of a four-year course that included Spanish (a foreign language to many), agriculture and handicrafts for the boys, and household skills and care of the home for girls. Some of the schools were excellent, some poor. The practical schools of agriculture were designed to train boys to farm, but some of them also prepared for entrance to an agricultural college. In addition, they were supposed to serve as centers for adult education and community services.

These schools could have done considerable good had there been enough good teachers to staff them. But there were not. In any case, such schools could not solve Mexico's basic agricultural problems because at best they were perpetuating old and inadequate information rather than producing adequate new information.

Intelligent Mexicans realized that better farming would have to come largely from the results of experimentation within the country, because the transfer value of foreign prescriptions is limited. It was easy to say, "We need better varieties, we need to fertilize this soil, and we must control pests and pathogens better." But what were the better varieties, what the best soil management practices, and what were the best pest and disease control measures for the many different conditions that existed? The general principles for improving agriculture were obvious, but it was obvious also that specific recommendations for so diverse a country as Mexico would have to be based on specific knowledge derived from adequate regional and

4 Jaime Torres Bodet, *Educación mexicana: Discursos, entrevistas, mensajes.* (Mexico City, 1944), pp. 99, 100. (The quoted material is from the translation on p. 409 in *Rural Mexico* by Nathan L. Whetten [Chicago: The University of Chicago Press, 1948.])

local experimentation. Unfortunately, however, the country had too few scientists to make the needed experiments.

What was being done to develop agricultural scientists? In 1941 there were three colleges of agriculture in Mexico, all on the undergraduate level only. The college at Ciudad Juárez was private, Antonio Narro at Saltillo was supported principally by the State of Coahuila, and the National School of Agriculture at Chapingo was under the management of the federal Ministry of Agriculture.

The National School, established in 1854, naturally had the widest responsibility. What was it like? One Mexican critic called it "a confused and unrelated series of events," and in 1934 Bernardo Arrieta wrote: "During the 80 years in which it has functioned as an institution of agricultural instruction . . . , the National School has not achieved a definition of its character . . . or determined the functions which its graduates are competent to perform in the country. . . ."5 *Germinal,* a magazine published by alumni of the School, had this to say: "In the National School of Agriculture students are admitted on the basis of recommendations with a carnival disguise of entrance examinations. The nephew of a Congressman, even though he be a Kentucky burro (and these are the biggest burros there are), can enter the school with greater ease than a candidate without patronage even though his preparation be good. May God give you letters of recommendation, my son!—the rest does not matter."6

These are severe strictures, but they were made by Mexicans themselves. The members of the Survey Commission were either more charitable or less realistic. In 1941 they wrote: "To judge these higher schools of agriculture by present standards in the United States would hardly be fair, although the comparison might be useful. It would be fairer to compare them with the agricultural colleges of forty years ago. . . . In fact, the best of the Mexican institutions might not suffer too much in comparison with some of the smaller agricultural colleges today, in which no graduate work is offered and little or no research is done."

The simple truth was that agricultural research and education were inadequate to the needs of Mexico.

5 Bernardo Arrieta, "La educación agrícola como fundamento de reorganización de nuestra economía rural," in *Los problemas agrícolas de México,* I. p. 250. (The quoted material is from the translation on p. 290 in *The Ejido—Mexico's Way Out* by Eyler N. Simpson [Chapel Hill: The University of North Carolina Press, 1937.])
6 *Germinal,* Feb. 15, 1934. (Quoted in Simpson, *The Ejido,* p. 290.)

What the Commission Concluded and Recommended

From the diverse views of three very different pairs of eyes and from the furnace of hot debate, the Commission unanimously drew some simple conclusions. They wrote: "Since Mexico is a country of violent contrasts, the emerging picture of Mexican agriculture has frequently been kaleidoscopic, changing with the experiences and impressions of each new day of travel. Nevertheless, the final views and conclusions of the Commission are unanimous in all essential details. As the members of the Commission differ widely in temperament, training, and experience, this fact lends some support to the hope that the picture which has finally emerged, and which is herewith presented, may be fairly accurate, at least in its broad outlines, and that the conclusions reached are reasonably sound."

There was hunger in Mexico in 1941. That "the country has many of the aspects of an overpopulated land" was evident to all who looked below the surface. The level of subsistence was low; dietary standards were bad. The average annual per capita consumption of meat was 25 pounds as compared with 145 pounds in the United States and 290 in Argentina; that of sugar was about 35 pounds as contrasted with more than 100 in the United States.

Although Mexico was capable of producing almost every kind of crop plant known to civilized man, "the people were hungry for food and for the land that produced it." What was wrong?

Mexico had a land problem. There was a great deal of land, but a great deal of it was not good agricultural land. Almost 80 percent of the country was classed as semiarid, nine percent as naturally humid, and less than 12 percent as irrigated, according to the data available in 1941. As only some 17.5 million acres were planted to crops in any one year, Mexico was trying to support her people on 0.9 acre of cultivated land per capita. Even though some areas produced two crops a year, Mexico simply had too little farm land; therefore, attempts had been made to increase the amount by constructing irrigation systems where rainfall was insufficient and by converting grasslands into plowlands where rain seemed sufficient. Hopes ran high, but then drought years, the ancient curse of Mexico, followed close on one another. On the former grazing lands, corn and wheat died of thirst where native grasses had earlier survived. The mountain tops were dry; reservoirs and rivers were dry; the sky was dry; the land was dry. There was blight in the land, with blighted crops and blighted hopes. Then came the rains, as intemperate as the drought had been. Many soils were washed away and many lands were so badly gashed by gullies that only the buzzards cared to cross them.

Had zeal for the quick use of new lands outstripped knowledge regarding their carrying capacity? If so, Mexicans themselves were accumulating necessary data for planning a safer expansion of the agricultural area. Meanwhile they continued to convert raw land into cropland, but this alone was not enough because most lands were not productive enough.

The efficiency of crop production was low. In 1941 corn, wheat, and beans together occupied about 80 percent of the croplands, but acre yields were only eight, 11, and three bushels, respectively. Corn and beans yielded only a third as much as in the United States, and wheat yielded about 70 percent as much despite the fact that most Mexican wheat had the advantage of being irrigated.

The efficiency of animal production, too, was low. Meat, milk, and eggs were scarce in amount and often poor in quality. Because Mexico needed her corn for human food, she could not afford to feed it to animals. There were too many scrub cattle feeding on scrubby lands. If they ever attained a weight of a thousand pounds, it took most of them four years to do it, whereas a well-bred, well-fed animal can do it in 16 months or less. Pigs and poultry too had to scrabble for what they got to eat. Although there were some good dairy herds near the larger cities, some good grass-fed cattle, and some good pigs and chickens, the average Mexican had to depend largely on the products of inferior animals, mostly poorly fed and often weakened by insects and diseases. Many of the poorer Mexicans could hardly have lived without goats and burros, for these animals required but little and gave as much as they could. The burros carried the poor man's burdens, and the goats provided his milk and cheese and meat. And at last they gave their hides. But more was needed.

So obvious and so urgent was the need to make Mexican lands more bountiful that the Commission stayed close to the earth in making recommendations but let hopes soar high and roam wide in visualizing expectations.

As the Commission saw it, "the most acute and immediate problems, in approximate order of importance, seem to be the improvement of soil management and tillage practices; the introduction, selecting, or breeding of better-adapted, higher-yielding and higher-quality crop varieties; more rational and effective control of plant diseases and insect pests; and the introduction or development of better breeds of domestic animals and poultry, as well as better feeding methods and disease control." They therefore recommended that the Foundation initially send to Mexico an agronomist and soils expert, a plant breeder, an expert in crop protection, and an animal husbandman as a working commission to cooperate with the Mexican Ministry in its agricultural improvement program.

The Survey Commission realized that they were not wise enough to blueprint in detail the activities of the proposed working commission, for ultimate success would necessarily depend on the wisdom of the collaborators in conceding to expediency when necessary and capitalizing on opportunities when possible. And so they wrote: "The proposed plan is not exclusive, nor does it contemplate final methods of procedure. It can be, and probably should be, amplified and expanded in several directions. It is presented merely as the most practical and effective to begin with."

The basic philosophy in making the specific proposals was stated thus: "The plan presented assumes that most rapid progress can be made by starting at the top and expanding downward. The alternative would be to start at the bottom and work toward the top. A program of improving the vocational schools of agriculture and of extension work directed toward the farmers themselves might be undertaken. But the schools can hardly be improved until the teachers are improved; extension work cannot be improved until extension men are improved; and investigational work cannot be made more productive until investigators acquire greater competence."

The ultimate aim was to help Mexico toward independence in agricultural production, in agricultural science, and in agricultural education. The design was joint participation, not preachment; the intent was to work with Mexicans in doing the things that needed to be done, not merely to tell them how they should be done. As independence would depend upon the number and quality of independent Mexican scientists, the Commission recommended "that provision be made for a special type of fellowship for outstanding investigators and teachers." Although clearly the primary obligation was to help improve agricultural materials and methods through research, the Commission was insistent on capitalizing to their limits the educational values of the researches.

It was assumed that the program would continue for at least a decade, as it seemed axiomatic that there seldom are miraculous solutions for complex scientific and social problems. And, although their hopes soared high and roamed wide, the Commission envisioned no easy agricultural miracles on the Mexican horizon.

Adoption and Evaluation of the Recommendations

In barest detail these were the viewpoints and recommendations of the Commission after about two months in Mexico, which included more than 5,000 miles of travel, numerous conferences, and the preparation of a report weighing 3.5 pounds and comprising 62 single-spaced typewritten pages and 143 photographs, taken by Mangelsdorf. The group had dispersed on the last day of August, one member remaining in Mexico about a week longer, editing the report for final typing and arranging to distribute copies prior to shipping them to New York, where they arrived on October 14, 1941.

In retrospect it appears that the Commission must have worked hard and with some degree of intelligence, for the recommendations were adopted unchanged by The Rockefeller Foundation's Board of Trustees as "the guideline for an action program in Mexico."

To those like Ambassador Daniels who may have thought in terms of an extension program of the Knapp type, the statement that "most rapid progress can be made by starting at the top and expanding downward" may have been a shock and a disappointment. To an experienced agriculturist like Vice-President Wallace, it meant that research might have to precede but should not exclude demonstration. To the Commission, it meant that research must precede effective extension under the conditions prevailing in Mexico.

Extension alone, and other forms of education, can make great improvement only when there is a great reservoir of potentially useful but unused information, and there was no such reservoir in the Mexico of 1941. Moreover, reservoirs usually run dry within a short time unless replenished constantly by the results of research, as has been painfully evident in many technical assistance programs in the fields of agriculture and public health, which deal with variable living organisms and changing situations. Of course, research alone does not alleviate conditions either unless the results are made practically effective through education and extension. Naturally, therefore, the Commission envisioned improvement through a combination of research, education, and extension—with research providing opportunities and furnishing materials for education and extension. This concept was neither novel nor profound, but it did have the merit of being sound and sensible. And it is equally sound and sensible today for other poorly developed areas.

As the viewpoint in most of this chapter is 1941, attempt has been made to black out the years between then and now. But in the interim many expectations have been met and some hopes have been fulfilled; there has been solid accomplishment. The evidence, however, lies ahead.

Chapter 3

Putting the Wheels in Motion
Pioneers Go to Work

The productivity of agricultural investigations depends on the conceptual wisdom and operational ability of the investigators, on the availability of necessary physical facilities, and on freedom to work without let or hindrance whenever, wherever, and however the work needs to be done. What most urgently needed to be done in 1941 in Mexico was fairly obvious; and it seemed that there would be relative freedom to do it, as both the Mexican Ministry and The Rockefeller Foundation were much more interested in doing useful things than in prescribing exactly how they should be done.

It was obvious that strong leadership would be needed to insure success of the contemplated program. So the Foundation set out to find a strong leader, and President Fosdick asked the Survey Commission, continued as an advisory committee, to help in the search. They found Dr. J. George Harrar, who seemed to be a natural for the position and later proved to be even more of a natural than he had seemed.

Harrar was born in Ohio in 1906. He earned the B.A. degree and many athletic honors at Oberlin College and was graduated in 1928. As an undergraduate he became deeply interested in botany and chemistry. Then, while a postgraduate student and teaching fellow at Iowa State College of Agriculture and Mechanic Arts at Ames, in the heart of the corn belt, he developed an interest in their application to agriculture. After receiving the M.S. degree at Ames, Harrar spent four years, in charge of botany and plant pathology, at the College of Agriculture, Mayaguez, Puerto Rico, then went to the University of Minnesota and obtained his doctorate in 1935.

From Minnesota Harrar moved to Virginia Polytechnic Institute, where he rose to the rank of professor in the Department of Biology. In 1941 he was appointed to succeed the eminent F. D. Heald as head of the Department of Plant Pathology of Washington State College, at Pullman, in the heart of the famous Palouse wheat country. From there, in 1943, he went to Mexico to put the wheels in motion in the first of the Foundation's operational programs in agriculture. There he stayed for almost nine years, constantly accelerating the motion of the wheels.[1]

At the outset, Harrar started those wheels quickly because he persistently studied the obligations and opportunities of the job, as he had done in every position that he had occupied. He was a versatile man, keen and resourceful in solving scientific problems, mechanical problems, and human problems. The prognosis for success in Mexico was good, for Harrar had specific qualifications in addition to his general ones. In Puerto Rico he had learned much about the Spanish language as various kinds of people liked to use it, had learned much about the Latin temperament, and was willing to learn more; he was "simpatico to Latinos."

Naturally, the head of a college department could not suddenly quit like a tramp printer, and, although appointed in 1942, Harrar did not go to Mexico until the next year. Excerpts from his early reports describe the beginnings of the program.

"The R.F. agricultural program in Mexico began as of February 1, 1943. At that time J.G.H. and Dr. E. C. Stakman came to Mexico. Subsequently, working with Dr. H. M. Miller, a memorandum of agreement was developed and presented to the Secretary of Agriculture of Mexico. Upon the approval by the Secretary and the R.F., the program was considered to be formally initiated."

Harrar wrote further: "During the ensuing three months Dr. Stakman and the undersigned made an effort to see as much of the agricultural activities of Mexico as possible and to familiarize themselves with the important agricultural problems and the personnel

---

[1] In 1951 he moved to New York to become the Foundation's first deputy director for agriculture, in the Division of Natural Sciences and Agriculture. Later he became director for agriculture, vice president, acting president, and, on July 1, 1961, president of The Rockefeller Foundation. Dr. Albert H. Moseman succeeded Harrar as director and served until July 31, 1965. Dr. Sterling Wortman became director on January 1, 1966.

of the Secretaría de Agricultura and its dependencies. To this end over twenty states were visited and agricultural activities in the production of cereals, legumes, fruits, vegetables, and special crops were observed in company with local representatives of the Secretaría de Agricultura y Fomento. In addition, a number of schools of agriculture in various parts of the Republic were visited. . . .

"Prior to Dr. Stakman's return to his position at the University of Minnesota a number of discussions were held and plans made for future developments in the cooperative agricultural program between the Secretaría and the Foundation. These plans were jointly developed by the representatives of the Foundation and the officials of the Secretaría de Agricultura."

It was agreed to cooperate initially in the following fields: (1) varietal and cultural improvement of corn, wheat, and beans; (2) soil improvement; (3) plant introduction and testing; (4) animal husbandry. The Foundation agreed to appoint and support financially several competent U.S. scientists for full-time work on these four projects and the Mexican Ministry agreed to place its facilities at their disposal. In addition, it was understood that the Foundation, if requested, might send scientific specialists to Mexico temporarily, to aid in the solution of specific problems. And it was mutually agreed to cooperate in capitalizing on the educational values of the investigational projects; accordingly the Ministry would commission young Mexican agrónomos to work as interns under the supervision of Foundation scientists, and the Foundation would provide scholarships for the further education of the best interns. Thus says the record.

Harrar went to work immediately recruiting staff, procuring housing and other facilities, and starting experimental work. It was a difficult time in 1943, for the United States was engaged in all-out war and it was hard to get scientists, scientific apparatus, motor vehicles, and needed machinery out of the country and into Mexico. But progress was made on all fronts except the animal husbandry program, later postponed indefinitely because a serious outbreak of foot-and-mouth disease necessitated a drastic quarantine and eradication campaign, with the slaughter of many cattle and work oxen. As the United States participated in this campaign, it was not a good time for Americans—or anyone else—to start an animal improvement program.

Manning the Works

CREATION OF THE OFFICE OF SPECIAL STUDIES

In October, 1943, the Mexican Ministry of Agriculture and Animal Husbandry authorized the establishment of an Oficina de Estudios Especiales—Office of Special Studies—commonly referred to as the *Oficina* or the Office and often designated by the letters OEE or OSS. The creation of this semiautonomous agency within the Ministry reflected the wisdom of its creators, for it developed into an exceptionally productive research and educational organization, comprising experienced scientists of the Foundation's staff and aspiring young Mexican associates or interns selected jointly by the Mexican Ministry and the director of the Office.

During its entire life span, from October, 1943 to December 31, 1960, the Office had only three directors; Harrar served from the beginning until 1951 and was followed by his associate, Edwin J. Wellhausen, who continued until February, 1959, when he in turn was succeeded by his assistant director, Ralph W. Richardson, Jr. This length of tenure and natural order of succession provided for continuity of effort by the Office, and sensible regulations provided reasonable freedom for all its operations. As the director of the Office was responsible directly to the Minister of Agriculture, policies and procedures were determined and expedited at the ministerial level. But in the fall of 1943 the Office still needed to be manned adequately.

FORMING A NUCLEUS OF PERSISTENT PIONEERS

One of the first jobs was to fill the key positions recommended by the Survey Commission and authorized by the Foundation. To find good scientists with missionary zeal is always difficult. It is always easy to find many who say, "Sure, I'd like to go: it would be good experience; but I wouldn't want to stay more than a year or two." It was harder to find the few men who said, "I don't want to go unless I can stay long enough to do some good."

The Foundation wisely sought relatively young men, men who had most of their careers still ahead of them, but enough experience behind them to enable them to function like veterans. Although the

Selective Service officials had prior claim to many such men, the nucleus of an extraordinarily good staff was quickly formed.

The man selected and appointed as corn breeder, after an exhaustive canvass by Mangelsdorf and Harrar, was Dr. Edwin J. Wellhausen, who was born in Oklahoma in 1907, went to country school with Danny Turnipseed in southern Idaho, was graduated from the University of Idaho, obtained his doctorate at Iowa State College of Agriculture and Mechanic Arts, and had been on the staff of Montana State College and of West Virginia University. Wellhausen was a happy choice, for he was a man of the soil as well as a man of science. From his experience as a farmer in Idaho he knew how to farm, and from his research experiences in Idaho, Iowa, Montana, and West Virginia, he knew how to apply science for the improvement of farming. He arrived in Mexico in September, 1943, and is still there, directing the Foundation's activities within the country and administering its Mexico-based international corn, wheat, and potato programs.

Not until the late summer and early fall of 1944 was it possible to get a soil scientist and a plant pathologist down to Mexico. The arrival of the soils man, Dr. William E. Colwell, antedated that of plant pathologist Dr. Norman E. Borlaug by a month or two. Borlaug, however, stayed longer and became a permanent pioneer. He helped to put the wheels in motion and to keep them moving; like Wellhausen, he knew what to do with a wheel if a spoke broke or a rim slipped off.

Colwell was born in Missouri in 1915, obtained the B.S. degree from the University of Nebraska, the M.S. from the University of Idaho, and his Ph.D. from Cornell University. He had been instructor in agronomy at Idaho and associate professor of agronomy and associate agronomist in the Experiment Station of North Carolina State College. Colwell knew soil on the farm and in the laboratory, and he knew how to find out what unproductive soils needed to become productive and what productive soils needed to become still more productive.

Borlaug was a native of northeastern Iowa, having been born in 1914 near Spillville, where Dvorak is reputed to have composed part of the New World Symphony. He studied forestry at the University of Minnesota, made the wrestling team and a good scholastic record,

The earliest pioneers of the Mexican program. *Top:* Mexico's Minister of Agriculture, Marte R. Gómez, who asked The Rockefeller Foundation for help; Raymond B. Fosdick, president of the Foundation, who made the help available. *Below:* J. G. Harrar, who started operations; Subsecretary of Agriculture, Alfonso González Gallardo, whose continual counsel was indispensable to success. (Chapter 1)

This Survey Commission studied Mexican agriculture in 1941 and recommended Foundation help in improving it (Chapter 2). Left to right: Stakman, Mangelsdorf, and Bradfield; on the extreme right, Richard Schultes, who accompanied the Commission on its travels.

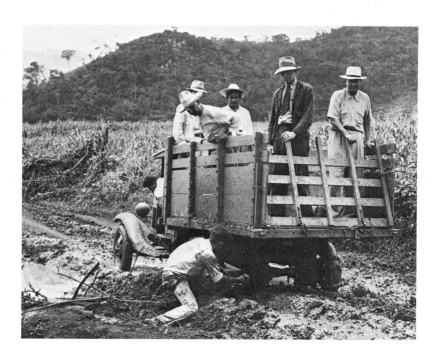

Mudbound while trying to learn how people farmed and lived in tropical Veracruz.

Farming and farm people were poor in much of the back country.

"The people could hardly have lived without goats and burros."
The goats furnished milk and cheese and finally gave their hides . . .

. . . and the burros carried the poor man's burdens.

Water was scarce in semiarid regions, and dry
land was scarce in humid areas.

J. George Harrar

"Putting the wheels in motion" (Chapter 3). The Persistent Pioneers who went to Mexico in 1943–1945, as they appeared about the time they went.

Lewis M. Roberts

Dorothy Parker

Norman E. Borlaug

Edwin J. Wellhausen

John J. McKelvey, Jr.

Primitive power preparing land for field experimentation; Wellhausen, "Pepe" Rodríguez pulling, and a willing helper pushing.

"Laboratories rose from rubble." The first plant pathology laboratory, at San Jacinto.

Developing an experiment station at Chapingo. Above, converting weedy fields into fields for experimentation. Below, the beginnings of a plant introduction garden and experimental plots; buildings of the National School of Agriculture in the background.

Conversion complete: The first modern experiment station in Mexico emerges.

Farmers soon see the results of experimentation.

Corn was everywhere in Mexico, even on these "vertical" farms (Chapter 4).

The tortilla was the Mexican's bread. In 1941 tortillas were hand-made, from the shelling of the corn to the shaping of the tortilla.

Corn gets top priority. In 1943 Mangelsdorf confers with Ings. Taboada (left) and Limón (middle), joint leaders of a Mexican corn improvement program started in 1941. Performance of United States hybrids had been disappointing.

In this test of Mexican varieties at Chapingo in 1944, Wellhausen observes some good varieties and some poor ones. It was decided to combine the good ones.

Improvement was urgent because too many fields yielded too little corn.

To speed progress, Wellhausen enlisted the help of young Mexican "interns" in the breeding work.

Better corns for the highlands were soon produced; they outyielded native varieties by a wide margin.

Corns especially suited to the hot country were produced at this tropical station. Below, Wellhausen preaches the gospel of better corn to farmers.

Improved corn, right, that helped increase acre yields of corn 70 percent between 1943 and 1963.

and was granted the B.S. degree in 1937. After working as a forester in various parts of the United States for two years he returned to Minnesota as an instructor and graduate student in plant pathology, obtaining the M.S. degree in 1940 and the Ph.D. in 1942. From 1941 to 1944 he worked as a plant pathologist in the fungicide testing laboratory of the E. J. du Pont de Nemours Company and once threatened to resign unless he could have freedom to work in the laboratory nights and holidays. He is still based in Mexico after twenty years of service, but his activities are worldwide.

Thus, the Foundation had formed an exceptional nucleus for the future staff by the fall of 1944. The oldest man in the group was 37, the youngest 29, and the average age was 33. All four were good scientists in laboratory and field, all knew how to establish and manage experimental fields, all had done some teaching—Harrar had taught for more than ten years with extraordinary success—and all were exceptionally dedicated workers.

In 1945 these original pioneers were reinforced by Dr. John J. McKelvey, an economic entomologist, Dr. Lewis M. Roberts, a corn breeder, and Dr. Dorothy Parker, a botanist with a flair for bibliographic work and the creation of good libraries.

Born at Albany, New York, in 1917, McKelvey did his undergraduate work at Oberlin College and obtained the A.B. degree in 1939. He then went to Virginia Polytechnic Institute, where he served successively as teaching assistant and teaching fellow until 1942; at VPI he did graduate work under Harrar and received the M.S. degree in 1941. From 1942 to 1945 he was an investigator in the New York State Agricultural Experiment Station at Geneva and a graduate student at Cornell University. After obtaining his Ph.D. in 1945, McKelvey went to Mexico to start the program of controlling insect pests and to help develop Mexican entomologists.

Roberts, who had been flying a B24 bomber during the war as a captain in the U.S. Air Force, was released just in time to fly to Mexico shortly before Christmas, 1945, and join Wellhausen in the campaign to improve corn production. Born at Terrell, Texas, in 1915, Roberts earned the B.S. and M.S. degrees at the Agricultural and Mechanical College in his native state and, in 1942, the Ph.D. degree at Yale. While doing his graduate work he had been assistant to two eminent corn geneticists: Dr. Paul Mangelsdorf and Dr. Don-

ald F. Jones, at the Texas and Connecticut Agricultural Experiment
Stations, respectively. (We will meet Roberts again when we go
to Colombia.)

Dorothy Parker was born in Indiana in 1910. She did her undergraduate work at Butler University, then earned the M.S. and Ph.D.
degrees at the University of Cincinnati. Afterwards she taught at
Brenau College, the University of Cincinnati, and St. Mary's College,
Indiana, where she was head of the department of biology from
1939 to 1942. After holding research fellowships of the American
Association of University Women for two years, she became assistant
curator of the herbarium and assistant editor of the *American Mid-
land Naturalist* at the University of Notre Dame. In 1945 she went
to Mexico as bibliographic assistant and subsequently became biblio-
grapher and librarian on the Foundation staff.

By the end of 1945, then, there were seven full-time staff members
in Mexico. All but Colwell are still in the Foundation, each with
wide international responsibilities in the Foundation's programs.
The record of these pioneers constitutes the best evidence of the
wisdom of the Foundation's policy of scrupulous care in selecting the
right kind of pioneers to blaze a trail that others might follow.

YOUNG MEXICANS JOIN THE PIONEERS

As soon as possible, the Mexican Ministry commissioned certain of
its younger scientists to the Office, their work with the Foundation
staff thus establishing a mutually beneficial internship system. As
there was a shortage of young agricultural scientists in Mexico in
1943, the only one assigned to the Office in that year was José
Rodríguez Vallejo, a recent graduate of the National School at
Chapingo, who was functioning as the first plant pathologist in the
Ministry. Rodríguez, 23 years old, became Harrar's right-hand man
and was his only regular helper until Wellhausen came in the fall
of 1943. And a great help young Rodríguez was; intellectually keen,
very urbane and diplomatic, he knew what to do and what to avoid
doing in Mexico. He was a good young scientist and a valued adviser.

In 1944 five additional Mexican recruits joined the Office, followed
by 21 the next year. Most of these early recruits were recent grad-

uates of the National School of Agriculture and still in their early twenties. Nearly all performed well when working under supervision, and some performed well when working under any conditions. All of the first six are still contributing to the improvement of Mexican agriculture, and four have attained distinction. Of the 27 in this pioneer group, 25 men and two women, all but four were still engaged professionally in agricultural activities at the latest canvass. Thirteen of the group were granted fellowships to study in the United States and 11 earned degrees, nine the M.S. and two the Ph.D. Some of the earliest fellows paid the penalty of pioneers; although they made brilliant records while obtaining the M.S., their services were so urgently needed in Mexico that they had to forego additional graduate study. Nevertheless, some of them have attained true distinction because of their long and outstanding services to Mexican agriculture. All honor to them, even though they may not have honorary degrees!

By the end of 1945 the Office of Special Studies comprised 32 members, seven scientists employed and paid by the Foundation and 25 Mexican "interns." The fields of science represented were genetics and plant breeding, soil science, plant pathology, entomology, and botany. Efforts were concentrated on projects for the improvement of corn, wheat, and beans; soil improvement; and the control of plant diseases and insect pests. A Foundation staff member was in charge of each project, aided by nine interns for corn, three for wheat, one for beans, five for soils, four for plant pathology, two for entomology, and one for botany. Besides their own work, the last three groups gave service to the others when necessary.

That a group of intellectually independent U.S. scientists and a heterogeneous group of young Mexicans were quickly welded together into an effective team is a tribute to Harrar's qualities of leadership and the wholehearted cooperation of virtually everyone in the group. Weekly staff meetings and seminars, in which freedom of speech was freely exercised, helped develop and maintain perspective on the major objectives and the best ways of attaining them. It was clearly understood that each one had a job to do and that all had a job to do together. And they did it by putting their shoulders to the wheels and pushing hard.

The Mexican Ministry and the Foundation realized the magnitude of the task they had undertaken and did their part to put the wheels in motion. Too much credit cannot be given to Minister of Agriculture Marte Gómez and his staff, for they put their faith in large-scale research and did what they could to furnish facilities and give orientation and guidance.

The Minister was a scholarly man who had been director of the National School of Agriculture and knew his way around in practical affairs. Subsecretary González Gallardo, a specialist in geology and soils, had also been a professor at Chapingo; scholarly and urbane, he knew how to get things done and was always ready to give sound advice and effective help. These men were wise, dedicated, and forthright; they were big men. They left the initiative in the Office of Special Studies to Harrar, but they supported him and expected other officials to give support also.

And others did, as Harrar testified at the time. In a report dated June, 1944, he mentions especially: "Oficial Mayor—Ing. Eduardo Morillo Safa, whose sympathetic, efficient assistance on many occasions has paved the way for the varied activities of the Oficina de Estudios Especiales; Director—Ing. Darío Arrieta L., who placed the facilities of the Dirección at the disposal of the Oficina and who has been continuously cooperative and helpful in its activities."

Harrar also acknowledges the helpful cooperation of Ings. Edmundo Taboada, Ricardo Coronado, and Damián Correu, plant breeder, plant pest specialist, and agronomist, respectively, in the Dirección General de Agricultura, roughly equivalent to a bureau of plant industry. He also thanks Dr. Carlos Figueroa, director of the Instituto Pecuario, or Bureau of Animal Industry, and his staff.

Relations were good.

Creating Facilities for Work

No matter how good a group may be, they need offices, experimental fields, tools and machinery, laboratories, and modern library facilities in order to work efficiently. As such facilities were not ready at hand in the Mexico of 1943, they had to be created.

LABORATORIES AND OFFICES RISE FROM RUBBLE

Harrar and his group did the best they could with the meager physical facilities originally available even as they worked hard to create better ones. At the beginning Dr. Payne of the Foundation's

International Health Division shared the space of his crowded quarters, but it soon became evident that the Office of Special Studies needed a home of its own, and the Mexican Ministry helped provide it. Space was allotted in an imposing but rather ramshackle building occupied by the Dirección General de Agricultura, once the home of the National School of Agriculture, near the San Jacinto outskirt of Mexico City.

At first there was space only, or space filled with junk, but then shovelers, masons, carpenters, and plumbers went to work under Harrar's general direction and converted much unused space on the ground floor and on the third floor into offices, laboratories, work rooms, and an embryo library. In Mexico, such work did not always progress as fast as an energetic person who wanted to use the space might wish, but Ing. Morillo Safa, Oficial Mayor (executive secretary and fiscal officer) of the Ministry, was a good expediter. One of the contractors for a plant pathology-entomology laboratory was pleasantly dilatory and failed to meet several successive deadlines, despite promises of completion. Harrar fumed with impatience but was reluctant, as a relative newcomer who was still feeling his way, to lodge an official complaint. While in the Oficial Mayor's office on other business, however, he was asked: "How is the new laboratory?" Harrar allowed that it was not finished. "Not yet? It was supposed to have been done six weeks ago, wasn't it?" asked the O.M. Assured that it was thus, he hesitated a moment, then peremptorily summoned a clerk, who brought with him someone from an outer room. "You're fired!" and "Bring me 2,500 pesos!" the O.M. barked almost simultaneously. The clerk had brought in the contractor, who quickly disappeared, and the clerk soon reappeared with a pained look and an armful of bills. "Here, take these and finish your laboratory," said the O.M. to J.G.H., setting him back on his heels for once in his life. But the laboratory was soon finished.

In that eventful first year, the Ministry also authorized the construction at San Jacinto of a greenhouse, especially for studies of races of wheat rust and other problems that cannot be studied outside—even in the salubrious climate of Mexico.

It was not long before the new quarters were fully occupied and only a little longer before they were crowded. But the crowds were good to see, because young and old together were doing something useful in a systematic and orderly way. The spirit always was informal, but no slovenliness was tolerated. If cleanliness is next to godliness, those plain quarters of the Office of Special Studies must have been pretty close to heaven. They certainly were a model for budding young scientists and a revelation to any older ones with an inclination toward untidiness.

SOWING THE SEEDS FOR A MODEL EXPERIMENT STATION

Pertinent to "Putting the Wheels in Motion" is the important fact that Harrar started field experiments almost as soon as he got to Mexico. During 1943 several hundred collections of wheat and corn were made; some wheats were planted during the summer, and in the fall more extensive test plantings were made. It had been necessary to improvise a great deal in starting this field experimentation because nothing was available to do it with except the fields themselves, and even they had been quite unprepared for their new task. Indeed, much of the land was a weed specialist's paradise. Mexico urgently needed an adequate agricultural experiment station.

In 1943 Mexico had no experiment station with the necessary combination of good land, buildings, machinery and apparatus, and experienced investigators. Ing. Edmundo Taboada, chief investigator in the Ministry, had developed experimental plots near Tlalnepantla, about an hour by automobile from Mexico City, where he was using side-hill caves of a former robbers' roost as seed and storage sheds. Being of an inventive turn, he too had improvised but was handicapped because he had to spend too much time in improvising. Nevertheless, the Tlalnepantla experimental fields were the nearest approach to a central experiment station. The Ministry had also established a number of regional stations, but they were relatively nonproductive, partly because of poor location and lack of facilities but mostly because there were not enough experienced men to operate them independently. The best-equipped station was at León, Guanajuato, about 200 miles from Mexico City as the crow flies but a hard day's drive and much farther as the roads then ran. There were good reasons for developing a central station near the City.

Harrar urgently recommended the establishment of a central station adjacent to the National School of Agriculture at Chapingo. This was the logical site because it was within about 20 miles of the

Ministry's headquarters in Mexico City, the Ministry already had the necessary land, and the National School, a dependency of the Ministry, could easily avail itself of the educational values of the station. The immediate purpose, of course, was to establish a functional experimental station; the ultimate purpose was to develop a combined research-educational center that might serve as a model for Latin America.

The Mexican Ministry and The Rockefeller Foundation quickly accepted Harrar's recommendations for the station. The Ministry allotted about 150 acres of land contiguous to the National School and provided what equipment it could. Harrar and Wellhausen immediately put themselves, their few helpers, and available machines to work in preparing the land for experimental purposes, and considerable progress was made before the end of 1943. But in the spring of 1944 difficulties began to mount. A well and pumping equipment for irrigation, building materials, motor vehicles, and additional farm machinery were urgently needed. But materials and equipment were scarce, costs were rising—prohibitively in some cases—there was an acute shortage of gasoline for motive power, and building costs were 50 percent higher than when estimates for station buildings had been made. In May, Harrar reported the situation to the Foundation officers in New York, and within two weeks they had allotted the additional money needed for buildings; but they could not relieve shortages of gasoline, machinery, and motor vehicles. As Dr. Hanson in New York wrote to Harrar: "Sorry, but we can't help now on station wagon or jeeps. The Government has added control of used-car market and tightened up entire situation regarding all cars."

Despite the birth pains of the station, however, Harrar could report before the end of 1945 that "the experiment station at Chapingo has been further improved and a station building has been designed. The acreage has been increased to approximately 65 hectares by the addition of a block to be used for seed increase. At the present time the station is being used primarily in connection with corn, wheat, and bean projects, the introduction nursery, fertilizer studies, rotation experiments, and miscellaneous smaller experiments."

Subsequently the Office of Special Studies also helped to develop three excellent regional federal stations and a state station at Toluca,

State of Mexico. Mexico is now well on the way to the completion of an experiment station system that is adequate for the needs of her very diverse agriculture. If Chapingo was not the first strictly modern agricultural experiment station in Latin America, it was close to it. It later served as a model for those that the Foundation helped build in Colombia and Chile. The hope that Chapingo might become a pioneer Latin American research-educational center is being realized (and is discussed further in Chapter 11).

DEVELOPING A MODERN RESEARCH LIBRARY

Another of Harrar's pet projects was the development of a modern research library. Those in the Dirección at San Jacinto and in the National School at Chapingo might have been of interest to an antiquarian but were of no use to a research worker. So Harrar started one and got Dr. Dorothy Parker to finish it—if a library is ever finished. By mid-1945, some 10,000 bulletins, reprints, and scientific periodicals and more than 150 books had been acquired. And Dorothy Parker went to work to make them accessible. As steel book stacks simply were not available when she started, wooden sectional stands were built and arranged with the greatest possible economy of space in the already crowded quarters at San Jacinto. These bookcases constituted the walls of a neat, attractive, and very useful young library, with an allotment of $5,000 to help it grow. But it had to move twice while growing.

The box-like wooden sections served well as carrying cases in two emergencies that forced the Office to move and threatened to annihilate the library. The first crisis came when striking students of the nearby normal school gave short notice that they would burn the San Jacinto building unless it was turned over to them for a dormitory. To meet the deadline, the library was carried out, wooden section by wooden section, between 6 P.M. and 1 A.M.; officials had advised this action, convinced that the students had real fire in their eyes. Along with other goods and chattels of the Office, the sectional library was moved to what was known as the glass palace, a poorly conceived and hastily constructed "look-of-tomorrow" building on Puente de Alvarado, one of the historic streets of Mexico City. When this building itself started to become historic because it was fast sinking into the ground and was suddenly condemned, with official orders to vacate immediately, the Office moved again, and the library was once more crated away sectionally in its wooden crates. The Office and the library finally settled in a more substantial building with the address Londres 40. The book stacks are now modern, the contents are modern and ample, and the library is almost as busy a place as the cashier's office.

Even in the early days the library began to attract the attention of Latin American visitors, and numerous requests were made for Dr. Parker's help in improving old libraries and starting new ones. The Foundation responded liberally, and many good libraries in Latin American agricultural institutions owe their present excellence to the example set by the original wooden-crate library at San Jacinto. Since 1958 Dorothy Parker has added Asia to her sphere of influence in library development, not only in agriculture but also in medicine. Books may not produce more food or conquer disease, but they can help.

The Wheels in Full Motion

Thus the machine had been built and the wheels were in full motion by the end of 1945. The joint staff, Mexicans and North Americans, was functioning in newly created and continually developing experimental fields, laboratories, and library. The development of better varieties of corn, wheat, and beans was in full motion, a beginning had been made in the improvement of certain forage crops, and new kinds of crops potentially valuable to Mexico had been introduced for testing. The basis was being laid for vast improvements in soil productivity and for the better protection of crops against pests and pathogens. The educational phase of the program was yielding perceptible results; the internship and fellowship program was functioning; and arrangements had been made for two young men from other Latin American countries to become interns as well. The hopes of the Survey Commission already had been exceeded.

In retrospect, twenty years later, the wonder is that so many hopes were realized so soon. That the program gained momentum so quickly is due to the cooperative efforts of two groups of pioneers, in the Mexican Ministry of Agriculture and in The Rockefeller Foundation. Minister Gómez and Subsecretary González Gallardo were true pioneers who did everything possible to help introduce the scientific age to Mexican agriculture, as did President Fosdick and certain other officers of the Foundation. Harrar and his early group were pioneers who became veterans without ever losing the pioneering spirit. These early pioneers merit an animated memorial involving revolving wheels that revolutionized the agriculture of a nation. Support for this opinion is to be found in succeeding chapters.

Chapter 4

Corn

Reshaping the Daily Bread of Mexico

There is no other country in the world in which corn is so revered, so much a part of the culture, traditions, and folkways, or so important in the nutrition of the people as it is in Mexico. Consumed in the form of the *tortilla,* a thin, flat, unleavened bread, corn is eaten three times a day, three hundred and sixty-five days a year. A Mexican laborer, when he can get it, will consume as much as a pound of corn a day.

To improve Mexico's food supply is first of all to improve corn production. Henry Wallace had seen this when he traveled by car from Laredo, Texas, to Mexico City in December of 1940 to attend the inauguration of President Avila Camacho. The members of the Survey Commission had seen it when they studied the problems and potentialities of Mexican agriculture in the summer of 1941. Corn received special attention in their report to The Rockefeller Foundation, and it received special consideration in the program that the Foundation initiated in 1943 as a result of this report. The first appointment in the program recommended by Harrar after he became director was that of a corn breeder. The first improved seed that the program developed and distributed to farmers was that of superior varieties of corn. In 1948, five years after the beginning of the program, Mexico, for the first time since the Revolution of 1910, had no need to import corn. This first success was soon followed by others. The social revolution was on the way to becoming an agricultural revolution.

Mexico's Is a Corn-fed Civilization

CORN IS EVERYWHERE IN MEXICO

The extent to which the Mexican people utilize every available spot of soil for the culture of corn is amazing. In the lowlands they plant corn between rows of bananas and pineapples; at high altitudes, among the pine trees. Near Mexico City the Indians grow corn among the flowers on the so-called "floating islands" of Xochimilco. Farther north in the region of Tamazunchale, corn is the principal crop in the "vertical agriculture"—cultivation on mountain slopes so steep that it is a wonder that farmers can till the fields at all. Small dooryard gardens are filled with corn, along with beans and squashes, and in front yards and public places in the cities it frequently grows as an ornamental plant. A stalk of corn appearing as a "volunteer" in a field of, say, alfalfa, or even in the lawn of a public park is seldom removed. Corn is much too precious in Mexico ever to be destroyed. There is a reverence for corn that has a long tradition and there is affection too.

The reasons for this reverence and affection are not far to seek, and anyone hoping to help Mexico improve her food supply will do well to seek them. If he would have his efforts succeed he must try to understand what corn means to Mexico today; what it has meant to Mexico in the past; and the many ways it is used for food and for other purposes. This is a general principle that applies as well to other crops in other countries: rice in China, Japan, and India; sorghum in the countries of Africa; the potato in Ireland and among the Indians at high altitudes in Peru. There are customs, traditions, and ceremonies associated with man's principal food crops that the plant breeder working in a foreign country can ill afford to ignore.

Corn is the basic food plant of Mexico and has been so since time immemorial. It has been said that no civilization worthy of the name has ever been built on any basis other than the growing of cereals. History seems to bear this out: Egypt, Greece, and Rome had their wheat and barley; China, Japan, and India their rice. All the advanced cultures and civilizations of the New World—the Inca of Peru, the Maya of Middle America, and the Aztec of Mexico—had corn for their basic food plant, and nowhere in America, north or south, was corn more important than it was, and still is, in Mexico.

MEXICO IS CORN'S HOMELAND

The people of Mexico take an inordinate pride in believing that Mexico is the homeland of corn—its center of origin. Botanists now agree, after some 400 years of debate, that corn is an American plant and that Mexico is undoubtedly one of its homelands. Fossil corn pollen estimated to be at least 80,000 years old has been identified. It was found in drill cores 200 feet below the present level of Mexico City by engineers preparing for the construction of Mexico's first skyscraper. The fossil pollen proves beyond any reasonable doubt that the ancestor of cultivated corn was corn and not, as some botanists have theorized, its close relative, teosinte. The ancient pollen also proves that corn is an American plant and not, as some botanists have argued, an Asiatic one. Thus Mexico's first skyscraper, an impressive 43-story building, is a monument not only to architectural and engineering progress but also to the solution of a centuries-old botanical mystery.

Even more convincing than the fossil pollen, which is microscopic in size and can be identified only by pollen experts, are prehistoric remains of all parts of the corn plant. These come from once-inhabited caves in the Valley of Tehuacán that were excavated by Dr. Richard S. MacNeish, the foremost authority on the beginnings of agriculture in America. In the lower zones of several of these caves MacNeish uncovered tiny corn cobs scarcely longer than a man's thumbnail, which Mangelsdorf and his associate, Dr. Walton Galinat of Harvard University, identified as cobs of prehistoric wild corn. The earliest cobs are dated by radiocarbon determinations of associated vegetal remains at about 5000 B.C. They represent not only the most ancient corn—except for the pollen from the Mexico City drill core—yet found, but also the first wild corn, living or prehistoric, ever to be discovered. Like the pollen, they show that corn is an American plant, that it had at least one origin in Mexico, and that the ancestor of cultivated corn is corn itself.

Other archaeological remains of corn from the Tehuacán caves, numbering more than 24,000 specimens and including all parts of the plant (roots, stalks, leaves, husks, cobs, kernels, and tassels), reveal a distinct evolutionary sequence. The findings show also that by 3500 B.C. corn had been domesticated and that a full-fledged agriculture comprising corn, beans, squashes, and chili peppers was being practiced. The cobs of this period, although somewhat larger than those of wild corn, were still small and quite primitive in their botanical characteristics. At this stage the squashes, with their starch and sugar-rich flesh and oil-rich seeds, may have furnished more food than the corn.

At about 2300 B.C., however, apparently as a result of hybridization with one of its wild relatives, teosinte or Tripsacum, corn suddenly began to evolve with almost explosive rapidity. Soon there developed two races, Chapalote and Nal-Tel, which are still recognized among the living races of corn in Mexico and are carefully preserved by the Indians in several parts of the country. These races, much more productive than the wild or early cultivated corn, furnished the major food supply for a greatly expanded population, which, outgrowing the caves, lived first in villages and later in cities. With an assured food supply came leisure, at least for some members of the population—leisure to study the sun, the moon, and the stars; leisure to invent a system of arithmetic and, combining this with wonderfully precise astronomical observations, to create a calendar more accurate than the Old World calendar of the same period. Along with these developments there grew a sophisticated religion that included, among its numerous deities, a maize god and involved solemn ceremonies associated with the planting, growing, and harvesting of corn.

Here, then, briefly told, are the reasons for the Mexican Indian's reverence for corn. It has been the source of his daily bread and that of his ancestors for thousands of years. Although he now has other cereals at his command (wheat, rice, barley, rye, and sorghum), corn is still for him and for the great majority of his countrymen the principal food; the nutritional basis of Mexico's modern civilization as it was of her ancient ones, the Maya and the Aztec. These are the reasons for the special emphasis given to corn in attempting to improve Mexican agriculture; these are the reasons, in part, for the reluctance of the Mexican farmer to adopt such new crops as sorghum; these are the reasons why the Mexican farmer, once he sees genetic improvement in his basic food crop, becomes ready to adopt cultural and other improvements—the use of fertilizer and pesticides —to help him produce more corn to make more tortillas.

CORN IS USED IN MANY WAYS

Tortillas, beans, and chili peppers—these comprise the principal constituents of diet for the majority of Mexicans, the corn providing the greater part of the energy, the beans providing the essential proteins, and the chili peppers providing not only several vitamins but also piquancy to a diet otherwise somewhat monotonous. Wrapped around meat, chicken, cheese, squash blossoms, or other delicacies and fried in deep fat, the tortilla becomes the basis for the more elaborate *taco*. Another corn dish, the *tamale*, is prepared by cooking a mixture of corn meal and meat wrapped in a corn husk. A kind of gruel, *atole*, is made by heating finely ground corn in water and flavoring it with cinnamon, pineapple juice, strawberries, orange leaves, or a kind of weedy herb related to wormwood. Roasting ears, *elotes*, are a favorite vegetable. In the cities an ice cream is made from the young corn grated from the cobs in the milk stage. Even the pests of corn are eaten. A disease of corn, *huitlacoche*, corn smut, is considered a delicacy; the fungus growths are eaten as a vegetable cooked with onions or garlic, tomatoes, and chili peppers. And should a plague of locusts devastate the corn field before the crop is matured, the farmer may still salvage a bit of food by setting fire to the remaining vegetation and consuming the toasted insects.

Nor is corn used only for food. The stalks are used for fodder, for thatching roofs, and for fences to contain small livestock; the cobs make an excellent fuel. When several hundred cobs are tightly bound together with twine or wire to form a thick disk with the ends exposed, they provide a rough surface over which ripe ears of corn are rubbed to remove the kernels. Thus corn is the only cereal that furnishes its own threshing device. The silks are used in an infusion as a remedy for dysentery. The husks are used as a filling for mattresses, and the thin inner husks are wrappings for cigarettes that are, like corn itself, one of ancient Mexico's gifts to the world.

Corn Improvement Receives Top Priority

Because corn is so overwhelmingly important in Mexico, comprising so high a proportion of the diet and utilizing so large a proportion of the labor (of the men in growing the crop and the women in preparing the tortillas), it did not require unusual perspicacity for the members of the Survey Commission to conclude that the greatest opportunity for immediate improvement of Mexican agriculture lay in improving the corn crop. And there was no doubt that improvement was desperately needed. While in the United States Corn Belt the average was then approaching 35 bushels and yields of 100 bushels were not uncommon, the average yield of corn in Mexico in 1941 was pitifully low, only about 8 bushels an acre. In spite of her large acreage devoted to the crop, Mexico was actually having to import corn—not only a drain on her financial resources, but also a grievous offense to national pride.

THE SEARCH FOR A CORN BREEDER

When Harrar assumed the leadership of the Mexican program in 1943 he enlisted the aid of Mangelsdorf in finding the best man available to serve as corn breeder or *maicero*, worker in corn. The Survey Commission in its report to the Foundation had emphasized the importance of staffing the program, if it were initiated, with the best men who could be found in the United States. The extraordinary effort that these two put into selecting the best man for this assignment illustrates their conviction that the Survey Commission had established a general principle and that the success of the program would depend more on the quality of the personnel than on any other single factor. Mangelsdorf spent substantial parts of May and June in seeking recommendations from geneticists, plant breeders, and agronomists throughout the United States, and during the first part of July Harrar and he made an extended trip to interview personally the five most promising prospects from an initial list of 25.

This trip also illustrated Harrar's talent for selecting the staff which was to make the program, almost from the start, a phenomenal success. He always made it a point to include the candidate's wife in part of the interview, explaining that a successful career in a foreign country depends as much on the wife as on the man. He knew this from his own previous experience in Puerto Rico, where he had observed that the men whose wives were unable to adapt themselves to living in a foreign country did not work effectively and were soon on their way home. Also, instead of describing the position only in its most attractive terms, he emphasized all the difficulties that a young couple and their children would encounter. The result, perhaps not a surprising one, was that even those candidates whose interest had initially been rather lukewarm began to recognize a challenge which they found not easy to resist.

As a result of their trip, Harrar and Mangelsdorf agreed that Dr. Edwin J. Wellhausen, then of West Virginia University, was clearly their first choice. Not only had he the technical training and experience needed for the job to be done, but also—and this proved to be a factor in the program's success—he was experienced in all aspects of practical farming. He could run a tractor, set a plow, and line out an irrigation ditch, and he could show others how to do these very practical things, without which a technical program of agricultural research can scarcely operate.

The selection of the first staff member thus represents a case history of the talents displayed and techniques employed by Harrar in enlisting the scientists who comprised his staff, and it also illustrates one of the principal factors contributing to the subsequent success of the program: finding not just good men but the best man for a particular job.

THE MAICEROS MAKE THEIR PLANS

Wellhausen arrived in Mexico in late September. Prior to his arrival, Mangelsdorf, now plant-breeder-geneticist member of the Foundation's agricultural advisory committee, went to Mexico to help lay the groundwork for the proposed corn project. He and Harrar spent considerable time with Ing. Edmundo Taboada, chief investigator in the Ministry of Agriculture, and Ing. Eduardo Limón, director of the León Experiment Station, who were jointly responsible for a corn-breeding program started two years earlier at the suggestion of Henry Wallace. Toward the end of August the four men made a ten-day car trip to the chief corn-growing regions of central Mexico, including a visit to the León station where they studied Limón's experiments with inbred strains of corn, some developed from Mexican varieties and others imported from the United States. It was apparent that the great majority of United States strains, among them some of the best that the United States had to offer, were not well adapted to Mexican conditions; and this observation played an important part in the plans for a program of corn improvement that Wellhausen and Mangelsdorf formulated. The program was based largely on the use of Mexican native varieties and not on the introduction of hybrid corn from elsewhere.

This program reflected other aspects of the background against which it was built: the primitive level of many of Mexico's agricultural methods and practices, the limitations of the average farmer, the urgent need for more corn, and the desire for cooperation with the existing program of Taboada and Limón. The long-term objective was to develop a hybrid corn for Mexico that might revolutionize her production as hybrid corn had already revolutionized corn production in the United States. But there had also to be a more immediate objective, because in 1943 the Mexican corn crop proved to be tragically short—1.8 million tons compared with 2.3 million tons the year before—and the government was forced to import 160,000 tons, the largest amount imported in any year of Mexico's history.

The program planned by these maiceros therefore had both short- and long-term objectives: the short-term, to meet Mexico's immediate needs as quickly as possible; the long-term, to develop productive hybrids especially adapted to Mexico's conditions. The plan included four main steps so arranged that each step would not only increase corn production and provide more food but would also contribute to the attainment of the final goal.

The first step was to collect corn systematically from all parts of Mexico to provide a comprehensive inventory of the genetic material available for breeding new and better kinds of corn. This emphasis on native stocks was based in part on the earlier observations that the majority of lines that Limón had introduced from the United States were poorly adapted to Mexican conditions. Step two in the program was to grow in the same field all the varieties thus collected and, under uniform conditions, to compare them for productiveness, disease resistance, and other important characteristics; and then to select the better ones and distribute the seed of these to the farmers as soon as possible. Step three was to inbreed among the better varieties and to use first-generation inbred strains in producing new synthetic varieties and modified hybrids which could be released to farmers while more highly refined double-cross hybrids, similar to those employed in the United States, were in the making. Step four was to continue inbreeding the lines collected from the better varieties and, with these and the inbreds from Taboada's and Limón's program, to produce conventional double-cross hybrids well adapted to the major agricultural regions. It was hoped that the first of these hybrids could be ready in five to six years.

In devising this program the maiceros made use of both old and recently published experimental results and also added innovations of their own. By intention the program was flexible so as to permit capitalizing fully on all new information and materials that might be obtained as the work progressed.

Hybrid corn, like many other practical developments, is the product of a long line of theoretical research including the nineteenth-century studies of Charles Darwin on the effects of self- and cross-pollination in plants and the early-twentieth-century work of the Danish botanist Wilhelm Johannsen on selection of pure lines from mixed varieties. William Beal of Michigan, who was familiar with Darwin's experiments, attempted to improve corn by crossing dent and flint varieties and in the process developed a method of producing crossed seed on a large scale by planting two varieties in the same field and emasculating one by removing the tassels.

Perhaps the most important single contribution was made by Dr. George H. Shull of the Carnegie Institution, who in 1908 published his discovery: when he crossed the pure lines that he had selected from several generations of inbreeding and combined them in single crosses (inbred A × inbred B), they produced hybrids that were more uniform and yielded more than the open-pollinated varieties from which they had been derived. Dr. Edward M. East of the Connecticut Agricultural Experiment Station made a similar discovery almost simultaneously when he crossed strains that had been inbred at the Illinois Experiment Station in connection with the famous experiments there on selection for chemical composition in which he, as well as two of Beal's students, Holden and Davenport, had participated. But seed produced by crossing one unproductive inbred strain with another proved to be prohibitive in cost. The major breakthrough came in 1918 when Dr. Donald F. Jones, also of the Connecticut Station, showed that by crossing two single crosses (A × B) × (C × D), thus combining them in a double cross, hybrid seed could be produced at a cost within the reach of progressive farmers.

As a result of these researches and many other experiments, hybrid corn had by 1933 come into commercial use on a substantial scale in the United States. From then on the acreage planted to

Campaigns against Hunger

hybrid corn increased rapidly, and by 1943, when the Mexican program began, more than half of the United States corn acreage was in hybrid corn and the average yields for the country as a whole had increased by more than 50 percent.

ADAPTING AMERICAN METHODS TO MEXICAN NEEDS

Could hybrid corn do for Mexico with its ancient folkways and traditions what it had done for the United States? The American maiceros believed that it could, but only if the methods of the United States were modified to meet the special problems of Mexico.

In the 1940's hybrid corns were usually produced by a process involving three steps: (1) the isolation of inbred strains by artificial self-pollination for four to six generations; (2) the testing of the inbred strains in various crossing combinations to determine their hybrid performance; (3) the combining of the selected strains into commercial hybrids, which in the case of field corn were predominantly double crosses. Corn breeders in the United States had learned to allow a minimum of ten years for the development and evaluation of a new hybrid combination, then another five years for its successful introduction to farmers. Certain experiments, however, had already shown that good materials could be made available in a shorter time.

In 1935, Dr. Merle T. Jenkins of the United States Department of Agriculture reported that hybrids of strains inbred only one or two generations were in some cases as productive as hybrids of strains inbred five or six generations. The same year Dr. T. A. Kiesselbach at the Nebraska Experiment Station showed that some combinations of more than four inbred strains—later known as synthetics—could be maintained as varieties and, unlike hybrids, did not require the production of fresh seed each year. Continuing this line of experimentation, Jenkins in 1939 suggested that synthetics could be produced with strains selfed only once. Wellhausen and Mangelsdorf adopted this method as offering the best opportunity for the rapid production of improved corn in Mexico, and they added a modification of their own to speed up the process still more. Because it was customary to test inbred strains in topcrosses (crosses with open-pollinated varieties), they decided to produce synthetics by directly combining the best topcrosses.

Implementing Well-made Plans

WELLHAUSEN BEGINS THE PROGRAM

The first two steps in the improvement program—collecting and testing corns from all parts of the country—were particularly important in Mexico, where a wealth of types had evolved over the centuries. In height, native corn plants ranged all the way from three feet to 20 feet and the ears that they bore might be as short as three inches or as long as 16 inches. While some varieties matured in three months, others took up to eight months, and there were countless other differences, an almost bewildering multiplicity of them. Variety testing on a limited scale had already been initiated by Taboada and Limón with promising preliminary results. This activity had now to be expanded.

Wellhausen took over the collection of ears that Harrar and Mangelsdorf had been picking up in their travels, and by March, 1944, he had assembled 413 samples, each consisting of 15 to 25 ears chosen at random from fields or granaries. The collection continued to grow and by 1950 included some 2,000 entries. (It became the basis for the classification of the races of corn of Mexico that is discussed in Chapter 15.)

Collecting was a major job in itself, and Wellhausen soon found it necessary to delegate this responsibility. As his assistant he appointed Efraín Hernández Xolocotzi, a native of the State of Tlaxcala and a Cornell graduate, who proved to be an ideal choice. Energetic, tough, and fearless and knowing Indian dialects, Hernández had no hesitation in going to any part of Mexico and before he was through had made his way—often on foot—into even the most remote villages.

On his trips, Hernández observed that different Indian groups had developed and still maintained their own particular type of granary. By noting changes in the granaries as he traveled, he knew when to begin collecting intensively, because the different groups had also maintained their own kinds of corn, some of them for centuries. Hernández began and later completed, as a graduate student at Harvard, a systematic description of Indian granary types, both prehistoric and contemporary.

TESTING NATIVE VARIETIES AND FINDING THE BEST

By the spring of 1944, Wellhausen was ready to test his first group of 805 samples: 413 Mexican varieties and 392 foreign corns obtained chiefly from the United States. His primary objective was to find superior varieties for the principal corn-growing areas of central Mexico: the Mesa Central, with elevations from 6,300 to 7,300 feet, and its extension, the Bajío, with elevations from 4,300 to 6,000 feet.

For his main testing ground, the San Martín Experiment Station provided a long-disused field at Chapingo, which at 7,200 feet was representative of the Mesa Central. The first planting here was an observation block; each sample was grown in a separate two-row plot about 30 feet long; every tenth plot was a *testigo*[1] or control variety with which the other entries could be compared. Fields were also available at the León and Querétaro stations in the Bajío, and in these Wellhausen planted observation blocks comprising 100 of the Mexican varieties collected at intermediate altitudes. Working with him were a group of young Mexican scientists commissioned to the Office by the Ministry of Agriculture as interns or trainees in corn improvement. Their services were much needed for there was much to be done.

An observation block is useful for making the initial coarse screening of a large group of varieties, but for precise determinations of yield each planting must be replicated or repeated at several different places in the experimental field so as to "average out" variations in soil fertility. Wellhausen selected 81 Mexican varieties at Chapingo for a replicated yield test. In addition, he and the interns graded the entries at each station for earliness of maturity because this is a character that determines at which elevation a variety is likely to do best.

Although poor soil and poor stands invalidated many of the comparisons, these 1944 tests established several important facts. First, of the 392 foreign varieties practically all were failures. This result was not entirely unexpected in view of Limón's experiences with inbred lines from the United States. Second, enough Mexican varieties showed promise to indicate that continued collecting and

[1] A Spanish word meaning "witness." Mexican agronomists are imaginative in choosing Spanish words to convey the meanings of technical terms for which their language has no exact counterpart.

testing would definitely be worth while. Third and still more encouraging, it would clearly be possible, as planned, to achieve a prompt increase in Mexico's corn supply simply by distributing superior varieties to farmers.

Wellhausen selected 135 of the native varieties for retesting in 1945. To these he added 313 new Mexican samples and sorted the entire lot into groups for testing at different altitudes. Those for the Mesa Central were again planted at Chapingo. Varieties for the Bajío were grown in fields at the León, Querétaro, Briseñas, and Pabellón stations and also on two private farms at Cortazar and Celaya in the State of Guanajuato.

Agricultural research workers, like farmers, are subject to the vicissitudes of weather and a variety of other hazards. One field was inundated for five or six days; in another weeds choked out the corn; on one of the private farms the major domo harvested the experimental plots before the data had been obtained. But many of the 1945 results were valid, and at the end of the season the maiceros had nearly a score of varieties that yielded more than those commonly grown in central Mexico.

The program was now reaching the point where Wellhausen and the interns could no longer handle it, and in December they were joined by Dr. Lewis M. Roberts, the former bomber pilot. Before going into the service, Roberts had completed the work for his Ph.D. at Yale University under the direction of Dr. Donald F. Jones, one of the inventors of hybrid corn. He thus became the final connecting link between the nineteenth-century observations of Charles Darwin on the effects of self- and cross-pollination in plants and the improvement of Mexico's basic food plant, corn (Darwin, Beal, Holden and Davenport, East, Jones, Roberts). Thus is added one more example to many previous ones that show how discoveries in strictly theoretical science so often contribute eventually to the improvement of man's welfare.

THE FIRST SELECTED VARIETIES GO TO FARMERS

During 1946 seed of the selected varieties was given out in small quantities to as many farmers as possible and some of the best selections were also grown in seed-increase fields so that larger amounts could be distributed. Two varieties of this latter group—selection

No. 7 from Hidalgo and selection No. 21 from Michoacán—performed so well that in the winter of 1947 they were turned over to the newly established Corn Commission for seed increase on a commercial scale.

Hidalgo 7 was a tall variety, nine to 12 feet in height, with an ear borne about two thirds of the way up the stalk. In the 1945 tests it produced more grain than the other late-maturing corns for the Mesa Central and provided about a fifth more forage for feeding to livestock. Its superiority was no genetic accident for one of its ancestors was the tropical lowland race, Tuxpeño, which carries some of the best germ plasm known in corn and is also one of the ancestors of Corn-Belt dent corn of the United States. From Tuxpeño, Hidalgo 7 derived not only high yielding ability but also tall stalks and a strong root system. Its excellent resistance to the corn rust disease came from another ancestor, Conico, which for centuries was the predominating corn of the Mesa Central.

Michoacán 21, also adapted to the Mesa Central, had ranked eleventh behind Hidalgo 7 in the 1945 yield tests, but the reason was soon evident: it was an early-maturing type. When it was compared only with entries of its own maturity class, its potentiality became apparent.

By the end of the 1947 season two other superior varieties—Nos. 216 and 221, especially adapted to the northern Bajío—were ready to join Hidalgo 7 and Michoacán 21 in commercial-scale seed increase. As a group, these four selections outyielded farmers' unimproved varieties by 15 to 20 percent. But even better varieties were in the making, for the maiceros had immediately begun to combine the superior qualities of the varietal selections into the higher-yielding synthetic varieties and hybrids.

The Program Makes Further Progress

SYNTHETICS REPLACE SELECTED VARIETIES

The first synthetics were produced in the simplest way: merely by growing the individual superior varieties close together in an isolated field so that they might intercross naturally among themselves. Next, the procedure was refined by first self-pollinating the selections to increase their purity and then planting these selfed lines close together in a field—two alternating lots that intercrossed. A further refinement was to test the first-generation selfed lines in topcrosses (crosses with open-pollinated varieties) and then combine the best into double-topcross synthetics.

During 1946 and 1947, as soon as each kind of synthetic appeared promising, seed was at once distributed among farmers so that it too could begin making its contribution to increased corn production. This contribution was a sizable one, because the synthetics could outyield the selected varieties by 10 to 26 percent. Moreover, the farmer did not have to learn any new techniques in order to realize this yield advantage. Beginning with his first harvest he could simply save seed, as many farmers had always done, from his best-looking plants. Now, however, his best-looking plants would yield more than before, and they would be more resistant to disease because the varieties and inbreds being used by the corn breeders had all been certified by the plant pathologists for resistance to ear rots, root rots, rusts, and smuts.

THE MAICEROS WORK DOUBLE TIME

In the summer of 1944, while the first varietal tests were in progress, approximately 2,200 first-generation self-pollinations in the Mexican samples planted at Chapingo were made by Wellhausen and the interns. This part of the work was greatly accelerated by the discovery, soon after Wellhausen came to Mexico, that winter crops of corn could be grown and self-pollinations successfully made at lower altitudes. Wellhausen arranged to plant most of the new lines in fields rented at Progreso, Morelos (6,340 feet), and by the spring of 1945 another 2,000 self-pollinations had been made.

In the United States corn breeders know that only one inbred strain in several hundred initially isolated will finally prove to be useful in commercial hybrids. They know, too, that the best hybrids are usually made up of inbreds derived from several unrelated open-pollinated varieties so they isolate inbred strains from a number of different varieties. This inbreeding is practiced on an extensive scale, but it is only the beginning. The inbred strains that are not discarded for obvious defects must be tested in hybrids—this is the only way their true value can be determined—for several years or in a number of different localities to even out the effects of variation in soil and water. In the 1940's, corn breeders in the United States were normally growing only one crop a year, with time from fall harvest to the following spring planting to analyze the results and select the inbreds to be crossed and the hybrids to be tested further. Not so in Mexico. The schedule of two crops a year was very demanding, and the work of analyzing and selecting had to be done in five or six weeks. Wellhausen, Roberts, and the trainees were therefore putting in very long hours but with the result—for Mexico an extremely important one—that the breeding of hybrid corn proceeded much more rapidly than was customary in the United States.

By the end of 1947, ten double-cross hybrids were ready for distribution in the Mesa Central and the Bajío, and still other hybrids, substantially better than these first ten, were being produced.

MEXICANS SEIZE THE INITIATIVE IN SEED PRODUCTION

As important as the improvement being effected in corn was the change in attitudes of the young Mexican interns as they participated actively in the program. Most of them, for the first time in their scientific careers, were working in the field and getting their hands soiled. They were learning that corn plants do not keep office hours, that when the pollinating season is at its height everyone is busy from early morning until dusk. They were working harder than ever before in their lives, and they were enthusiastic, even thrilled, by their results and what they were helping to accomplish. When one of the swivel-chair officials of the Ministry chided several of the trainees for being always in field clothes and putting in such long hours—"You are not much better than the peons"—they were able to reply with dignity: "If the American doctors can do these things, then we too can do them."

In October, 1945, the Foundation's agricultural advisory committee, upon hearing from Harrar that the success of the technical aspects of the corn improvement program was already assured, had recommended that immediate steps be taken "to work out a system for distributing seed of new and improved varieties of plants to provide for rapid use while avoiding exploitation of individual farmers." Before this recommendation could be implemented in any substantial way, however, the Mexicans themselves had seized the initiative.

The young interns were not the only Mexicans who were following the corn work with avid interest, learning new ways and seeing new opportunities. Señor Ricardo Acosta, whose farm near León was one of the yield-test locations in 1945, had seen in tests on his own land that some of the entries were far superior to the varieties commonly grown in the Bajío. Enlisting the support of Lic. Gabriel Ramos Millán, then president of the Mexican Senate, he proposed to President-elect Miguel Alemán the establishment of a special commission to produce, process, and distribute seed of the improved varieties being developed. President-elect Alemán was not hard to persuade, and even before his inauguration he had designated a four-man corn commission that included Sr. Acosta.

The Corn Commission was officially established on January 17, 1947. With a generous budget—three million pesos for the first year and seven million for the second and succeeding years—it could secure land and engage personnel on a scale far beyond that possible for the Office of Special Studies. Harrar and Wellhausen cooperated wholeheartedly by turning over to the Corn Commission all the seed of the improved varieties and by releasing some of the young Mexican interns to man the new organization.

The Corn Commission rented land in the State of Morelos for the winter crop and began the work of increasing the seed stocks. This continued with spring and summer plantings in other localities. By 1948 approximately 1,400 tons of seed of selected varieties, synthetics, and double-cross hybrids were ready for distribution to farmers. It was agreed that this seed should carry a distinctive label and since the work of the Office was already favorably known to many farmers in the central region, the name chosen was coined from the first syllables of Rockefeller and Mexico: "Rocamex."

IMPROVED CORN SPARKS THE AGRICULTURAL REVOLUTION

The first large-scale distribution of improved seed could not have been made at a more favorable time. Not only was the growing season of 1948 excellent, but there had been an increase in fertilizer production in Mexico and the more progressive farmers were beginning to use it freely. The combination of good seed, more fertilizer, and good weather produced spectacular results on some farms and attracted wide attention from the neighboring farmers. For the first time since the Revolution of 1910, Mexico had no need to import corn; indeed, as a gesture of confidence, she actually exported a small amount to her less fortunate neighbors.

According to the Corn Commission's estimate, approximately 270,000 acres were planted to the improved corn varieties during 1948. Because this represents only a small fraction of the country's corn acreage, the success of the crop was due only in part to the use of improved seed; there was not yet enough of it. But the impact of the seed went far beyond the actual quantities distributed. Government officials, from the President down, visited the demonstration fields and convinced themselves that Mexico's food problem could be solved and that the key to its solution lay in more research, more education, and more extension work among farmers. The general public became aware of these new developments through articles in newspapers and magazines and radio reports. There was a new spirit of progress and hopefulness in the land. A drastic change in his basic food plant had awakened the Mexican farmer, traditionally one of the world's most conservative individuals, making him receptive to other changes: soil improvement through the use of fertilizers, crop rotation, and erosion control, which, in the long run, are even more important objectives than grain improvement through breeding.

The Mexican experience suggests that one of the most effective ways to start an agricultural revolution is to improve the basic food plant by the application of genetic principles. It is this drastic change, accompanied by soil improvement and the control of pests, that brings new hope to the tradition-bound farmer of the underdeveloped countries and prepares the way for other, even more far-reaching changes.

Extending the Program

The selected varieties yielded 15 to 20 percent more than open-pollinated varieties commonly grown by farmers, and the synthetics pushed this increase 10 to 26 percent higher. During 1949, hybrids were being distributed in central Mexico that could outyield unimproved varieties by nearly 50 percent.

These hybrids had been produced in a remarkably short period of time, but unfortunately only the relatively few progressive farmers in Mexico were ready to use them. The process of producing and maintaining the seed was really a job for an expert, and the seed was too expensive for most farmers. Also, hybrids had to be grown from new seed each year, and the Mexican farmers were accustomed to using seed from the previous crop.

Under these circumstances it was clear that the best prospect for rapid improvement in corn production lay in increased distribution of synthetics. Accordingly, in 1950 the breeding program was revised to put more emphasis on synthetics. At the same time the breeders began making up hybrids in such a way that farmers could use the advanced-generation seed to create their own synthetics. Thus, while the best farmers obtained high yields by planting new hybrid seed each year, the ordinary farmer obtained better yields by using seed of synthetics and modified hybrids, and the existing corn germ plasm was being upgraded by a wider distribution of better germ plasm.

The first superior variety for the tropics, Rocamex V–520, had been released in 1947, and demand for seed had been increasing each year. But hybrids well-adapted for growing at low altitudes (0 to 3,250 feet) were needed to help the tropics contribute their share to the national corn crop. The work of isolating inbred strains from tropical varieties had been under way for some time at the winter breeding station in Morelos, and by 1950 a very large number of lines were available. Because the selecting had been done during the dry season, no one knew whether these lines were resistant to the major diseases prevalent in the rainy season. Therefore, in 1950 the tropical breeding work was transferred to new headquarters at San Rafael, Veracruz, where the climate is hot and humid the year round and ideal for determining resistance to many pathogens and pests.

Under these rigorous conditions the majority of the tropical lines from Morelos fell victim to diseases and had to be discarded. But of the many inbred lines that had been developed, some proved resistant, and the maiceros, working closely with the pathologists, were ready to release seed of their first tropical hybrids to the Corn Commission at the end of 1952. Beginning in 1953, Gulf Coast hybrids and experimental materials were tested at an increasing number of locations in the tropics and subtropics of Mexico. As information was obtained on the particular conditions in each new area, the maiceros developed hybrids adapted to each and eventually achieved full geographical coverage.

Wellhausen's principal associates during this period were Dr. Sterling Wortman, who had succeeded Roberts in 1950 when Roberts was appointed head of the Foundation's newly established agricultural program in Colombia, and Dr. Robert D. Osler, who replaced Wortman in 1954. Dr. Elmer C. Johnson, still stationed in Mexico today, joined the program later. When Ing. Gilberto Palacios, who had been commissioned to the Office of Special Studies in 1947, took charge of the corn project in 1963, there were at his disposal hybrids and synthetics for growing at altitudes ranging from 0 to 7,300 feet in areas extending from the Pacific Northwest to the Yucatán Peninsula.

Successes and Disappointments

Mexico has trebled her corn production, from two million tons to six million tons, since 1943. This increase is due in part to expanded corn acreage, but more important is an increase of from 8 to 14 bushels in average yield per acre. This, in turn, is largely the result of the efforts of the corn project, supplemented by the efforts of other projects in the Office of Special Studies. The maiceros showed the way to improved yields by selecting superior varieties from the native corns and using them to create more productive varieties. The pathologists helped to incorporate disease resistance into the new varieties; the soil scientists demonstrated the importance of good fertilizers and improved cultural methods; and the entomologists devised better methods for protecting the increased crops against destruction from insects and rodents during storage.

Hybrid corn, however, which has been available for 18 years, has come to occupy only 14 percent of Mexico's corn acreage, and this is a real disappointment when compared with progress in the United States. There, in a similar 18-year period, from 1933 to 1951, hybrid corn expanded to 80 percent of the total acreage, including even the smallest farms. But in the United States progress was stimulated by the competition of private enterprise. For various reasons the Mexican government preferred to maintain complete control of the production and distribution of improved seed, and private enterprise was excluded. One consequence has been that, once hybrid corn became established on the larger farms managed by the more progressive farmers, the expansion slowed down. Hybrid seed is not yet reaching the small farmer in Mexico in substantial amounts, and it probably never will until private enterprise is allowed a part in its promotion. Whether this will ever happen in Mexico remains to be seen. In the meantime, other countries can learn from Mexico's experience that government monopoly has not proved to be successful in getting hybrid corn into the hands of small farmers.

Nevertheless, the impact of the improved seed has been greater than might appear on the surface. Improved varieties have reached small farmers in appreciable amounts. An estimated 36 percent of the corn acreage is now planted to selected varieties, synthetics, and modified hybrids that have been distributed or created by the farmers themselves. And this is progress, even though a revolution in corn production has not yet been achieved.

The corn-growing areas with dependable rainfall or irrigation probably offer the best prospect for further improvement. The knowledge necessary for doubling yields on these lands is available and needs only to be applied. In parts of Central Mexico, where drought is an ever-present threat, land that is marginal for corn production might profitably be devoted to sorghum, a plant requiring considerably less moisture. The substitution of sorghum for corn is already taking place, but the rate of change is slow because of the traditional importance of corn. (Sorghum's potential for Mexico is so great, however, that it is discussed further in Chapter 7.)

In addition to the concrete results, the corn project made important scientific contributions that promise to have even more far-reaching consequences. The classification of Mexican races of corn may prove to be of great value in the future improvement of corn wherever it is grown. (This is discussed more fully in Chapter 15.) But the concrete results are clear evidence that the original plan for corn improvement in Mexico was well conceived. It was also well carried out, and where circumstances indicated the expediency of deviation, the maiceros had the good judgment to make changes. There were some disappointments, but they were due less to scientific than to political causes.

Chapter 5

The Wheat Revolution
More Bread for the Hungry

Mexico has revolutionized its wheat production since 1943. During the past twenty years there has been more progress than in all the four hundred years after the Spaniards first brought wheat into the country about 1520 and established it as a Mexican crop plant during the following decades. Acre yields have trebled and the area of cultivation has been expanded by one half, now that wheat growing is profitable in regions and in seasons in which it was a very risky business two decades ago. Mexico has answered the plea of her people for more bread, not by a miracle but by hard work and persistent use of science and common sense.

"Give us this day our daily bread" had for centuries been the fervent prayer of many devout and hungry Mexicans. It is true that the traditional daily bread was the tortilla made from corn. But Mexico wanted wheat bread also. She wanted it badly enough to spend about 20 million scarce and hard-earned dollars a year to get it, for she was importing about 10 million bushels of wheat annually when the cooperative wheat improvement program was started in 1943.

No longer is it necessary to import wheat to satisfy the hunger for bread. Mexico has supplied her own needs since 1956. Twenty years ago there was about three fourths of a bushel of home-grown wheat for each Mexican; now there is a bushel and a half, even though there are 15 million more Mexicans now than then. Wheat production has won the race with human reproduction; while the population was increasing from 20 million to 35 million, wheat production was increasing from 15 million bushels to more than 60 million bushels a year. The present population is about 170 percent of what it was in 1943, but wheat production is at least 350 percent of what it was then. The area has expanded from less than 1.5 million acres to more than two million, and average yields have increased from a scant 11.5 bushels an acre in 1943 to more than 30 bushels in 1963.[1] Moreover the average has risen each year since 1952, an indication that the upward trend is based on a firm foundation and not on mere luck. Indeed, luck had no part in it, but science and hard work did.

The Causes and the Beginnings of the Revolution

The beginnings of the wheat revolution came in February of 1943, when George Harrar went to Mexico. The first thing for him to do, of course, was to decide what to do first. The decision was not too difficult because Minister of Agriculture Gómez and his Subsecretary, González Gallardo, knew what they wanted. They wanted scientific help in producing more wheat, corn, and beans— Mexico's basic food crops. Although they may not have put wheat at the head of the list, that is where it naturally belongs in a chapter on wheat. They did say that wheat rust was one of their worst agricultural enemies and asked for help in suppressing it. And so the commitment was made.

The project for increasing and insuring wheat production was a bold undertaking, because wheat was generally such a poor crop that some agriculturists asserted that Mexico simply was not and never could be a wheat-producing country.

In 1943 there was no reason for pride in the performance of Mexican wheat. The average yield was a scant 11.5 bushels an acre, as contrasted with almost 19 in Canada, 18 in Argentina, and about 15 in Chile and the United States. Because Mexican wheat was produced under irrigation during the winter dry season, it was less subject to damage by drought, floods, and certain humid-weather diseases than in many other countries. And yet, in yields per acre, Mexico was close to last among the 60 countries for which data were available. What, then, was wrong? The problem was to find out, and there seemed to be no better way than to seek the answers in the wheat fields themselves.

During the first three months of 1943 Harrar and Stakman visited 20 Mexican states, including the principal wheat-producing areas.

---

[1] Preliminary estimates are for 34 bushels per acre in 1963 and for a total production of some 60 million bushels.

They studied hundreds of wheat fields and talked with scores of Mexicans. Rich farmers and poor farmers, intelligent farmers and unlettered farmers, scientists and teachers contributed whatever information they could; even if they could contribute nothing, they contributed it with dignity and courtesy. And, of course, wheat itself was the best teacher about wheat.

There were many obvious reasons for poor yields: mediocre varieties; worn-out soils in some areas; the scourge of stem rust in the most fertile areas; occasional blighting weather in most areas; and skepticism and resistance to change among some growers in all areas.

"As ye sow so shall ye reap." Mexico was sowing too many scrub wheats, and so she was reaping too many scrub harvests. Most varieties were a hodgepodge of many different types, tall and short, bearded and beardless, early ripening and late ripening. Fields usually ripened so unevenly that it was impossible to harvest them at one time without losing too much overripe grain or including too much underripe grain in the harvest. Consequently, the small farmer was a slave to the hand sickle, which he had to use in the slow and tiresome job of selective harvesting. He worked hard to get all he could from his poor fields, but he usually got pathetically little because his poor varieties were grown on equally poor soil.

The "tired" soils of northern and central Mexico were of little help to any wheat variety, poor or good. Long-time cropping had sapped their fertility, because little had been done to maintain it by proper manuring. Many farms were too small to support larger animals so barnyard manure was scarce; the use of clovers or other legumes for green manure was almost unknown; and the use of chemical fertilizers was considered completely impracticable. Too many small farmers were neither conserving nor fertilizing their land; they simply did not understand the soil. They gravely explained that it was tired and needed rest. But they could not afford to let it rest because they had so little of it, so they kept on working it until it was worn out or washed away. Wheat had to struggle so hard for existence in most of Mexico that it could yield only five to eight bushels an acre on the poorer soils and seldom more than 15 bushels on the better soils.

Only on the newer, well-irrigated lands in the Pacific Northwest was the soil generally fertile enough to yield 20 bushels or more an acre. But there stem rust often blasted the wheat just before harvest and turned the fields of golden grain to a sickly gray. Wheat growing was a gamble with rust, and most growers in that area had been wise enough to stop gambling with it.

Tragically, stem rust generally was deadliest in exactly those areas where wheat was potentially most productive. Because of ruinous epidemics in Sonora for three consecutive years, 1939 to 1941, and heavy damage in certain other areas, many farmers had reduced their acreage or stopped growing wheat entirely. Two other kinds of rust, orange leaf rust and yellow stripe rust, sometimes were destructive also, but they were seldom as devastating as stem rust.

Stem rust is caused by a microscopically small mold-like fungus plant that lives as a parasite in many species of the grass family and has its sexual stage on several species of the barberry family, *Berberis* spp. Known scientifically as *Puccinia graminis*, this species comprises varieties, such as *Puccinia graminis* var. *tritici* (= of wheat), *Puccinia graminis* var. *avenae* (= of oats), etc. The wheat variety, var. *tritici*, can thrive on wheat, barley, and many wild grasses but not on oats. And the oats variety, var. *avenae*, can thrive on oats and some wild grasses but not on wheat and barley.

Within each variety there are parasitic strains, commonly called physiologic races because they look alike under the microscope but differ in their virulence and other physiologic characters.

To determine the physiologic races in collections of wheat stem rust, seedlings of 12 "differential varieties" of wheat are inoculated, in a properly equipped greenhouse, to determine the effect of each rust collection on each wheat variety. A variety may be resistant, susceptible, or mesothetic (intermediate) to various samples of rust. The race in the sample is then identified by means of a "Key for Identifying Races . . ." and assigned the number which designates that race, as illustrated below:

Variety	Rust race and varietal reaction					
	59	19	38	56	11	15B
Little Club	S	S	S	S	S	S
Marquis	R	R	R	S	S	S
Kanred	R	R	S	S	S	S
Mindum	R	S	M	R	S	S
Vernal Emmer	R	R	R	R	R	S
Khapli Emmer	R	R	R	R	R	R

S = susceptible; R = resistant; M = mesothetic.

All vertical columns in the table are different because each rust race differs from all others in its effects on one or more wheat varieties; likewise, of course, all horizontal lines are different because each wheat variety differs from all others in its reaction to one or more rust races.

The resistance or susceptibility of a wheat variety, then, depends on the rust races present when and where the wheat is grown. As an example, Marquis was resistant for ten years in central Mexico because the races that predominated there, 59, 19, and 38, cause only weak infection on it; but it was completely susceptible in northern Mexico because race 56 and certain others that can attack it heavily were abundant in that area. But Marquis became susceptible in central Mexico also when that area was invaded by race 56 and later by 11 and 15B. Khapli has thus far been resistant to the prevalent North American races but is susceptible to some that occur in South America, Africa, and Asia.

More than 300 races of wheat stem rust are known, and new ones are continually being produced by mutation, by hybridization between existing races in the sexual stage of the rust on barberry, and by other kinds of genetic changes. Thus, while man breeds new wheats, nature breeds new rust races, and occasionally she spawns virulent ones that can attack varieties that had been resistant to those previously prevalent.

Rust races may spread fast and far, for the rust multiplies by means of spores, "fungus seeds," which are only one-thousandth of an inch long and so light that the wind can carry them indefinite distances. As there are about a quarter of a million spores in each rust pustule and 50,000 billion on an acre of well-rusted wheat, they can quickly spread infection to distant areas if wind and weather are right at the right time.

Bad weather often added to the woes of wheat. Grown at elevations of a few feet to almost 10,000 feet above sea level, the crop suffered somewhere every year from heat, frost, wind, hail, or scarcity of irrigation water. Some "native" varieties were capable of yielding well under favorable conditions but not when faced with adversity. And, unhappily, there was too much adversity and too little knowledge about ways of overcoming it.

Much of the wheat was poor because many wheat growers were poor. Because they had sometimes been misled by bad advice, many small farmers were skeptical of good advice. The better growers wanted information and knew how to use it, but there was little information to give. Therefore the Ministry and The Rockefeller Foundation put science to work on the problem, and together they started the wheat revolution.

Mapping the Strategy of the Revolution

Early in 1943 Harrar formulated the basic creed and code for the wheat revolution. Because a fatal weakness of Mexican bread-wheats was their susceptibility to stem rust, a primary need was to develop resistant varieties. Many soils badly needed fertilizer, but why invest money to produce better wheat fields only to see them destroyed by rust? And why produce rust-resistant varieties if they were to be starved on the poor soils of central and northern Mexico? Harrar saw that the fight against rust had to be won before the fight against poor soils could be won, but that both fights must be won before the campaign for enough bread could be won. So he went to work under the terms of a cooperative project entitled, "Small grain improvement (wheat, barley, oats), through selection, testing, breeding, and disease and pest control." Brave words, these, in the Mexico of twenty years ago. But not only words, for deeds were done as soon as the program was begun.

Not Only Words, but Deeds

Harrar promptly started implementing the wheat program. Where, though, were the experimental fields, the greenhouses, the laboratories, the equipment, the scientific assistants, the labor, the organization? Many men would have waited until they could be provided. But Harrar used whatever facilities were available while working hard to provide better ones.

Some wheat improvement work was already in progress when the cooperative program began. Ing. Edmundo Taboada, geneticist in the Ministry, had purified some Mexican varieties, had imported some rust-resistant ones, and had made several crosses designed to produce good hybrids with resistance to stem rust. Ings. Eduardo Limón and Antonio Marino also had a wheat improvement program at the experiment station at León, Guanajuato. And in 1942 the Ministry, in informal cooperation with the United States Federal

Rust Laboratory at St. Paul, Minnesota, had started testing 25 varieties of several wheat-species groups in uniform rust nurseries at 18 places in the various wheat areas of the country. These nurseries were designed to determine varietal reaction to stem rust and to provide material for the identification of parasitic races of the rust. Samples were sent to Minnesota for race identification; the requisite facilities and trained personnel were not then available in Mexico.

Worthy as were these early efforts, they had produced only limited practical results. As Ing. José Rodríguez Vallejo wrote in retrospect: "In conclusion it can be affirmed that all of the experimentation prior to 1943, as concerns the problem of stem rust in particular and of wheat improvement in general, was deficient, principally because of lack of continuity in the experimentation." This was a fair appraisal by a young Mexican who saw that a big job like national wheat improvement could be done only by working on a big scale and keeping everlastingly at the work.

Young Rodríguez, an honor graduate of the National School of Agriculture, was the first of many outstanding young Mexicans whom the Ministry commissioned to work and learn in the cooperative program. And Rodríguez, pioneer Mexican plant pathologist, learned fast and helped much.

A spotless white laboratory coat was standard garb for young Mexican scientists in 1943—the younger the scientist, the whiter the coat. On the first joint field trip Rodríguez left his laboratory coat at home but did appear in a snow-white shirt, well-polished low shoes, and a well-pressed suit. When reminded that he might spoil his good clothes, he remarked with a touch of pride, "Oh, I've got plenty of others at home." When it was suggested that he might not care to cross a muddy ditch into a sandy wheat field, he answered with a touch of defiance, "I can go any place you can." And he went; his low shoes followed knee boots into what just happened to be the worst places in the field, and he came out with his shoes full of mud and sand, his ankles covered with cockleburs, and his eyes full of smouldering fire, but with this apparently casual remark: "We Mexicans are used to little things like this." The next time, however, he wore new khaki trousers tucked into new boots; and where those first new boots went many other pairs of boots followed.

One of Harrar's major accomplishments was his ability to inspire many bright young Mexicans to follow where he led—into heat and dirt and dust and grime, when that was necessary to help improve wheat or whatever else grew in the earth from which 75 percent of the Mexicans made their living.

In the spring and summer of 1943 the Harrar team collected seed of many wheat varieties for fall plantings, prepared land for experimentation at Chapingo, studied the wheats in eight of the 18 uniform rust nurseries, and collected many samples of stem rust to be used for identifying physiologic races and mapping their geographic distribution.

The Wheat Revolution Gains Momentum

FIRING THE FIRST BIG GUN

The first big gun of the wheat revolution was fired in November, 1943. It was aimed at stem rust, because "in the case of the rusts, resistant varieties are the only answer," as Harrar put it. Accordingly, some 700 native and imported varieties and selections were planted at Chapingo and artificially inoculated with local races of stem rust to assure a good test of varietal resistance. Smaller plantings were made at two other places, in the states of Mexico and Puebla. In June, 1944, about 500 survivors of this first test were planted for their second trial, with the addition of a considerable number of varieties that were new to Mexico.

Harrar and his colleagues spent long hours examining each variety or line, saving seed from those that were good enough to test further and discarding those that had no special virtue.

THE FIRST YIELD TESTS

To determine the yielding ability of the 100 best-looking wheats selected during 1943 and 1944, they were planted in two separate fields at Chapingo in December, 1944. As there were three three-row plots of each variety in each field, there were 1,800 individual rows to study, more than five miles long if placed end to end. Tedious and painstaking work this was, not glamorous, but highly fruitful because it established a base for further operations.

Fortunately, there was enough stem rust in the 1944–1945 season to distinguish between rust-resistant and susceptible varieties but not enough to reduce yields. Consequently, the varieties could be grouped according to time of ripening, rust resistance, and inherent yielding ability. Many Mexican varieties ripened early, by May 12, but all were susceptible to stem rust; most of the foreign varieties ripened late, about May 30, but were resistant to stem rust. Yields ranged from 15 to 38 bushels an acre. The six highest yielders were susceptible to rust, and only three of the 13 that yielded more than 30 bushels were resistant. Evidently, very few lines or varieties combined earliness, stem-rust resistance, and inherent yielding ability. Twenty of the best, however, were selected for further use, and Borlaug used them well.

BORLAUG TAKES COMMAND

The first phase of the wheat revolution was over. Harrar had clarified numerous problems, evaluated hundreds of wheat varieties, laid the basis for varietal improvement by selection and hybridization, initiated projects on soil fertility, and found a fine group of young Mexicans—José Rodríguez, Leonel Robles, Benjamín Ortega, and José Guevara—to help do the jobs ahead. Wellhausen, in charge of corn improvement, had also helped by word and by deed. But expanding needs required additional personnel, and in October, 1944, Harrar brought to Mexico Dr. Norman E. Borlaug, farm boy, college wrestler, forester, plant pathologist, and future genius of the far-reaching wheat revolution.

Borlaug immediately started helping in the wheat program and was put in command of it in March, 1945. He had not been trained as a wheat specialist, but he had been well educated as a biologist. Borlaug and wheat seemed destined for each other. Or, possibly, it was the Mexican people who destined Borlaug for wheat. He was wont to say: "On a job like this our science has to be good, but it has to be good for something; it has to help put bread into the bellies of hungry Mexicans." And he knew that it would take teamwork to furnish the bread quickly. As he expressed it: "The wheat program has to be a package deal. We can't get anywhere if we split it up into a lot of splinter programs. And we can't wander off on a lot of scientific sideshows or go chasing academic butterflies; we have to do first things first."

And Borlaug did things. Dedicating himself to the cause of more bread for more Mexicans, he lived with wheat and absorbed a vast knowledge about it by fraternizing with thousands of kinds, from the seedbed to the seedbin. Work was not just a word to him; it became a code of honor. If genius is "an infinite capacity for taking pains," Borlaug had it. And so he worked day in and day out, from sunup to sundown, in the heat and dust and wind and rain—always in the fields and experimental plots. Once, after a hard day's drive, nearing a town where there was an experiment station, Borlaug said, "How about going over and taking a quick look at the wheat plots?" His companion asked, somewhat testily, "Tonight? It's way after midnight; we can't see wheats now." The rebuttal came quickly: "There's a good moon; we could at least see what the plots look like."

Borlaug's fanatical devotion to wheat paid big dividends. Many of his young Mexican associates caught the "wheat fever" from him, and together they carried the wheat revolution to a successful conclusion.

Creating New Mexican Wheats for Mexico

MANY WERE TRIED, BUT FEW WERE CHOSEN

It was evident by the spring of 1945 that there was no perfect wheat for Mexico among the hundreds of reselections from kinds that had been tested. But there were two rays of hope: five reselections from imported lines were enough better than the varieties commonly grown to justify the expectation that they might be useful until still better varieties could be produced by the slower process of hybridization; also, five Mexican varieties and a dozen imported ones apparently had the parental stuff to make good hybrids. Accordingly, the wheat group started to convert the reselections into varieties as quickly as possible; and they crossed the promising parents in 38 different combinations. Better wheats for Mexico were on the way.

Four of the five reselected lines chosen as potential varieties performed so well in extensive regional tests that they were multiplied, christened, and distributed to farmers in the fall of 1948. These are the pertinent data regarding them:

Varietal name	Material from which selected[2]	Type of resistance to stem rust
Supremo	McFadden hybrids	Hope
Frontera	McFadden hybrids	Hope
Kenya Rojo	Burton lines	Kenya
Kenya Blanco	Burton lines	Kenya

Although these four new varieties were good wheats in general, their outstanding virtue was resistance to stem rust.

The keystone in the Hope-type resistance was the variety Hope, which McFadden had produced by crossing Marquis, an excellent spring wheat, with Yaroslav emmer, a sort of cousin of true wheats. McFadden likened a wide cross such as this to a nickel cigar "because only one in a thousand is worth a nickel." Although worth little as a commercial wheat, Hope had been so resistant to stem rust in the northern United States that shortly after it was first released as a variety in 1927, some seedsmen had offered a dollar for every rust pustule that could be found on it; and as a parent it had transmitted its presumably universal rust resistance to a number of good commercial spring-wheat varieties. McFadden himself had crossed it extensively with other wheats, principally of the Mediterranean winter-wheat group, and had obtained a very numerous and diverse hybrid progeny, among them the progenitors of Supremo and Frontera.

The Kenya-type resistance may have been derived from *Triticum turgidum,* poulard wheats. From an extensive hybridization program in Kenya an English plant breeder, Burton, had obtained a number of stem-rust resistant varieties and lines, but he was not sure of their parentage because a fire had destroyed his records and burned the family trees of his wheats.

Mexico now had four superior varieties of wheat, each adapted to certain areas, and all resistant to stem rust. But Supremo and Frontera had one type of rust resistance, the Hope type, and the two Kenyas had another, the Kenya type. This later proved to be valuable insurance.

Supremo and Company gave a tremendous boost to wheat pro-

[2] The "McFadden hybrids" had been obtained directly from E. S. McFadden of the U.S. Department of Agriculture and the Texas Experiment Station at the suggestion of Dr. Mangelsdorf, who had been vice director of the Texas station. The "Burton lines" came from Kenya, East Africa, one by way of Minnesota and the other by way of Australia and Minnesota.

duction. For the first time Mexico had good bread-wheats that defied stem rust and yielded well when rust destroyed the older varieties. And for the first time Mexicans felt safe in growing wheat during the summer rainy season. The wheat boom caused some misgivings, however. As an experienced observer wrote in 1949: "The spectacular performance of the new wheats has created enthusiasm among Mexicans which is almost frightening because of danger of disillusionment."

Fear of disillusionment was natural enough, for stem rust was a very shifty enemy that had wrecked the career of many a wheat variety by attacking it with physiologic races that were unborn or unknown while the variety was in the process of creation or in the early flush of its success on millions of acres in farmers' fields. Would Supremo and Company escape a similar fate? Nobody knew, but Borlaug and his wheat group took no chances. They knew better than to rely completely on these four varieties in so diverse a country as Mexico and in the face of so resourceful an enemy as stem rust. And so they were pushing the development of still better varieties in the hybridization program.

NEW VARIETIES IN CREATION BY HYBRIDIZATION

In the hybridization program, the first crosses were made in April, 1945, and by the end of 1947 the number of combinations had reached 1,500; consequently the telling of what begat what would run into as many words as the tales of the ancient kings. What came out of these combinations is more important practically than what went into them, but what went into them is important scientifically and practically because good parents are known by their progeny.

New varieties can be created by nature in a haphazard way or by man in a scientific way. When different kinds of wheat grow close together, the wind may occasionally carry pollen from one kind to the ovaries of another kind, and the seed that results from fertilization has some of the genes, the units of heredity, from both kinds. This, then, is a natural cross, and chance determines what crosses with what. When a scientist makes a cross, he eliminates chance; he chooses the parents. He removes the stamens or male organs from the young flowers of one parental variety, A, to prevent self-fertilization, then takes ripe pollen from parental variety B, places it directly on the ovaries of variety A, and then protects them against wind-carried pollen by covering the heads with "pollinating bags" so that he can be sure of the parentage of the resulting hybrid seed. He then has a hybrid (A × B), but his work has just begun when the hybrid seed is ripe.

When hybrid seed is planted, a first-generation hybrid plant grows from it, but it may not show that it is a hybrid; it may look like one of the parents. When its seed is planted to produce second-generation plants, however, and their seed is planted to produce third-generation plants, many different types may appear because of "hybrid segregation." Then the breeder has the job of selecting good plants and discarding poor ones. He plants seeds of the good plants and thus establishes hybrid lines for further testing. He again selects the best and keeps on saving and discarding until the lines settle down and stop their segregating. Then he has the job of increasing the seed of the best lines and testing them on a larger scale in various regions. The best lines are then given a varietal name. Where only one generation can be grown each year, it takes about ten years to create and establish a new variety. Where two generations can be grown each year, as in Mexico, the time can be shortened. And it was shortened in Mexico.

Among the Mexican varieties that looked like good parents were Marroquí, Mentana, Aguilera, Candeal, and Pelon Colorado; among the foreign ones were Newthatch, Kenya, Regent, Renown, as well as several others. Contrasting characters in the two groups are illustrated by Marroquí and Newthatch:

Characters	Marroquí	Newthatch
1. Adaptation to Bajío region	Good	Poor
2. Yielding ability	Good	Poor
3. Ripening class	Early	Late
4. Shattering (dropping of seed)	Susceptible	Resistant
5. Reaction to stem rust	Susceptible	Resistant[3]
6. Reaction to stinking smut	Susceptible	Resistant
7. Quality of flour	Fair	Excellent

[3] Newthatch, produced jointly by the University of Minnesota and the U.S. Department of Agriculture, resulted from a series of crosses, double crosses, and backcrosses involving Marquis, a spring bread-wheat; Kanred, a winter bread-wheat; Iumillo, a durum; and McFadden's Hope. Combining several types of resistance, including the Kanred type, the Hope type, and a generalized type derived from Iumillo, it was one of the most resistant of all known spring bread-wheats to stem rust, with its special "Newthatch-type" resistance.

The aim in crossing these two varieties was to produce a hybrid variety with characters 1, 2, and 3 from the Marroquí parent and 4, 5, 6, and 7 from Newthatch. Other varieties were crossed with the same general kinds of objectives.

It usually is about ten years from the breeding nursery to the breadbox, but Borlaug took the shortest way; he grew two generations a year—heresy then, but accepted practice now. By the end of 1949, therefore, he could write: "In El Yaqui, La Laguna, the Bajío, and Chapingo, the four principal wheat regions of Mexico, seed was sown for increase of the best lines that resulted from the crosses made in Chapingo in 1945. . . . In the summer of 1949 seed of four new varieties was increased for the second time, in order that they may be available to farmers as soon as possible."

THE FIRST VARIETIES PRODUCED BY HYBRIDIZATION

The four pioneer hybrid varieties were Yaqui, Nazas, and Chapingo, from Marroquí × Newthatch crosses; and Kentana, from a Kenya × Mentana cross. All were early-ripening spring wheats—resistant to lodging and shattering; resistant to stem rust, yellow rust, and certain other diseases; high-yielding; and with red grain of acceptable milling and baking qualities. Yaqui was recommended for the Yaqui Valley and the other Pacific Coast areas; Nazas for the Laguna; Chapingo for the Mesa Central; and Kentana for the Pacific coastal area, the Bajío, the Mesa Central, and northern Coahuila.

Mexico now had eight superior Mexican-made varieties, four each from the selection and the hybridization programs. But they were not yet perfect wheats, and Borlaug was a perfectionist. So he kept on importing, crossing, recrossing, and backcrossing lines and varieties. The number of crosses soon reached 2,000, and there were 50,000 varieties and hybrid lines in the breeding nursery.

VICTORY ALMOST IN SIGHT

By 1951 it looked as if the wheat revolution was almost won. The new varieties constituted 70 percent of the total wheat acreage, farmers were beginning to fertilize their fields, yields were increasing, acreage was expanding on the rich lands of the Pacific Northwest, the acreage of summer wheat was increasing in the high valleys of the Mesa Central, and stem rust seemed under control. But then the rust made a terrific counterattack.

STEM RUST FIGHTS BACK

Race 15B of wheat stem rust, found occasionally in small quantities near barberry in northern United States since 1938, suddenly exploded in the United States and southern Canada in the summer of 1950 and ruined late fields of varieties that had been almost immune from rust for more than a decade. High winds carried race 15B into Mexico in the fall of 1950; it survived the winter on fall-sown wheat in a few places, then multiplied fast on spring-sown wheat in the exceptionally wet summer of 1951, and ruined late-sown fields of Supremo and Chapingo that had promised 40 bushels an acre.

Race 15B had smashed the Hope and the Newthatch types of resistance, but Kentana 48 and Lerma 50 were ready to fill the breach with their Kenya-type resistance. Both had resulted from crosses between Mentana and Kenya Rojo.

The wisdom of the broad and diverse breeding program was highlighted in the summer of 1951. Some 60,000 varieties and lines from the Mexican program and another 6,000 from the World Wheat Collection of the United States Department of Agriculture were grown and evaluated at Chapingo and three other places in three Mexican states. In this vast test, only four varieties grown commercially in North America were resistant to stem rust, and all were Mexican made: Kentana 48, Lerma 50, Kenya Rojo, and Kenya Blanco. With their Kenya-type resistance, these varieties were checkmating race 15B in Mexico.

But in the summer of 1953 race 139, an unexpected enemy, struck them down. Known for 20 years in the United States, this race had been rare and unimportant practically, although it had excited curiosity because of its exceptionally weak parasitism and its persistence in minute quantities in northern Mexico. But it now demonstrated far more strength than it had shown previously; it knocked out varieties that the generally stronger race 15B could not hurt. Race 139 (and possibly the closely related 49) had the weapons for breaking through the Kenya-type resistance, just as 15B had the weapons for breaking through the Hope-type and Newthatch-type resistance.

Taking one variety to represent each resistance group, then, here was the situation: Kentana 48 had the Kenya-type defense against race 15B but none against 139; Yaqui 48 had the Hope- and New-thatch-type defense against race 139 but none against 15B. What to do was clear: cross Kentana and Yaqui to unite their defenses. And the wheat group had already done it, thus producing the varieties Chapingo 52, Chapingo 53, Bajío, and Mexe with resistance both to 15B and 139 and to other known Mexican races.

But stem rust was not yet finished. Races 29 and 48, long known in certain areas of the United States but not in Mexico, made threatening gestures in 1953, provoking Borlaug to write in 1954: "The varieties now being grown commercially must be replaced by newer varieties with different types of stem rust resistance. This is necessitated by three major changes in rust races which have occurred since 1950. Races 15B, 49, and 139, and 29 and 48 are serious threats to the present commercial varieties. . . . Varieties resistant to some or all of these new races, as well as to the races formerly prevalent, have been developed by the cooperative program." He then listed as promising new varieties in seed increase plots the four derived from Yaqui × Kentana and seven others of diverse parentage. He concluded: "The constant shifting in populations of stem rust races illustrates the necessity of a continuous breeding program to combat this parasite which is constantly a threat to the wheat crop." By 1957, however, he could write: "Despite two changes in stem rust races since 1950 the breeding program has successfully kept pace with stem rust by having new resistant varieties available when the changes occurred."

And thus it has been. Between 1950 and 1960 a group of virulent races almost completely replaced a relatively weak group in central Mexico. But the population of wheat varieties had been changed almost completely also, as a succession of rust-resistant varieties replaced the susceptible *criollos,* native varieties. Had this not been true, stem rust would have caused a catastrophe in 1959. What would have happened if resistant varieties had not replaced the criollos is shown by what did happen to Coquillo, a criollo variety that a few farmers still grew; stem rust simply annihilated it. And what would have happened if still better varieties had not replaced the early improved ones is shown by what did happen to Kentana 48, which had held the line against race 15B but was retired when it could not resist races 139, 29, and 48. The few farmers who persisted in growing Kentana despite its official retirement watched sadly while stem rust ruined their fields in 1959.

Rust-resistant varieties have not completely thwarted stem rust in Mexico, but they have blunted its killing edge. Farmers no longer ask, "Why spend money to fertilize wheat, only to see it ruined by stem rust?" Improved varieties gave fertilizers their chance to help win the wheat revolution.

Efforts to Increase Soil Fertility

The campaigns for varietal improvement and soil improvement went hand in hand. After preliminary experiments by his predecessors, Dr. John Pitner, in charge of soils work in the Office of Special Studies from 1947 to 1954, demonstrated the great value of commercial fertilizers for wheat in certain areas. In 1952 he entrusted the wheat work to Dr. Reggie Laird, who was given charge of all soils work when Pitner resigned in 1954.

Laird and his associates showed that nitrogen was a miracle food for wheat in many areas and that phosphorus often was a strong booster. In typical experiments on properly irrigated soils in the Bajío, the addition of 125 pounds of nitrogen an acre raised yields more than four-fold, from nine bushels an acre without nitrogen to 40 with it. Dry soils yielded only eight bushels an acre without nitrogen and 20 bushels with it; and when phosphorus was added also, yields often were increased five- or six-fold. By 1954 many farmers were getting 45 to 60 bushels an acre from lands that had given them six to 10 bushels before they started fertilizing.

Borlaug could write in 1956: "Soil fertility studies . . . have firmly demonstrated the soundness of using chemical fertilizers to increase wheat yields. Experimental work by the Soils Section of the Office of Special Studies has established the proper formulas and rates of fertilization for wheat on most of the major soil types in the most important wheat-producing areas of the Republic. It has also led to modifications in planting and irrigation methods in some areas and in this way too has contributed to increased yields at lower costs." And so it was. The average national yield of wheat was 20 bushels an acre in 1956, contrasted with less than 12 bushels 10 years previously, even though most farmers were using only half the recommended amount of fertilizer and many were not yet using any.

The wheat revolution was succeeding. For more than a decade Borlaug and his staff had been weaving the manifold results of cooperative experimentation into a pattern of procedures for producing three ears of wheat where only one had grown before. And they did it so well that Mexico gained her wheat independence in 1956.

Wheat Independence and Its Problems

Mexico became independent of foreign wheat for the first time in 1956. That year she produced about 40 million bushels, enough to satisfy market demands with some to spare. Early-ripening, rust-resistant varieties had made it possible to expand the acreage of the winter crop in the fertile areas of the Pacific Northwest and of a summer crop in certain mountain valleys of Central Mexico. Better varieties, better farming methods, and better soil fertilization had almost doubled the average yield in northern and central Mexico. Improved varieties had suppressed stem rust, and improved soil had raised the acre yields of the improved varieties; the fight against stem rust and the fight for soil fertility had been largely won. But victory was not complete.

Independence brought new problems in its wake, as it so often does. Because wheat plants tend to lodge on rich soil, it became increasingly important to develop varieties that could stand up while taking the richer nourishment from the progressively better-fertilized soils. And as combine machines were replacing the hand sickle, there was increased need for nonshattering varieties that would hold the kernels until they were ripe enough for the mechanized harvesting-threshing operation. Moreover, the Mexican-made wheats had low "baking strength," which formerly had been raised by blending with the stronger imported wheats. Now that bakers were using flour from all-Mexican wheat, however, milling and baking quality assumed new importance.

To shorten and strengthen the stems had been one objective of the breeding program, but it became a major one in response to greater need and desire. The increased use of fertilizer created the need for stiff-straw varieties that could remain erect while utilizing it, and it created the desire to convert as much of the fertilizer energy as possible into grain instead of wasting it in building more straw than was needed or wanted. Accordingly, the wheat group set out to create varieties with long heads containing many kernels and with short, stiff straw to support them properly. They accomplished their purpose by crossing Japanese dwarf varieties with the best Mexican-made varieties, thus combining the best characters of both groups of parents. The varieties Sonora 63, Sonora 64, and others recently developed have captured the fields and converted Mexico into a country of superior "semidwarf wheats" that resist lodging and shattering. They hold their heads up off the ground, and the heads hold the kernels tight to keep them from falling to the ground.

Bread-making quality is continually improving also. A well-staffed modern "Quality Laboratory" at Chapingo tests the quality of hybrid lines early in their careers; those that do not make good bread are eliminated and those that do are saved, provided they survive the rigid rust test in the greenhouse. Thus, all lines that are saved for further testing have passed stiff qualifying tests as rust-resisters and as good bread-makers.

In 1958 Mexico became independent in respect to wheat scientists as she had become independent in respect to wheat production in 1956. Young Mexicans had participated effectively since the beginning; now some of them had finished their apprenticeship, obtained their doctorates, and earned the dignity and rights of independent scientists. Borlaug was their advocate as he had been their guide. "Give the young fellows a chance" was part of his basic code; and when he said, "Nacho could run this wheat program as well as I can," he acted accordingly. He recommended Nacho for the job, and Nacho—Dr. Ignacio Narváez—got it.

These young Mexicans and their associates began running the wheat program and running it well. Borlaug worked himself out of one job and worked "his boys" into it; but he is still in Mexico, cooperating with them and operating the Foundation's international wheat program (which is described in Chapter 16).

Past, Present, and Future

While trying to live again in the Mexican wheat fields of 1943, it was necessary to write: "Wheat has to struggle so hard for existence in most of Mexico that it can yield only 5 to 8 bushels an acre on the poorer soils and seldom more than 15 bushels on the better soils." But that referred to the spring of 1943. In the spring of 1963,[4] it was "85,000 tons more wheat this year—the 1962–63 harvest will be a million and a half tons," according to front-page headlines in the May 20, 1963, edition of *Excelsior,* a leading Mexico City newspaper. This article was based on a news release by Ing. Emilio Gutiérrez Roldán, in charge of the Ministry of Agriculture's seed multiplication and distribution service. According to later estimates, the production actually was 1.8 million tons—about 66 million bushels. According to Roldán and others, higher acre yields due to better varieties and better methods accounted for this record-breaking crop.

Higher yields per acre! Vitally important this is for countries that have relatively few arable acres, and highly important for all countries that care anything about efficiency in land use.

"The Mexican wheat revolution" may sound hyperbolic, but may those who think so ponder the facts and figures.[5] In 1943 wheat yielded 11.5 bushels an acre. In 1963 it yielded 88 bushels an acre at Santo Domingo, Baja California; 50 to 75 bushels near Ciudad Obregón, Sonora; and 50 to 60 bushels in the Bajío, the one-time breadbasket of Mexico that could not fill the basket with bread because of worn-out soils and low yields of 8 to 15 bushels an acre 10 years before. The average yield in 1963 was about 30 bushels an acre, almost three times that in 1943. There is a new and full breadbasket in Mexico. The Bajío still is doing its share, but its share has shrunk, for two thirds of the wheat is now produced in the Pacific Northwest instead of in central and northern Mexico, as it used to be. The dream of expanding the acreage in that fertile area by reducing the rust hazard has come true. And the dream of increasing acre yields in the Bajío by means of soil enrichment has come true.

Lest we forget, however, there always is danger that stem rust or other insidious parasites may make sneak attacks with new or secret

[4] This chapter was written in the spring of 1963 and is based on data then available, as the original intention was to measure the progress of twenty years.

[5] Through Dr. Theodore Schultz of the University of Chicago, N. Ardito Barletta, Jr., has authorized publication of the following statement from his study "Cost and Social Return to Agricultural Research in Mexico": "The financial value of Mexico's increased wheat and corn production that has been contributed by research is the equivalent of about 400 percent annual interest or return on the total amount of money spent for all research in the cooperative program from 1943 to 1962. The returns to the wheat program alone, resulting from comparing wheat research expenditures and benefits, are at least 800 percent per year."

weapons. Indeed, stem rust races 11, 32, 87 and a few other snipers recently have been taking pot-shots at some of the newest and best wheat varieties. But the new generation of Mexican scientists are watching with trained and knowing eyes and are preparing to thwart major attacks. They will do it if it can be done; they know that they must fight constantly to preserve past gains and make future progress. And they know how to fight intelligently, for they became seasoned veterans while helping to win the wheat revolution.

The Mexican wheat revolution may not have been "a miracle of science," but it was a tremendous scientific and educational accomplishment. Its most conspicuous feature, of course, was its conspicuous success. And it was conspicuously successful because those who wrought the revolution were extraordinary men who worked together as an extraordinary team. To them wheat was not just *Triticum aestivum;* it was bread for hungry Mexicans. Wheat improvement was their purpose, more bread was their ideal, devotion to the cause became their tradition, and hard work became a habit.

The "wheat boys" worked as only zealots can work. They had to work hard and they had to work intelligently to accomplish what they did. They had to study thousands of kinds of wheats and cross them in thousands of combinations, then study and select the best of thousands of hybrid lines. In a single season, they made 6,000 individual crosses, and during each of many years they studied the performance of 40,000 varieties and lines at several places, a total of 400 miles of wheat plants, a few inches apart in the rows. And they scrutinized these plants carefully, for "the kernels in some of those plants may be gold nuggets; sure, some of them are only gold-plated, and many are only brass, but we have to find all of the gold ones and save them, because a few gold nuggets can make a lot more bread for Mexico," as Borlaug said. And they did find a lot of the gold nuggets; they created and distributed more than 75 new varieties, each of which contributed its share to the revolution in wheat production.

It took scientific brains to understand the complex composition and behavior of wheat, the complex composition and behavior of hundreds of kinds of enemies of wheat, and the intricate interrelationships between wheat and the soils in which it grows. And it took practical intelligence and ingenuity to piece together hundreds of bits of information into coherent procedures for producing more and better wheat.

The results of the Mexican wheat revolution may not be as spectacular as shots into space, but to millions of human beings they bring a better life. And simple human beings do not yet disdain simple human values, even though they may not fully understand how those values were created. The values to Mexico are fairly obvious;[6] those beyond her borders are discussed in Chapters 13 and 16.

[6] Among the Mexican scientists who participated in the wheat program and got some of their education in it are: Aristeo Acosta, Ph.D.; Arnoldo Amaya, Ing. Agr.; Alfredo Campos, Ph.D.; Federico Castilla Chacón, Ing. Agr.; Genaro Cruz, Ing. Agr.; Silvestre Espino, M.S.; Alfredo García, Ing. Agr.; José Guevara, Ph.D.; Antonio Marino, M.S.; Rodolfo Moreno, Ing. Agr.; Ignacio Narváez, Ph.D.; Manuel Navarro, M.S.; Benjamín Ortega, M.S.; Jacobo Ortega, Ph.D.; Leonel Robles, M.S.; José Rodríguez, M.S.; Ricardo Rodríguez, Ing. Agr.; Gregorio Vázquez, M.S.; and Evangelina Villegas, M.S. Those who contributed especially to soil improvement were: Nicolás Sánchez, Ph.D.; Enrique Ortega, Ph.D.; Roberto Núñez, M.S.; and Ramón Hernández.

Chapter 6

Beans

Improving the Meat of the Poorer Mexicans

In 1941 beans of various kinds represented—as they still do—the principal source of protein in the Mexican diet. Millions of Mexicans were subsisting day after day, year after year on a diet of corn, beans, and chili peppers, supplemented at times by squashes and peanuts but only rarely by food of animal origin: milk, meat, eggs, and the like. It was largely because the national diet was essentially a vegetarian one that Mexico could even begin to support so large a population on so little agricultural land. Anthropologists estimate that a given amount of land can support roughly ten times as many vegetarians as meat-eaters. This figure may be a bit too high but not by a wide margin; we know that it takes roughly ten pounds of feed to produce a pound of beef, slightly less a pound of pork, and much less to produce a pound of broilers, the cheapest of meats in terms of transforming feed for animals into food for human beings.

Recognizing the role of beans in the Mexican diet and recognizing, too, that beans represented Mexico's second most important crop in terms of acreage devoted to them, the Survey Commission recommended that high priority be given to bean improvement both through breeding and through the control of diseases and insect pests.

Tradition Proves to Have a Scientific Basis

Extensive researches have shown that an adequate diet must contain carbohydrates, fats, proteins, minerals, and vitamins. The first three constituents are sometimes called "fuel" or "caloric" constituents because their value can be measured largely, although by no means entirely, in terms of calories. The last two are called "protective" constituents because while they have little or no fuel value they are quite essential, sometimes in exceedingly minute quantities, to various metabolic processes that protect health and well-being.

It turns out that beans and corn complement each other almost perfectly with respect to certain of the building blocks of proteins —amino acids—that the body cannot produce for itself but must obtain from foods consumed. For best results, these "dietary essential" amino acids, eight in number, should be available in the diet each day; a deficiency incurred in one day is not made up completely by a surplus consumed sometime later.

In the amino acids tryptophane and lysine, corn is low whereas beans are medium and high, respectively; in threonine, valine, and methionine, beans are low and corn is medium, high, and medium. Because, furthermore, beans are high in total proteins, a diet of beans and corn is adequate in both quantity and quality so far as proteins are concerned.

This complementation of beans and corn goes further: it involves also the minerals and vitamins. Beans are an excellent source of two important minerals, phosphorus and iron, in which corn is low. Beans can also remedy corn's notorious deficiency in the vitamins riboflavin and nicotinic acid, lack of which has been responsible for pellagra in certain cultural groups. In Mexico, pellagra is almost unknown.

How the Mexican Indians, with no knowledge of chemistry, discovered that beans and corn together provide an adequate diet is still a mystery; but somehow they did and they did it thousands of years ago. The evidence comes from the refuse excavated in once-inhabited caves in northeastern and southern Mexico. In Tamaulipas in the northeast, runner beans, *Phaseolus coccineus*, probably wild, were found in zones dated at 7000–5000 B.C., and cultivated kidney beans, *P. vulgaris*, in zones dated at 5000–3000 B.C. But an agriculture capable of furnishing an adequate and balanced diet did not make its appearance until cultivated corn was added to the complex in the period 1400–500 B.C.

In southern Mexico, in caves in the Valley of Tehuacán, wild corn occurred in the zone dated at 7200–5200 B.C., while in the next period, 5200–3400 B.C., there were remains of an early form of cultivated corn and the tepary bean, *P. acutifolius.* Here, a full-fledged agriculture did not come into existence until the period 1500–900 B.C., when a productive corn, resulting from hybridization of the early form with its wild relative, Tripsacum, became part of a complex that included the common bean, *P. vulgaris,* and the summer squash or pumpkin. The squashes were a valuable addition for two reasons: they provided an increase in calories, and in their edible seeds they contributed an increment of fat, in which component a diet of corn and beans alone is barely adequate.

This complex of corn, beans, and squashes spread out from Mexico far and wide and became the basis of virtually all prehistoric Indian agriculture in all parts of America. It formed the nutritional foundation of the prehistoric civilizations of the Western Hemisphere: the Inca of South America and the Maya and Aztec of Middle America and Mexico. It was a highly successful complex, not only because it was adequate in both quantity and quality, but also because it made efficient use of the land, especially for a people who lacked draft animals to perform the various tillage operations. The beans climbed and twined on the stalks of corn, exposing their leaves to the sun without drastically shading the leaves of the corn plants; and the squash vines spread out over the ground between the hills of corn, choking out weeds.

The abundance of food produced by this agricultural complex was responsible for tremendous increases in population in Mexico during prehistoric times. To take one example, the Valley of Tehuacán, which at 7200 B.C. supported not more than three wandering microbands of four to eight people each, living a hunting and food-gathering life, had an estimated population of over 100,000 people when the Spaniards arrived in the sixteenth century.

Varietal Improvement Gets under Way

The Mexican Ministry of Agriculture and The Rockefeller Foundation were agreed that bean improvement would have to include control of diseases and insect pests and the development of better varieties. Accordingly, as soon as possible after the initiation of the cooperative program, pathologists and entomologists began studying the problems. The insect work, particularly, got off to a good start with the appointment of John McKelvey to the staff in 1945. Even before this, Wellhausen, the geneticist, and his assistants had begun collecting beans throughout Mexico in conjunction with their corn-collecting trips.

MANY KINDS OF BEANS

There is a great diversity of beans in Mexico with respect both to species and to varieties. The predominating species is *Phaseolus vulgaris,* which is grown for string beans and shell beans in the United States and also includes kidney beans, navy beans, and other types. Ranking second in Mexico is the runner bean, *P. coccineus;* the scarlet runner is used in the United States as an ornamental for its brilliant scarlet flowers. These two species, *P. vulgaris* and *P. coccineus,* together constitute the Mexican *frijol.* Grown to a somewhat lesser extent is the lima bean, *P. lunatus.* The tepary bean, already mentioned as one of the earliest to be domesticated in Mexico, has now almost disappeared, although it is still grown by Indians in the southwestern United States, to which region it spread in prehistoric times.

Also known as "beans," although they belong to other botanical genera, are the horse or broad bean (*haba* in Spanish), *Vicia faba,* an Old World legume introduced into Mexico after the Conquest; the chickpea, *garbanzo,* another Old World legume, which is especially relished by Mexicans in a soup, *sopa de garbanzo;* and finally the soybean, *Soya max,* a most versatile legume about which more will be said in Chapter 7.

The bewildering diversity of varieties and forms of beans in Mexico is botanical testimony to their long history of domestication. In 1953, recognizing the need for some kind of classification of the extensive collections of Mexican beans, the Foundation employed George F. Freytag, then a doctoral candidate at Washington University, for two years to study the taxonomic relationships within the genus *Phaseolus.* Freytag concluded that the common bean, *P. vulgaris,* and an intermediate type, *P. multiflorus,* are closely related and have both come from hybridization of the true runner bean, *P. coccineus,* with two ancient and as yet undescribed native species of *Phaseolus.* There are still wild beans in Mexico, indeed, several kinds. One form, growing on the slopes of an extinct volcano in the State of Colima, has tiny speckled seeds quite similar in shape to modern cultivated beans but much smaller, a miniature version of certain cultivated varieties. These wild beans can be hybridized with their cultivated counterparts, but such hybrids are still to be intensively studied to determine their part, if any, in the ancestry of domesticated beans. In the meantime, Freytag's classification of the cultivated beans was helpful to the breeders in planning their improvement work.

The Mexican frijol comes in many varieties, and the Mexican consumer makes distinctions among these on the basis of color, flavor, and cooking characteristics. Among the obvious color types are the Canario (yellow), Negro (black), Bayo (tan), and Pinto (spotted). Mexicans living at higher altitudes tend to prefer the relatively quick-cooking Canario, even though it is less productive and contains less protein than the Negro, the type preferred in the tropics where it is recognized as *mas fuerte,* or "stronger."

COLLECTING AND TESTING VARIETIES

An obvious first step in any crop improvement program is to take an inventory of the breeding material available. Collections are assembled from all parts of the country and grown under controlled conditions for comparison of their productiveness, disease resistance, and other characteristics.

During the first active year of the cooperative program, 392 samples of beans were collected from 20 different states in Mexico and others were imported from Colombia, Cuba, and the United States. In the summer of 1944 these were all grown in the experimental field at Chapingo, adjoining the National School of Agriculture. Each sample was classified with respect to growth habit: whether bush type, low and spreading; pole type, or climbing; or intermediate between these types. In addition, the samples were scored for their reaction to the two most prevalent diseases, rust and anthracnose.

Some samples proved to be quite resistant to rust while others were wiped out; and the same was true in the case of anthracnose. The varieties from the United States and Colombia did poorly, an indication at this early stage that bean improvement in Mexico, like corn improvement, would probably have to rely strongly on selection within Mexican varieties and hybridization between them. It was therefore encouraging to find that great variation existed among the Mexican samples, not only in degree of resistance to various diseases but also in yielding ability. Moreover, this variation occurred both between samples from different parts of the country and within single samples. This latter observation made it clear that few, if any, of the Mexican varieties were "pure."

PURIFYING MIXED VARIETIES

The next step was to choose from the 392 samples those which seemed, on the basis of disease resistance and yield, the most worthy of increase for possible distribution to farmers. In order to "purify" these, at least three individual plants were selected from each sample.

The procedure known as "pure-line selection" is based on the results of experiments on selection conducted by the Danish botanist, Wilhelm Ludwig Johannsen, and published in 1903. Johannsen originally thought it might be possible to control heredity through the selection in successive generations of extreme variation. He tested the possibility by selecting unusually large and unusually small beans and growing them for several generations. Although selection apparently was effective in the first generation, it had no effect in subsequent ones. He concluded that in self-pollinated plants like the bean the progeny of a single plant represents a "pure line" in which all individuals are genetically identical and the observable variation is environmental in origin. Johannsen postulated that an unselected race like the ordinary garden bean, with which he had started his experiments, was a mixture of pure lines that differed among themselves in many characteristics but were each one genetically uniform. This pure-line theory has been widely applied to the improvement of cereals and other self-pollinated plants. Many of the varieties of wheat, oats, barley, rice, sorghum, and flax grown in the world today are the result of sorting out pure lines in mixed agricultural races and identifying and multiplying the superior ones.

The first year's work with the Mexican beans had shown that each of the samples collected from various regions was mixed. Whether these mixtures were the product of previous mutations or of hybridization or of the careless mechanical mixing of one race with another was of no particular importance. The important point was that each sample could be presumed to be a mixture of pure lines. It was therefore necessary only to save the seeds from individual plants in order to sort out these lines and propagate them.

From the 1944 tests a total of 706 individual plants were selected. In 1945 all of these were grown at Chapingo and at three other locations—Cortazar, Aguascalientes, and Briseñas—in Mexico's most important agricultural region, the Bajío. Also grown at these four stations were the countrywide collections, which by now had grown to 492 in number. The tests at the three Bajío stations were failures for various reasons, but the test at Chapingo was highly successful in showing, even more convincingly than had the preliminary test in 1944, that great variation existed among the samples and that some were quite promising with respect to yield. At this time, the average yield in Mexico's good bean-growing areas was about 500 kilograms per hectare. The 30 most promising collections in the 1945 test yielded from 1,628 kilograms, the lowest, to 3,235 kilograms—or three to six times the then average yield. While part of this increase was obviously due to improved cultural practices, a substantial part could be attributed to inherent characteristics, including built-in yielding potentiality and resistance to certain diseases.

Among the pure lines, selected from individual collections, variation in yielding ability was not so great as in the case of the countrywide collections, but still it was large enough to suggest that substantial progress could be made through the method of pure-line selection. In some collections, the highest-yielding pure line produced almost twice as much as the lowest yielder.

The results of these first two years of work with beans laid the basis for continuing along these lines: Collect beans all over Mexico wherever they are grown; compare them in controlled experiments for resistance to disease, productiveness, and other characteristics; select the best performers for prompt increase; purify the best performers to improve their productiveness and render them more uniform.

FIRST RELEASES TO FARMERS

By 1946 the number of collections had risen to 700, and two selected varieties had undergone seed increase and could be released to farmers. Guanajuato 10A, a Negro type, was adapted to growing at altitudes of 6,500 to 13,000 feet; Mexico 38A, a Canario, had about the same adaptation. Six other promising selections were increased during the year.

It was clearly recognized that none of these selected varieties was perfect in all respects. But with beans, as with corn and wheat, the policy in these early years was to give the farmers something better as quickly as possible, not only to relieve the current food shortage but also to show the Mexican people, farmers and politicians alike, what the application of scientific methods could accomplish in the improvement of agriculture. In both respects, the early work with beans can be counted a success; refinements came later.

Varietal Improvement Gains Momentum

HYBRIDIZATION ASSUMES A ROLE

One refinement, introduced soon after the breeding of beans began, was to employ hybridization as well as selection. In a self-pollinated plant like the bean, selection alone can do no more than isolate the best from among the variation already present; but hybridization can create new variation, sometimes on a grand scale. It can also create new genotypes that combine the best features of both parents. For example, a cross between a bean resistant to rust and one resistant to anthracnose can produce in later generations at least a few individuals with resistance to both diseases.

By 1953 the collections of beans from Mexico numbered about 1,600, and additional collections from other parts of the world, assembled in a search for resistance to various diseases, totaled 400. The breeding work had been extended from the Bajío into the tropics, and hybridization had largely replaced pure-line selection as a method of improvement. Nearly 150 crosses had been made, and from these crosses more than 4,000 promising new lines in the fourth, fifth, and sixth generations had been selected and were being compared in yield trials with the improved varieties Rocamex 1, 2, and 3. These latter varieties, produced by pure-line selection, had been released to farmers of the Mesa Central and the Bajío in 1949.

More than half the crosses had the Mexican variety Canario as one parent. Canario is a bush type that bears large, yellow seeds roughly cylindrical in shape; it matures fairly early, in about 90 days, and is strongly resistant to rust and moderately resistant to anthracnose. As noted earlier, many Mexican consumers prefer

Canario, partly because it is tasty and nutritious and partly because it takes only a short time to cook. Its yield, however, is low, owing in some measure to its susceptibility to root rots and to bacterial blights. To combine the good qualities of Canario with higher yield as well as resistance to root rots and bacterial blights therefore seemed to offer a promising line of attack.

Bean improvement had now become a major activity of the Office of Special Studies. In recognition of this fact, during the spring of 1953 all phases of the work, including breeding and studies on disease and insect control, were established in a separate bean project, under the direction of Dr. William D. Yerkes, Jr., a plant pathologist from Washington State University.

The first hybrid varieties could not be ready until several more years of testing, but pure-line selections superior to Rocamex 1, 2, and 3 were available to bridge the interval and contribute to steady improvement in bean yields. The best of these selections was Canario 101, a bush type, which yielded up to 1,800 kilograms per hectare and was adapted to growing zones ranging all the way from sea level to 7,000 feet. It proved immediately popular and within two years had come into widespread use.

The first three hybrid varieties, each one a bush type, made their debut in 1956 under the names Canocel, Bayomex, and Negro Mecentral. These varieties not only possessed high yielding ability but also had considerable resistance to anthracnose, rust, and bacterial blights. In 1957 they were joined by three hybrid varieties developed for the Gulf tropics, and by 1963 varieties superior in terms of both yielding ability and disease resistance could be recommended to farmers in each of the principal bean-growing regions: eight different ones for the Mesa Central and several each for the Bajío, the northern zone, the Pacific Coast, and the tropics.

These improved varieties not only produced more beans, but they also produced better beans.

QUALITY SUPPLEMENTS QUANTITY

Besides working to improve plant characteristics that can be observed in the field, the agronomists gave attention to other less apparent but equally important qualities that can be determined only by laboratory tests. One of these is length of cooking time.

Some beans take very little time to cook, others take two or three times as much. This is an important consideration in Mexico, especially at high altitudes where any cooking tends to be prolonged because of the low temperature at which the water boils and where, in addition, fuel is both scarce and expensive. A popular feature of Canario 101 and the later hybrid bean lines has been the fact that even at 7,300 feet elevation they can be cooked in only two hours.

Another characteristic measurable only by laboratory tests is protein content. Since beans were—and still are—the principal source of protein in Mexico, it was obviously important to maintain protein content while improving yields. In beans, however, as in the cereals, there tends to be an inverse correlation between yield and protein content, the latter going down as the former rises. Why this should be so is not clearly understood. Some agronomists have speculated that a given crop tends to elaborate only so much protein per acre regardless of total yield; thus, if the total yield is high, the amount of protein in percentage of the total constituents is low, and vice versa. Whatever the true explanation, plant breeders, whether they are working with beans, corn, or wheat, have to pay attention to protein content; otherwise it is likely to decline as productiveness rises.

In the case of beans, plant breeders must be concerned not only with total protein content but also with the quality of the protein, in terms of its constituents, the amino acids. Especially is this true as regards tryptophane, the amino acid in which corn is most deficient and in which it most needs to be complemented by beans. Let the tryptophane content of beans decline and they can no longer serve as corn's near-perfect dietary companion.

In the early years of the bean improvement work no attention was given to tryptophane content. Indeed, no facilities were available for determining tryptophane amounts. Such facilities became available, however, with the establishment in Mexico in 1947 of a modern nutrition institute, supported in part by the Kellogg Foundation and supervised in part by Dr. Robert Harris of the Massachusetts Institute of Technology. In 1949 tests made by the institute on the improved bean varieties that had been distributed to farmers showed that protein quality had suffered to some extent: both protein and tryptophane content had declined slightly. Fortunately, no real damage had been done to Mexican dietary standards through the release of these varieties, because the considerable increase in yield more than compensated for the slight reduction in protein content. But in the improved varieties that were subsequently released, protein content and protein quality were required to meet high standards. Nor was this all.

Disease and Insect Control

From the beginning of the bean improvement work, the plant pathologists had been giving attention to the diseases of beans in Mexico and the entomologists had been studying ways of controlling the considerable number of insects that produced injuries on beans.

In the early years anthracnose, root rots, and rust appeared to be the most serious diseases, but later it became evident that bacterial blights, mosaic, and several other virus diseases were also important. As none of these could be easily controlled by treating the seed or by spraying the foliage with chemicals, the development of resistant varieties seemed to offer the best solution. Accordingly, the plant pathologists early began to cooperate with the plant breeders in the selection of disease-resistant lines, and to study the causes and nature of the diseases.

In the case of both rust and anthracnose, the disease situation proved to be complicated by the existence of a number of different physiologic races of the pathogen; by 1963, 31 races of bean rust had been identified and 20 of anthracnose. Nevertheless, the pathologists were able to be of real service in the selection of resistant lines and, as already noted, the improved varieties released to farmers had considerably more resistance to both rust and anthracnose—and also to bacterial blights—than did the older varieties they replaced.

In the case of root rots, the pathologists found that several organisms, especially *Rhizoctonia,* were involved. By 1957 it was clear that none of the bush-type (*Phaseolus vulgaris*) lines in the breeding program had a significant amount of resistance to these organisms, and efforts were therefore begun to incorporate the root-rot resistance of climbing beans (*P. coccineus*) in a commercial bush-type variety.

Of the considerable number of insects producing injuries on beans, six were early recognized as being among the most important:

the Apion pod weevil, the Mexican bean beetle, and, in some areas, white flies, leafhoppers, thrips, and leafminers. Breeding of beans, or any other crop, for resistance to insects was still largely untried, and because many insect pests could be satisfactorily controlled by spraying or dusting with insecticides, the entomologists concentrated on measures of this kind for Mexico.

In 1945, McKelvey began an extensive series of tests with both old and new chemicals, and at the same time initiated basic research on the major pests of beans in terms of taxonomy, biology, and geographic distribution. The first bean insect pest studied thoroughly was the Apion pod weevil. The entomologists collected specimens of the weevil from all the bean-producing areas in Mexico and sent them to Dr. J. Balfour-Browne, a world-recognized authority, who identified three known species—*Apios dalea, A. rynchosia,* and *A. tephrosia*—and described seven other species as new. With 10 different species attacking beans in Mexico, there is little wonder that this weevil was a ubiquitous pest.

Experiments on chemical control of both the weevil and the beetle soon showed that the regular application of insecticides, when the stands of beans were good and there was sufficient moisture, often resulted in yields twice as high as the current average yield obtained by farmers. Later experiments indicated that there might be differences among bean varieties in degree of susceptibility to attacks of the weevil.

By 1963, practical control measures were available for use against most of the major pests of beans. In the meantime, the agronomists had been working to improve methods of cultivation.

Improved Cultural Practices

With the establishment of the separate bean project in 1953, the scope of the effort was at once enlarged to include experiments concerned with cultural practices.

One such experiment involved determining the effects of 10 different fertilizer mixtures on nine different bean varieties. Like other legumes, the bean plant has the capacity to live in symbiotic relationship with nitrogen-fixing bacteria which capture atmospheric nitrogen and make it available to their host plant, which in turn supplies the bacteria with carbohydrates. But Mexico's soils, after centuries of intensive cultivation, were so depleted of nitrogen (see Chapter 8) that even beans with their associated nitrogen-fixing bacteria showed the effects of nitrogen deficiencies in their growth. Preliminary experiments on a small scale had indicated that beans, like wheat and corn, would respond to nitrogen fertilizer and that, if higher levels of nitrogen were utilized, there might also be responses to higher levels of phosphorus and potassium. Hence the testing of 10 different fertilizer mixtures. This experiment was followed by a number of others, but it will still be some time before the best fertilizer practices can be prescribed for all the different areas of Mexico because soil conditions vary so widely.

A second experiment initiated in 1953 was designed to compare the productiveness of beans growing with corn and of beans planted alone. As pointed out earlier, the agricultural complex of corn, beans, and squashes that originated in Mexico centuries ago utilized beans of the climbing type, which twined on the stalks of corn. In the 1940's and 1950's this practice of interplanting corn with climbing beans was almost universal among small farmers in Mexico. At first glance this way of growing beans might seem to make the most efficient possible use of the land, but actually it made control of diseases and insects on the beans very difficult; and there was, furthermore, a question as to whether maximum yields could be produced by this system. The time had come to find out, and the finding was that when grown alone, beans produced about three times as much as when grown in association with corn. Better control of insects and diseases was certainly one factor; freedom from competition with the heavily feeding corn during stalk production was probably another.

Besides investigating fertilizer practices, the agronomists determined optimum planting dates and planting rates for the improved varieties in each region and also showed that herbicides were promising as aids in reducing the number of cultivations needed to control weeds.

Two Decades of Progress

That Mexico has made substantial progress in bean production is clear from the record: in 1963 production totaled nearly 500,000 tons as compared with only 150,000 tons two decades earlier. And that this progress has been achieved to a considerable extent through an increase in acre yields is also clear: within the same twenty years average yields almost doubled. Whatever all of the reasons for this increase may be, use of improved varieties—improved in yielding ability, in adaptation to the different regions, and in resistance to some of the major diseases—has certainly been a major factor, and for this contribution to greater yields the Office of Special Studies deserves full credit. Better cultural practices and a reduction in losses caused by pests and diseases undoubtedly have played their part too, even though it would be difficult to measure this exactly.

Without any question, bean yields can be raised still higher if the information now available is utilized more widely. This is primarily a problem of extension and demonstration. To increase yields to the maximum will require much more research, however, and no one appreciates this fact more fully than Dr. Alfonso Crispín, who was first commissioned to the bean project in 1954 and is now head of bean improvement in the National Institute of Agricultural Research. Working with him are several other "graduates" of the Office of Special Studies, and continued progress in the decades ahead thus seems assured.

Chapter 7

Mobile Reserves

Potatoes and Other Vegetables,
Soybeans, and Sorghums

The dramatic improvement in Mexico's food supplies between 1943 and 1963 involved mainly Mexico's three principal food plants: corn, wheat, and beans. Considerable attention was given, however, to three other potentially important food plants: potatoes, soybeans, and the sorghums. They had been of minor importance or had only recently been introduced from the Old World and therefore were virtually unknown to the majority of Mexican farmers. The combined results of the research on these plants, though not yet significantly affecting Mexico's total food production, have yielded a body of technical knowledge and a diversity of new varieties that justify, we believe, the title given to this chapter.

New varieties of potatoes resistant to the diseases most prevalent in Mexico and new varieties of soybeans and sorghums adapted to the Mexican climate represent potential sources of food that can now be exploited when and as the need arises. If their history in other parts of the world is any criterion, each of these three crops will find its place in Mexico and will become increasingly important as the pressure of population becomes more acute and as the agriculture of Mexico necessarily becomes less traditional, less provincial, and more functional.

The Potato: Mexico Discovers Its Value

POTATOES WERE PRIMARILY FOR TOURISTS

When the members of the Survey Commission wrote their report to The Rockefeller Foundation in 1941 they made no mention of potatoes because at that time potatoes were not a major source of food in Mexico. Consumption was only about five kilograms per person per year—a mere fraction of that in Great Britain, 114 kilograms, or Germany, 600 kilograms—and a substantial share of even this small fraction was being consumed, not by the Mexicans, but by resident Americans and Europeans and by tourists. Official production statistics did not even refer to potatoes by name but lumped them in the 25 "other crops" that altogether occupied only six percent of Mexico's cropland.

The limited production of potatoes was in the hands of a few relatively prosperous farmers who could afford to import high-quality seed from abroad and who had the means to control, through the regular application of fungicides, a serious disease called late blight, which afflicts cultivated potatoes in virtually all climates suitable for their production. Moreover, since late blight is at its worst in Mexico during the summer rainy season, the relatively small acreage of potatoes was confined mainly to crops grown under irrigation during the dry winter season.

The following account of how the potato was started on the road to success in Mexico and had repercussions in potato-growing countries around the world, belongs to current history, but it may perhaps be better understood if we first take a look at the past history of the cultivated potato.

POTATOES ARE AMERICAN

The potato, *Solanum tuberosum*, originated as an American plant and has many wild species—at least 148, according to Dr. J. G. Hawkes, the British botanical authority on the cultivated potato and its relatives. These occur at high or intermediate altitudes all the way from New Mexico to Chile. Some 26 wild species exist in Mexico alone, but most of these are inedible. Tubers of the few edible wild species are sometimes gathered by the Mexican Indians, as they undoubtedly were in prehistoric times, but they have never been brought into cultivation.

The cultivated potatoes belong to a section called *Tuberosa*, which comprises (according to Hawkes) 64 species, all of them native to various countries of South America: Colombia, Ecuador, Peru, Bolivia, Argentina, and Chile. It was in this Andean region, probably in what are now Bolivia and Peru, that the potato was first domesticated centuries ago. There it became, and still is, the principal food plant of Indians living at high altitudes.

It was in this same Andean region, probably in present-day Colombia or Peru, that the Spanish explorers first encountered the potato, and from here it was carried to Europe, by the Spaniards about 1570 and perhaps again by Sir Francis Drake in 1586. After some initial reluctance on the part of the people to accept it, the potato was finally generally adopted by all the countries of northern Europe. The increase in production of food that potato culture provided to these countries is considered by some historians to have been the principal factor in the spectacular increases in population that occurred in Europe in the seventeenth and eighteenth centuries.[1]

Soon after becoming naturalized in Europe, the cultivated potato made a return voyage to the Western Hemisphere and landed in Mexico, probably during the seventeenth century. Corn and beans, however, had been there since prehistoric times, and even by comparison with wheat the cultivated potato was a latecomer. It therefore could not compete with corn for the affection and reverence, of the Mexican people.

HOME-GROWN SEED GIVES POTATOES A BOOST

Although in the early 1940's the potato was of little significance as a food crop in Mexico, several members of the Office of Special Studies soon began to wonder whether its status could not be raised, and so they made a few preliminary test plantings at Chapingo. Then in 1947 potatoes demanded special attention because the growers near León, Guanajuato—the one established area of winter potato production—ran into trouble and besieged the Office for help.

The help provided took the form of a visit to León by Dr. John S. Niederhauser soon after he had joined the Office as associate plant pathologist in the summer of 1947. While a graduate student and later an extension pathologist at Cornell University, Niederhauser had acquired considerable knowledge of potato diseases. It did not take him long, therefore, to recognize that many of the plants at León—in some fields 100 percent—were infected with viruses. As many potato viruses were known to be transmitted through seed

[1] W. L. Langer, "Europe's Initial Population Explosion," *American Historical Review*, 69(1963), 1–17.

tubers, Niederhauser immediately set about selecting seed from healthy plants, which he then grew alongside the growers' unselected seed in a comparative test. The results were spectacular: the selected seed outyielded the growers' seed by nearly two to one.

If this could be done on a small scale, why not on a larger one? A local source of good inexpensive seed not only would benefit the León growers by eliminating the cost of importing seed from abroad, but might also improve the chances for encouraging potato production in other areas of Mexico. But could a seed crop be produced in the summer for fall planting? In 1950 two farmers cooperated in the first attempt at summer seed production. With late blight controlled by spraying, they obtained excellent yields, and by 1953 about 1,200 tons of locally grown seed were being sold to León growers for winter planting. Thus a basis had been laid for a local seed-potato industry, and Niederhauser had given the potato its initial boost on the road to success.

THE KEY TO A GOOD SUMMER CROP

Meanwhile Niederhauser had also been making some experiments in the high valleys of the State of Mexico, where summer conditions were ideal for potato growing provided late blight could be controlled. Experimental plantings at Texcoco, near Chapingo, and on a private farm in the Toluca Valley proved highly successful because of the use of good seed and regular spraying for control of blight. But for most farmers the sizable investment that spraying required— in machinery, materials, and labor—was almost as great a barrier to potato growing as late blight itself.

From the beginning it had been realized that the ideal solution to the problem would be to find blight-resistant varieties that could be grown with a reduced number of spray applications or, still better, with none at all. Along with his other work, therefore, Niederhauser had each year been screening a limited number of reportedly resistant varieties.

Ever since the catastrophic outbreak of late blight in Ireland in the early 1840's, small, less spectacular outbreaks had continued to occur somewhere each year, and application of fungicides for control of the blight fungus, *Phytophthora infestans*, had become almost a universal practice. Systematic attempts to produce blight-resistant varieties by hybridization had been in progress since about 1920, but every resistant variety that breeders developed sooner or later proved to be more or less susceptible to a new parasitic race of the fungus. R. L. Salaman in England and Donald Reddick at Cornell University had found that the Mexican wild species, *Solanum demissum,* was immune from all races of *P. infestans* known to them and were trying to incorporate its resistance into cultivated potatoes.

By 1951, although Niederhauser had not yet found any varieties that could be grown in Mexico without spraying, he had found four European varieties that showed enough resistance at both Chapingo and Toluca to justify the expectation that they could be grown with a reduced number of sprayings. The prospects for increasing potato production in Mexico now seemed rather bright; accordingly, Harrar elevated the potato improvement work to the status of a major project in 1952, and an intensified search for blight-resistant varieties became its first order of business.

VIRULENT PARASITES PROVIDE THE ACID TEST

For his headquarters in this search Niederhauser chose the newly established State of Mexico Experiment Station in the Toluca Valley, both because conditions there during the summer were highly favorable for the development of blight and because the results of earlier tests suggested that the parasitic races of the blight fungus present there might be much more virulent than those previously known.

In the summer of 1952 several thousands of varieties were planted in the field at the Toluca station and allowed to grow without spraying. All these had come to Mexico rated as "immune" or highly resistant in their own countries, but by harvest time all had been blighted and killed.

In 1953 came the first hopeful sign for Mexico: although most of the entries that year succumbed completely to the pathogen's withering attack, a few managed to survive. After several more years of testing, Niederhauser had some 250 clones or lines that had passed the most severe test of blight resistance yet known.

By 1956 three "elite" varieties had been selected from the clones with proven blight resistance and the other qualities of a good potato. Seed tubers were distributed to farmers in 100-pound lots with the stipulation that each farmer would, from his first harvest, give 100 pounds of seed to some other farmer.

These first blight-resistant varieties were accepted eagerly and in a short time had spread far from the original villages to which they were introduced. At very low cost, small farmers could now put in a small plot of potatoes in their dooryard garden and obtain a measure of freedom from virtually complete dependence on corn and beans. One element in this measure of freedom, as many of the new growers were quick to recognize, is the fact that the potato crop is underground and so protected from frost. Thus, an early frost that might mean complete failure to corn and beans would merely terminate the aboveground growth of potatoes; the half-grown tubers underground would still represent half a crop, and to a hungry farmer and his family half a crop is a good deal better than none. Meanwhile, the potato team was already at work trying to improve these already improved varieties.

WILD POTATOES CONTRIBUTE DISEASE RESISTANCE

Although the Mexican wild species, *Solanum demissum,* seemed to be the best source of resistance to late blight, the procedure for producing a good commercial potato using this species as one of the parents was long and laborious. In Mexico one step in this lengthy procedure could be shortened because at least some of the clones that had shown resistance at Toluca were already the product of crosses involving *S. demissum.* The potato team therefore went directly to making a series of crosses involving these resistant clones in the hope of increasing their blight resistance and of combining as many other desirable characters as possible.

The results exceeded expectations. Within the brief period of three years a number of promising new selections had been created, and dozens more were on the way. Most of these new varieties, which were christened with appropriate Spanish names—Anita, Bertita, Conchita, Dorita, Elenita, Eréndira, Florita, Gabriela, and Greta—derive their blight resistance from material furnished by Dr. Wilhelm Rudorf of the Max Planck Institute in Cologne, Germany. (Eréndira, for example, has the following pedigree. Parent A was derived from a cross made by Rudorf between two hybrids resulting from crosses between *S. demissum* and cultivated potatoes; it was sent by Rudorf to the United States Department of Agriculture, from whom Niederhauser obtained it. Parent B also was obtained from the USDA and was the result of crosses involving the recently produced American varieties Chippewa and Katahdin and some German material. Niederhauser crossed parents A and B and selected Eréndira from the progeny. Presumably, therefore, Eréndira owes at least some of its resistance to S. *demissum*.)

THE SECRET OF THE PROVING GROUND

Soon after it became apparent that the Toluca Valley provided the most severe test of blight resistance yet known, efforts were begun to find out why this was so. Cultures of the fungus collected in the Valley promptly revealed one reason: all the known parasitic races of the blight fungus were present there. Using a series of differential clones containing the four known dominant resistance genes, singly and in all combinations, plant pathologists had postulated the existence of 16 races, but before 1954 only nine had been found and identified. Cultures of the fungus collected at Toluca yielded all 16 races and gave strong reasons for believing that still other races exist that cannot be identified by present methods.

Other important discoveries followed in quick succession. In the wheat rust and many other fungi, virulent new races arise mainly from sexual crosses. The potato blight fungus, however, had never been known to reproduce other than asexually—"pinching off" some of its cells wrapped in thin protective membranes and propelling them into the air to produce a veritable fallout cloud of infection. Many other fungi reproduce in this manner, but most of them also produce male and female cells that fuse to form larger and more thickly walled sexual spores. For scores of years many investigators had painstakingly searched for these sexual bodies in cultures of the blight fungus, but they had never found more than a few and these never germinated. The blight fungus seemed to be sexually sterile, and, as any biologist knows, sex *is* necessary if an organism is to have great diversity through recombination of characters.

The solution to the puzzle began in October, 1955, at the Chapingo station when Niederhauser and his co-workers, Dr. Jorge Galindo and Ing. Sebastian Romero, noted that certain cultures of the blight fungus from the Toluca Valley were producing large numbers of sexual spores that *would* germinate. These spores originated mainly in "mixed" cultures (subcultures arising from a single asexual spore rarely producing them), and at first it was thought that some nutritional element vital to the production of sexual spores had been carried into the original mixed cultures and then lost when these were broken down into pure subcultures. However, a parallel investigation by Dr. John J. Smoot and his associates, working at Camp Detrick, Maryland, and using cultures sent to them from Mexico, revealed that the Toluca isolates could be separated into two "sex-compatibility groups." Only when a representative of each group is present in the culture can the fungus reproduce sexually. The two groups are not themselves "sexes" in the ordinary sense; Galindo has shown that cultures of each group can produce both male and female organs containing the equivalent of sperms and eggs. The male cell of one group, however, can fertilize only a female cell from the other group. It is as though two tribes living in the same area observed taboos against marriage within the tribe. Except for this biological taboo there is no observable distinction between the groups, both having the same capability to infect given potato varieties.

With respect to the sex-compatibility groups, Central Mexico is probably unique in that both groups are present there in approximately equal numbers; elsewhere in the world where studies have been made, all cultures of the blight fungus apparently belong to a single compatibility group. It is the presence of both groups in Central Mexico and sexual crossing between them that provide an explanation for the many virulent races that have arisen in this area and that in turn have eliminated all but the highly resistant species of wild potatoes.

INTERNATIONAL IMPORTANCE OF THE MEXICAN DISCOVERIES

The program begun at Toluca to find blight-resistant varieties for Mexico has evolved into an international cooperative project for late-blight research. Potato breeders the world over now send their varieties to Toluca for testing. The assemblage of indigenous races of the pathogen prevalent there eliminates most of the susceptible plants at once and enables the breeder to concentrate his attention on the relatively few resistant survivors. Since 1956 the Mexican potato program has also been sending certain selections to other countries for further testing. Uniform sets of 10 elite strains have gone out to collaborators in 47 different countries on five continents. Reports on these international trials show that the Toluca-screened potatoes are at least as resistant as they were in Mexico, and most of them appear to be immune to the races of blight prevalent in those countries. In Guatemala, Costa Rica, Haiti, Panama, Chile, and Kenya certain of the Mexican varieties have proven commercially acceptable as direct introductions and are being multiplied and distributed there.

MEXICAN POTATO PRODUCTION DOUBLES

Although the potato is not yet making a major contribution to Mexico's food supplies, it has, through the efforts of the Office of Special Studies, changed in status from an insignificant crop to a potentially important new food source. Between the five-year period 1948–1953 and 1962 the area planted to potatoes in Mexico increased from 87,500 to 137,500 acres and the national average yield rose from about 66 bushels to nearly 120 bushels per acre, although better growers are getting nearly five times that much. The total potato production during this period has more than doubled (342,000 tons vs. 134,000), and this does not take into consideration the thousands of small home garden plots whose product does not enter commerce and is not counted in the statistics.

This substantial increase results from the fact that some of the principal barriers to potato production have been removed. Mexico now produces her own seed potatoes under a seed certification program regulated by the Ministry of Agriculture, and potato growers' associations have been organized in the five main growing areas. No longer does seed have to be imported from abroad at considerable expense. And no longer is the potato a luxury crop because of the need to control late blight with costly fungicides. Blight-resistant varieties have not only made potato growing more profitable for the large farmers but have also made it safe for thousands of small farmers.

Now that fertilizers are available at moderate cost and Mexican farmers are recognizing their value, potato production may be expected to increase at an even more rapid rate. Already the best yields in the Toluca Valley, at León, and in the vicinity of Navidad, a new area for potato growing, are around 600 bushels per acre. Such yields compare with the best in Europe and the United States.

With the establishment of the National Institute of Agricultural Research in 1961, leadership of the potato project in Mexico passed to Dr. Javier Cervantes and Santiago Delgado, M.S., two of Niederhauser's former colleagues. At the same time, Niederhauser stepped into a larger job.

THE PROGRAM GOES INTERNATIONAL

The international aspects of the potato program took a new turn in January, 1961, when the Foundation established an Inter-American Potato Improvement Project and appointed Niederhauser as director. In a sense, the initiation of this new project was no more than an official recognition of hemispheric activities already established: the collaboration in testing promising new clones, the interchange of ideas among potato workers at the triennial congresses of the Asociacíon Latinoamericana de Fitotecnia, and the visits of Niederhauser to Central and South America and of scientists from those areas to Mexico.

The Inter-American Potato Project now has three principal aims: (1) to promote closer cooperation in potato research in Latin America, particularly on a regional basis; (2) to encourage the establishment of selected basic studies on internationally important problems involving potatoes and the development of "germ plasm banks" in Mexico and Peru; and (3) to assist in the education of young Latin American scientists interested in potato improvement. It is perhaps too soon to evaluate the progress that has been made, but it can at least be said that the project has got off to a good start.

The Mexican potato program, which had its modest beginnings in efforts to help the growers at León, has not only helped all of Mexico to discover the value of potatoes but has also grown up and become truly international, both in scope and in importance.

Other Vegetables: Improved Sources of Vitamins and Minerals

What has been done with potatoes has also been done, on a somewhat lesser scale, with other vegetables. The Mexican diet today not only has more calories than it had in 1941; it is also richer in vitamins and minerals.

Peoples in all parts of the world have somehow learned that an adequate diet must usually include fresh vegetables, and the Indians of the prehistoric cultures of Mexico were no exception to this general rule. Corn and beans provided them with adequate amounts of carbohydrates, fats, and proteins and also, of course, furnished some minerals and vitamins. A daily diet of corn and beans is hopelessly monotonous, however, and the Indians learned long ago to add piquancy to it with chili peppers. Seeds of these were found in the once-inhabited caves in Tehuacán in cultural zones dated 5200 B.C. Even today no Mexican meal is complete without its chili peppers, either fresh or preserved in a sauce of some kind. At an early stage the Indians also learned to make use of the squashes, of which the majority of known species are native to Mexico. Wild squashes all have somewhat bitter flesh, and it is supposed that prehistoric man first used them primarily for their seeds, which are rich in a palatable and wholesome oil. Now, however, the squashes are grown for both seed and flesh, and even the blossoms are sometimes eaten, wrapped in tortillas and fried in deep fat.

A third widely grown vegetable in Mexico is the tomato. While the modern, large-fruited tomato of commerce probably had its origin in South America, Mexico is the home of the related species, the small-fruited *Lycopersicon pimpinellifolium.* Tomatoes are used both fresh and in many sauces, often in combination with chili peppers. Nutritionists today recognize tomatoes as being approximately equal to citrus fruits as a source of Vitamin C (ascorbic acid). Also widely used in Mexico is the so-called husk tomato.

In addition to the vegetables that the Mexicans regularly grow under cultivation, there are a large number of species growing wild or as weeds in the corn fields that are gathered and used as pot herbs or eaten raw on the spot. Some of the wild plants and weeds that the Mexican Indians consumed are extraordinarily rich in vitamins and minerals.

It appears that the Mexican Indians, living on the land and eating their corn, beans, and chili peppers supplemented at times by tomatoes, by the seed and flesh of squashes, and by wild plants and weeds, may have had not just an adequate diet but a near-perfect one. But in the 1940's the poorer people in the cities, whose traditional culture pattern had been disrupted and who no longer had access to the wild plants of the countryside or the weeds of the field, were definitely subject to malnutrition, often in chronic form.

By the terms of the original agreement the cooperative program that led to the creation of the Office of Special Studies was confined to the principal field crops—corn, wheat, and beans. But as Harrar and other members of the staff saw how restricted was the diet of many urban and rural Mexicans with respect to fresh vegetables and how inferior the quality of many vegetable products coming on the market, the desirability of initiating experimental work with vegetables became apparent. Preliminary trials in producing good vegetables safe to eat were made at Chapingo early in the program. It was not until 1951, however, that a major project was begun, under Ralph W. Richardson, Jr., a Ph.D. graduate from the University of Minnesota. The main objective was to stimulate the development of home gardens, with secondary emphasis on improving commercial production.

PROMOTING HOME GARDEN PRODUCTION

Richardson, a naturally energetic young man, immediately set about testing numerous vegetable varieties introduced from the United States and other areas to identify those best adapted to the environmental conditions in several parts of Mexico. During the first year, trials were carried on in the Bajío and the states of Mexico, Jalisco, and Morelos. Included were varieties of radishes, carrots, onions, beets, chickpeas, lettuce, cabbage, mustard, spinach, chard, cauliflower, broccoli, tomatoes, string beans, and lima beans. By the end of the second year, well-adapted varieties of these vegetables had been found for year-round production in the Valley of Mexico and for winter production in Morelos. The best planting dates had also been determined. Richardson promptly established demonstration plots to show extension workers as well as farmers the performance of these varieties and the proper methods of cultivation.

By this time he had also begun experiments on seed production, starting with cabbage, onions, and tomatoes, three widely used vegetables. Seed from the United States not only was expensive but often represented varieties that were not well suited to Mexican conditions. Developing local sources of inexpensive seed of adapted varieties was therefore of great importance.

Further progress in varietal testing was rapid, and by 1954 promising varieties of the major vegetables could also be recommended for the Bajío, the Toluca Valley, and the coastal plains of Veracruz. The accumulated information was made available to the public in a bulletin, *Verduras en el Huerto Familiar* (Home Garden Vegetable Production), in which Richardson and his assistant, Oscar Brauer Herrera, listed the varieties best adapted in each region and provided detailed information on proper cultural practices as well as methods for controlling the common garden pests and diseases. This bulletin subsequently proved to be the most popular ever issued by the Office of Special Studies.

With the preliminary stage of the vegetable program thus completed, emphasis now shifted to breeding work and disease- and insect-control studies. The experimental work was also extended to additional regions, including the Pacific Northwest and several localities in the State of Durango.

NATIVE VEGETABLES RECEIVE SPECIAL ATTENTION

As a practical matter, special attention was given to improvement of the three vegetables traditional in Mexico—tomatoes, chili peppers, and squashes.

Because the large-fruited tomatoes of commerce apparently are not native to Mexico, trials were confined largely to varieties introduced from the United States. This procedure quickly paid off. In a planting of 13 tomato varieties at the Cotaxtla Experiment Station in January, 1955, a line designated S-1, which Richardson had brought with him from the United States, proved to be outstanding not only in yield but also in resistance to sunscald and to damage by the "northers," cold winds that periodically afflict almost all parts of the tropics during the winter months. This line was named Cotaxtla 1, and seed production was immediately begun. By 1957 seed was being distributed to growers in the Gulf Coast region by extension agents and seed dealers. Cotaxtla 1 has continued to be one of the best varieties available to tomato growers in this region.

In the case of the native chili peppers and squashes, collections were made throughout the country and elsewhere and compared under controlled conditions for yield, disease resistance, and other characteristics. All cultivated plants are subject to diseases caused by fungi, and even the hot chili pepper is no exception. For many years a destructive disease had troubled growers in all of the principal pepper-producing regions of Mexico. The disease had been attributed to the attack of a species of *Fusarium,* but careful study under greenhouse conditions revealed that the causal organism was actually a species of *Phytophthora, P. capsici,* related to the fungus responsible for late blight of potatoes. Within three years, the Ancho pepper had been identified as outstanding in disease resistance and other characteristics.

MEXICANS NEED NEVER LACK FRESH VEGETABLES

By 1961, ten years after the vegetable improvement program had begun, home gardens had become much more numerous, although by no means universal, and there was noticeable improvement in the quality of the vegetables available in the city markets. Improved seed was available of tomatoes, peppers, squashes, cabbage, onions, and peas as well as propagating material of sweet potatoes. The program had clearly demonstrated what could be done, and because Richardson had from the outset made the training of personnel one of his main goals, there were Mexican scientists qualified to carry on.

With the knowledge of vegetable production that has now been gained, and with a climate in which a great variety of vegetables can be grown at almost any time of year, there is no reason why Mexico should not have an abundance of fresh vegetables at all times, both in the cities and in the rural areas.

The Soybean: A Most Promising Old World Legume

SOYBEANS WERE ABSENT IN MEXICO IN 1941

Grown as a vegetable in many parts of the world, but in others even more important as a source of raw materials for industry, is one of the world's most versatile and valuable plants, the soybean. The members of the Survey Commission were well aware of these facts, and in their report to The Rockefeller Foundation they called special attention to soybeans: "In this connection mention should be made of the complete absence of soybeans in Mexico. The soybean occupies in China and other Asiatic countries the same position in the diet as the bean in Mexico. It has, however, many more uses and, where it is adapted, is far more productive. There is some question whether soybeans can be satisfactorily grown in Mexico; certainly in the central plateau the altitude is too high and the nights too cool for the varieties of soybeans grown in the Corn Belt. There are, however, hundreds of varieties of soybeans in Asia, and among these may be types which will prove to be at home in Mexico. At any rate, a thorough test of all available soybean varieties is needed."

The common bean has been described in Chapter 6 as "the meat of the poorer Mexicans," their main source of protein. The soybean, however, represents an even better source. Not only does it have a higher protein content—34 percent as compared with 22.5 percent for the common bean—but the quality of its protein is also superior. In addition, it surpasses the common bean in fat content—16 percent as against 1.8 percent. Any plant product so rich in proteins and fats is certain to be used in a great many ways, and the soybean has amply proved its versatility. As a food it is used green in salads or for canning; the dry beans are boiled, baked, roasted, or sprouted. Soy sauce, made by fermentation with a fungus, *Aspergillus oryzae,* is an indispensable part of the daily diet of millions of Asiatics and a constituent of all Worcestershire sauces. A vegetable milk made from soybeans is not only similar in composition to cow's milk but can also be used in similar ways: fed to infants, condensed, or made into curds or cheese, fresh, dried, or smoked. To Asiatic peoples the soybean is second in importance only to rice.

Aware of the highly nutritious qualities of the soybean and having seen it become an important crop in the United States Corn Belt in a relatively short period of time, once its commercial planting began, the Survey Commission strongly recommended that the soybean's potentialities for Mexico be given early consideration.

THE VALUE OF SOYBEANS IS QUICKLY DEMONSTRATED

The Office of Special Studies acted on this recommendation almost as soon as it initiated the program on beans. In 1944 eight varieties of soybeans obtained from the United States and other sources were tested at Chapingo, Querétaro, Torreón, and Matamoros in preliminary plantings, which provided a considerable amount of field information. Additional introductions were tested in the next two years, and by 1947 some 125 varieties had been found to be more or less well adapted to various parts of Mexico and several were being increased. During 1948 yields of between one and two tons per hectare were obtained in tests of 25 of the better varieties. As soybeans demonstrated their potential value for Mexican agriculture, farmers became increasingly interested in the new crop, and in 1949 many requests for seed were received. The soybean was not replacing the common bean in the Mexican diet, but there appeared to be a developing market for soybeans for use in animal feed, oil production, and industrial products.

That Mexican consumers would quickly abandon their traditional frijoles in favor of the more nutritious and more productive soybean was, of course, hardly to be expected. Food habits developed over centuries tend to be highly resistant to change. Moreover, it is axiomatic among economic botanists that to introduce a new food plant into a country is very difficult when one already available serves essentially the same purpose, even though less adequately.

But in its other roles as a legume to be used in a system of crop rotation and as a source of edible oil, the soybean continued to gain in popularity, especially among the progressive farmers in the Pacific Northwest, who, having achieved spectacular success with Borlaug's rust-resistant wheat varieties, were ready to try other new things. In 1961, 8,363 hectares were planted to soybeans in the Yaqui Valley of Sonora, and the production of 11,655,688 kilograms brought an income to the region of 16,318,103 pesos. By this time the bean program had been giving increased attention to soybeans for several years, and in 1962, while still better varieties were being developed through hybridization, seed of the varieties Hood and Hill was released to meet the need of Yaqui Valley farmers for soybean varieties that can be planted relatively late, after the wheat harvest, and still mature satisfactory crops.

SOYBEANS ARE READY FOR ACTIVE SERVICE

Given enough time, the soybean may yet become one of Mexico's most useful crops. After all, it took more than a century to become established in the United States, where dietary traditions are much younger and less rigid than in Mexico and where progressive farmers are usually ready to try anything. First grown in Pennsylvania in 1804, the soybean did not come into its own in the United States until automobiles and tractors replaced horses; the resulting drastic reduction in the market for oats, formerly the principal horse feed, released millions of acres for other purposes. Many of these acres came to be planted in soybeans and today production in the United States exceeds that in the soybean's native home, China.

This same pattern of events is beginning to appear in Mexico. Varieties adapted to Mexican conditions are now available, cultural practices have been perfected, production has been shown to be profitable, and the acreage planted, although still limited, is gradually expanding. As the pressure of population increases and the need for new sources of protein becomes more acute, the soybean, now figuratively speaking a mobile reserve stationed behind the lines, will almost certainly be brought into active service as a reinforcement for the traditional frijoles.

Sorghum: A Potential Auxiliary to Corn

SORGHUMS PRODUCE WHERE CORN SUFFERS

A mobile reserve with even greater potentialities for Mexican agriculture is sorghum, an Old World cereal whose resistance to drought makes it a much more dependable crop than corn for those parts of Mexico where drought is an ever-present threat. If subjected to prolonged drought at the critical stage in its development, corn may be a complete failure. Under similar conditions sorghum simply stops growing and goes into a kind of dormancy; when the rains come, it resumes growth and produces a crop.

There are many varieties of sorghum, ranging from low-growing, early-maturing types to tall, late sorts especially adapted to the tropics. Some varieties are grown primarily for their forage; these include the sweet-stemmed kinds from which the juice can be extracted and boiled down to a palatable syrup well known in the southern United States as "long sweetnin'," a substitute for "store-bought" sugar. Other varieties are grown primarily for their grain, which in chemical composition is quite similar to corn and has about the same nutritive value.

Because sorghums are so much better adapted than corn to growing in semiarid conditions, they are now the principal grain crops in such regions in many parts of the world. Originating in Africa, they spread to India and China in prehistoric times and became the basic food plant of millions of people. On a world basis the sorghums today rank fourth among the major cereals, being exceeded only by rice, wheat, and corn. In the United States, where sorghums were introduced from Africa toward the end of the nineteenth century, they provided a dependable feed crop that in turn became an important factor in opening up the Great Plains to agriculture.

With these facts in mind, the members of the Survey Commission were concerned to see so little culture of sorghums in Mexico in 1941, especially in those parts where corn was clearly a marginal crop, producing a satisfactory harvest only about one year out of three or four. Particularly concerned was Mangelsdorf, who had seen at first hand the ability of the sorghums to produce dependable crops of forage and grain under the semiarid conditions prevailing in the southwestern United States. During his years in Texas he had persuaded Robert Karper, in charge of sorghum improvement, which was then largely confined to western Texas, to join him in a series of experiments to make direct comparisons of corn and sorghum throughout the eastern part of the state where corn was the principal grain crop. These experiments, which were planted side by side in the same fields, with each crop planted at its own optimum date, showed in almost all instances that the best-adapted varieties of sorghum produced more grain than corn and two or three times as much forage.

In his conversations with Mexican agronomists in 1941, Mangelsdorf received little support for his suggestion that corn should be replaced by sorghums in many parts of Mexico. "The Mexican people are by tradition wedded to corn," he was told. "It would take at least fifty years to introduce sorghums into Mexico on a substantial scale." To which his reply was: "If it is going to take fifty years, we had better get started at once."

SORGHUMS PRODUCE FORAGE AS A BONUS

Harrar agreed with Mangelsdorf's opinion, and the Office of Special Studies began the testing of sorghum varieties on a small scale soon after Wellhausen arrived to take charge of the corn improvement program. By 1947 more than 150 sorghum varieties had undergone preliminary evaluation, and the next year 25 of the most promising were put into field plots at Chapingo, Vista Hermosa, León, and Pabellón. The best-adapted varieties produced yields of two to six tons of grain per hectare or, if cut green for fodder, 50 to 70 tons of green forage per hectare.

This ability of the sorghums to produce a good crop of forage in addition to the grain is a characteristic of particular importance to Mexico, where forage for livestock is often in short supply. One of the most common sights in Mexico during the summer months is that of burros going to market carrying bundles of corn fodder so large as to virtually obscure the bearers. These are the tops of still-green corn plants removed immediately above the ears. This decapitation of the growing plants actually removes a part of the food-manufacturing leaf area and causes substantial reductions in yield of grain. The farmer is much better off to leave his corn plants intact and to plant a small patch of sorghum especially for forage.

In 1950 Harrar was able to say to the Foundation's agricultural advisory committee: "It is evident that the sorghums have a real place in Mexico's agricultural economy." He reported that seed stocks of several varieties had been increased and turned over to the recently created Committee for the Increase and Distribution of Improved Seed and that there was a demand for seed of these varieties from farmers interested in animal husbandry.

Beginning in 1950 the experiments with sorghums were turned over to John Pitner and were continued on an expanding scale, taking in additional regions. In Torreón sorghum grown under irrigation yielded four to five tons per hectare in 1951, and to meet the heavy demand for seed 15 tons of foundation seed stocks were produced in the winter planting for distribution to farmers in the summer of 1952.

By 1954 the important potentialities of the sorghums for Mexico had become so generally recognized that a full-fledged program of research on this crop was initiated, with Dr. Robert D. Osler, who had joined the corn program, in charge. Testing of varieties was extended into additional areas, including the Gulf Coast tropics where a new research center had recently been opened at Cotaxtla in Veracruz. A program of breeding new varieties was begun and experiments on the use of fertilizer applications, especially nitrogen, were conducted. Other experiments involved dates of planting and spacing between rows and between plants in the row.

By this time it had also become evident that the sorghum varieties available had limitations with respect to the altitudes at which they could be grown. None were well suited to altitudes above 2,000 meters, although there are large areas of Mexico above these altitudes where rainfall is a limiting factor to corn production and where the drought resistance of sorghums would be a valuable asset if only they could be grown. Dr. Kenneth O. Rachie, who took charge of the sorghum work in 1955, recognized the desirability of developing sorghums adapted to high altitudes and asked Foundation officers in New York to look into the possibility of obtaining high-altitude varieties from India. Such varieties were subsequently obtained from both India and Africa, and under Rachie's successor, Dr. Elmer C. Johnson, these became the parents of new hybrids developed for Mexican conditions.

The sorghum work in Mexico received immeasurable benefits from the research on sorghums conducted in Texas by Robert Karper and J. Roy Quinby of the Texas Experiment Station. These two experts, who had collaborated closely in developing new sorghum varieties for different parts of Texas, had hundreds of hybrids growing in their experimental fields and made the most promising of these available to the Mexican program. They also visited Mexico on several occasions to confer with the workers there.

DESPITE FOOD PREJUDICES, SORGHUMS HAVE A FUTURE

Sorghum production is now well established in several Mexican states (especially Oaxaca and Nayarit), in the areas around Torreón and Matamoros, and in the Pacific Northwest. Although production is still small compared with that of corn, it is definitely on the increase. Most of the crop is used as a feed for livestock and, to a lesser extent, for industrial purposes. Wherever a considerable amount of sorghum is grown, the hog-raising industry has expanded. Many poultry raisers have also found sorghum to be as satisfactory as corn for feed, and indeed it is quite probable that the spectacular growth of Mexico's poultry industry (mentioned in Chapter 10) is partly the result of the greater amounts of feed available through the growing of sorghum. Thus the sorghums, converted to eggs and meat by feeding to chickens, are contributing to an increase in Mexico's supply of protein.

The industrial uses of sorghum in Mexico are only beginning, but these also may be expected to increase. In the United States sorghum grains are now recognized as approximately equal to corn in the production of starch, glucose, syrup, oil, and gluten feed. A special kind of grain that occurs in sorghum, and in corn as well, is also used in the manufacture of tapioca, adhesives, and other products.

So far, however, the sorghums have made no substantial headway in replacing corn in the making of tortillas. Although experiments indicate that sorghum can be substituted for corn up to about 40 percent without appreciably affecting the flavor of the resulting tortillas, the Mexican consumer remains unconvinced. Food preferences and prejudices are, of course, deeply ingrained, and many people in all parts of the world would rather go hungry than adjust themselves to eating strange foods with unaccustomed flavors. However, when hunger becomes acute enough, approaching the level of starvation, such prejudices tend to disappear. It is to be hoped that this stage will never be reached in Mexico and that instead sorghum will find its place through the increasing recognition of its productive capacity under conditions not altogether suitable for corn, of its value as a feed for livestock, and of its potential usefulness as a supplement to corn in the human diet. In Mexico's campaign against hunger, the contribution that sorghum is capable of making will sooner or later be fully recognized and utilized.

Mexico has revolutionized her wheat production (Chapter 5). Above, a typical wheat field in 1943. Below, better wheat a few years later and three of the men who helped make it better; left to right, Rupert, Borlaug, and Harrar.

The development of rust-resistant varieties was a key to wheat improvement; "native" variety killed by stem rust, flanked by resistant varieties bred in Mexico.

Semidwarf varieties that combine "standability" with rust resistance and other virtues have largely replaced the tall varieties with weaker straw. Adoption by farmers followed observation; superior varieties have been their own best extension agents.

The CIANO experiment station, near Ciudad Obregón, Sonora, where most
of Mexico's superior wheats were created.

The payoff of the wheat revolution. Before 1943, wheat was poor and harvest hard; now, wheat is good and harvest easy.

...duction of beans, the meat of many Mexicans, has almost doubled since 1943 (Chapter 6). The program starts: young and old seek better beans in experimental plots.

Better varieties of several types were bred.

Threshing an improved bean variety and sacking seed for distribution.

Better control of bean pests and diseases has helped to increase and insure production. Front, a good variety injured by leafhoppers; rear, the same variety protected by spraying.

Mexico has learned how to produce more potatoes at lower cost (Chapter 7).

enty years ago costly spraying was necessary to control the late-blight disease.

In the hope of avoiding the cost of spraying, blight-resistant varieties were imported and tested in the Toluca Valley. But the Mexican blight was so virulent that it killed almost all the plants.

From a few plants that survived, however, varieties were produced that withstood the blight when those on the right were killed.

In larger plots at Toluca the new varieties yielded about 600 bushels an acre, even though they had not been sprayed.

Farmers helped harvest the plots and took as pay seed potatoes for their own farms.

Varieties of soybeans, above, and of sorghums, below,
have been developed for Mexican conditions. Along
with potatoes, they are "mobile reserves."

Soil scientists have contributed much to agricultural improvement in Mexico (Chapter 8). Mexican soils are very diverse in origin, and many of them have been modified by the action of volcanoes, such as Paracutín, which appeared without warning in 1943 and covered the land for miles around with volcanic ash.

Mexico had a land problem in 1943. Many agricultural lands had been ruined by water erosion, and vast areas had scarcely any water at all.

Although the construction of irrigation systems had increased the amount of cultivated land considerably, still more was needed because of the low fertility of most Mexican soils.

About 90 percent of Mexico's soils needed nitrogen. Supplying it to corn at the rate of 80 pounds an acre has a tremendous effect on plant vigor and on yield.

Soil cultivation was slow and inefficient with the old wooden plow.

The steel disk plow was better.

But modern machines are better still.

"In the tropical zones Mexico has valuable land and water resources awaiting development." The potentialities of large areas seem enormous; if wisely developed, they can become one of Mexico's most valuable agricultural assets.

Chapter 8

Soils, Water, and Man

How Mexico Learned to Use Them Better—
An Example for Emerging Countries

Improving the Soils

The increase in soil productivity was one of the Big Three that helped Mexico to win her agricultural revolution. Better varieties, better plant nutrition through better soil tillage and fertilization, and better protection against pests and pathogens were, as we have seen, the principal factors that boosted acre yields of corn, wheat, beans, and certain other crops. In addition to the specific benefits mentioned especially in connection with the improvement of corn and wheat, however, the soils program helped Mexico to understand and utilize her soils better than ever before. She has learned that her soils can be a permanently productive resource if properly conserved and cultivated, and she has learned much about how to conserve and cultivate the many kinds that lie within her borders.

DIVERSE SOILS CREATE DIVERSE PROBLEMS

Of all the diverse features in the Mexican scene, not one is more diverse than Mexico's soils. The vast variety in her surface rocks—weathered under wide ranges of temperature and rainfall, then transported, mixed, and again laid down on river flood plains and in lakes, or blown up on hillsides by wind—has formed the basis for this diversity. In addition, there is nearly always a volcano visible someplace on the Mexican horizon—an old volcano, inactive for thousands of years, or a new one, like Paracutín, which appeared without warning in a corn field near Uruapan in 1943. All these volcanos have contributed a blanket of ash fresh from the hot interior of the earth's crust and often covering an area of 400 to 500 square miles. In places, repeated deposits of this kind have rejuvenated the soil, supplying all the elements needed by plants except nitrogen. Primarily because of this lack of nitrogen, however, ash-covered areas remain barren for several years until the natural processes of soil building have done their work.

The extent to which the minerals in these varied deposits have been weathered is greatly influenced by the extent of their contact with water. Annual rainfall ranges from three inches in Baja California to 175 inches in many tropical areas near the Gulf of Mexico.

If to this natural variety of soil and water we add the changes made by man in the past 2,000 years, we can get some idea of the complexity of the problems that confronted soil scientists in Mexico when they began studying the practical management of these soils for crop production.

In 1941 a few Mexican soil scientists were already grappling with various of these problems. Some of the best-trained men were employed by the Irrigation Commission to classify the soils to be irrigated with the water impounded by the many new dams then under construction. Because there was only enough water to irrigate a small fraction of the land available, it was important to use it on the best soils. The Subsecretary of Agriculture, Ing. Alfonso González Gallardo, understood the importance of soil science and had written a textbook on the subject that was used in many schools. Some elementary soil science was taught in the agricultural colleges, and there was some research under way at the regional experiment stations maintained by the Ministry of Agriculture. But the amount of reliable information available was woefully inadequate for a rapidly growing country. Arrangements were made, therefore, to get more information.

FINDING OUT WHAT MEXICO'S SOILS NEEDED

The Rockefeller Foundation had made provision for a soil scientist in the first group to start work in Mexico, but it took some time to find a suitable candidate for this important job. In 1944 a man with the right combination of personal qualifications, scientific training, and practical experience was found in Dr. William E. Colwell, who tackled his new job with enthusiastic vigor. He quickly learned Spanish and assembled an energetic team of young graduates of the National School of Agriculture at Chapingo to work with him.

This team worked hard at many jobs, some of which many Mexicans considered too lowly for college graduates. But Colwell worked with them, and morale was high. Hard work was fun once you learned the art of it. The group traveled together a great deal, and as they traveled they talked, they sang songs, they swapped stories. His new colleagues taught Colwell the Spanish language and Mexican farming practices and social customs; Colwell taught them English, soil science, and the farming practices of the United States. Theirs was a type of relationship between Mexicans and Gringos that both enjoyed. Years later, when asked what he would rate first in his Mexican experience, Colwell replied: "My contacts with the Mexican boys, working with them, learning with them, and becoming friends." Essentially the same answer was given by all his successors.

In 1946, just as the soil research was getting off to a good start, Colwell was enticed back to the United States, and Dr. Robert F. Chandler, Jr., obtained a short leave from Cornell to continue the work. In 1947 he was succeeded by Dr. John B. Pitner, who had had farm experience and undergraduate work in Mississippi and graduate training at the University of Wisconsin. Pitner continued much of the fertilizer research and assumed the main responsibility for managing and developing the enlarging research station at Chapingo. Later, he was assisted for a few years by Eiliff Miller and then by Reggie J. Laird, a Mississippian with a Ph.D. from the University of California. In 1954 Pitner resigned to accept an attractive position in the United States, and Laird was put in charge of the soil program. He has had a longer term of service than any of his predecessors and is still in the Foundation. Since much of the following story is continuous despite these staff changes, no attempt will be made to break it up and allocate credit for the resulting segments.

Three major projects were started during the first few years: a series of soil management studies in the field, a laboratory for analyses of soils and crops, and research on forage crops. These projects were closely integrated and tended to supplement one another.

The soil management project included studies of cultural practices for different crops, crop rotations, and studies to determine the economic value of commercial fertilizers in each of the more important centers of production in Mexico. Most of these experiments were made with wheat and corn.

In spite of the diversities of soil and climate referred to above, it was found that most of the soils had one property in common: they were deficient in nitrogen. The early experiments, supplemented by hundreds of later ones, showed that between 90 and 95 percent of the soils of Mexico would produce higher yields of practically all crops if given a suitable application of a nitrogenous fertilizer. The magnitude of the response on the same soil varied widely from year to year, however, an indication that some other management or seasonal factors were exerting a modifying influence. Because subsequent research elsewhere has given similar results, and because nitrogen fertilizers have contributed so much to the consistently high average yields obtained in the United States and other countries in the past twenty years, it may be of interest to review the fascinating story of nitrogen in a little more detail.

NITROGEN NEEDED, IN MEXICO AND EVERYWHERE

On 90 to 95 percent of Mexico's soils, corn and wheat were yielding only eight to 12 bushels an acre because of a shortage in the soil of nitrogen in a form they could use. But in the atmosphere enveloping the entire earth there are about 11 pounds of nitrogen gas per square inch. What an anomalous situation! While Mexico's corn and wheat were starving for nitrogen, above each acre was a free supply sufficient for a 100-bushel crop every year for 500,000 years.

The vast significance of the nitrogen cycle to human existence everywhere is seldom fully appreciated. People, as well as plants, may suffer nitrogen deficiency. If soils are poor in nitrogen, farmers tend to grow starchy foods that supply calories but are deficient in protein. Although adults can survive and work on such diets for an extended time, growing children need protein to build muscles. As long as they are nursing and getting a little milk each day, children often manage fairly well; but once they are weaned and placed on the same starchy diet as their parents, many of them—often up to 50 percent—die before they are five years old from a protein-deficiency disease called kwashiorkor. Dying from lack of nitrogen! Yet these children take into their lungs and then exhale over 100 times as much nitrogen each day as they need for healthy growth. What tricks nature plays on us—or better, perhaps, what challenges and rewards she has provided for those who take the pains to learn and apply some of her basic laws. Emerging countries in general have not yet learned how to obtain these rewards.

Nitrogen is ordinarily a rather inert gas. Mixtures of nitrogen and either hydrogen or oxygen can be kept in a bottle for years at ordinary temperature and pressure without any combination taking place between them. But nature has methods, not yet fully understood, for combining nitrogen and hydrogen into ammonia and for combining nitrogen and oxygen into nitrates. Once ammonia or nitrates have been formed, the biological cycle can proceed, because plants can use either form in their growth processes and can synthesize them into amino acids and proteins that animals can use for their growth processes. Just how this nitrogen cycle, so intimately involved in all life processes, plant and animal, got started is not yet clear. It is known that when a bolt of lightning passes through the atmosphere some nitrogen unites with oxygen to form oxides and that these dissolve in water to form nitric acid, which in turn forms salts, such as potassium, calcium, and magnesium nitrates, when it comes in contact with the rocks on the earth's surface. These nitrates probably accumulate in depressions and set the stage for the initiation of plant growth by primitive plants such as algae.

When these primitive plants die, their remains decay and part of their nitrogen is released as ammonia and nitrates, the simple forms that can be reused immediately to feed the next generation. The rest of the nitrogen is converted into more stable colloidal compounds, often called "humus," which accumulate in the soil and form a reserve of nutrients for an increasingly diverse flora of bacteria, fungi, algae, and eventually of the higher plants.

Some of these bacteria and algae have a secret formula for converting nitrogen from the air into proteins needed for their own growth; this frees them, in part at least, from dependence on the soil reserves. Certain of these nitrogen-fixing bacteria have developed a mutually beneficial or symbiotic relationship with certain types of higher plants, the most important of which are members of the legume family—peas, beans, clover, and alfalfa, for example.

Living in the nodules they have made on the roots of legumes, these fortunate organisms have access to a living source of high-quality food, plant sap, which enables them to thrive and multiply and fix more and more nitrogen. Since a part of this nitrogen can be absorbed by the host plant, it too becomes less dependent on the soil's supply of nitrogen. As a result, legumes are able to grow on soils with very little organic matter or nitrogen and so serve as pioneers among the higher plants. Like most pioneers, they prepare the way for their successors.

Within a period of five to ten years legumes can build up enough nitrogen in the soil to provide for the vigorous growth of competing non-legumes like grasses. The proportion of legumes in the vegetative cover then declines. In time, however, the non-legumes deplete the supply of available nitrogen in the soil to a level at which their competitive ability is reduced, and the legumes again increase. Such cycles are common in pastures, meadows, and forests.

All these natural methods for converting the free nitrogen gas of the atmosphere into combined, solid, biologically active forms are relatively slow processes. But they are of great importance because they seldom stop. Even slow processes can accomplish much over centuries if they are operating continuously and if a substantial part of their product accumulates in a rather stable form in the soil. This rate of accumulation of nitrogen has been studied in many places and under a wide range of conditions. It seems to vary from about 20 to about 100 pounds of nitrogen per acre per year in the early stages. In only a few centuries the nitrogen content of the soil can reach a maximum or an equilibrium value, often ranging between 3,000 and 10,000 pounds an acre.

This appears to be a dynamic equilibrium in which the rate of destruction of humus just equals the rate of formation. As long as man lives by gathering his food from wild sources, the equilibrium is not seriously disturbed. But when he becomes dissatisfied with wild foods and decides to grow, by crude methods of cultivation, more of the food he prefers, the nitrogen equilibrium in the soil is quickly disturbed, because cultivation accelerates the depleting and retards the accumulating processes. As a result, the nitrogen and humus content of the soil starts to decline, the rate at which this occurs being affected by a number of factors and consequently varying widely with different locations and with different methods of cultivation. Some soils with a large reserve of fertility can be cropped continuously for half a century without any decline in productivity. At the other extreme, some tropical forests often lose up to 50 percent of their productivity in two to four years. Farmers have learned to manage such soils in different ways.

NITROGEN IN RELATION TO CROPPING SYSTEMS

In Mexico and most of the developing countries soils are managed in various ways, which can be classified on the basis of their effect on the nitrogen-supplying capacity of the soil:

1. Continuous cropping, in which there is no effort to maintain the productivity of the soil.
2. Shifting cultivation, in which the soil is cleared, cropped for two to four years, and then abandoned, as in the *milpa* system of Mexico.
3. Mixed farming rotations, in which the soil produces a crop each year but one or more of the crops in the rotation are nitrogen-fixing legumes. Some of the crops are fed to livestock and their manure returned to the land.
4. Supplementing the soil reserves by means of chemical fertilizers containing nitrogen.
5. A combination of mixed farming rotations (No. 3) with the use of chemical fertilizers (No. 4).

A large proportion of the cultivated land in the world is still cropped continuously, without any conscious effort by the farmer to offset the accelerated depletion of the nitrogen reserves in the soil. If these reserves are large, as in the rich, black soils of the United States Corn Belt, the farmer may continue to get fair crops for 50 years or even longer before yields start to decline. In time they do decline, to about eight to 12 bushels of corn or wheat per acre per year, but if the soil is rather level, fairly deep, and non-erosive, these low yields can often be maintained for even a few centuries through the operation of the natural nitrogen-fixing processes. Grain yields reached this stage in medieval Europe, and much of the commercial agriculture of Mexico and many other countries still falls in this category. Much of the fertilizer research in Mexico has been done on soils so depleted, hence the responses usually observed after nitrogen fertilization.

Shifting cultivation is practiced largely in tropical forests. There most of the farms are small and communally held. A small patch in the existing forest is cut down, allowed to dry, and then burned, the ashes and unburned litter serving to enrich the soil. Crops are planted, usually with a pointed stick, among the debris without further preparation. Although the cropping pattern is frequently complex, yields decline quickly because soil reserves of fertility are low, and after two to four years the area is abandoned, the jungle moves back, and soil-building forces again predominate. After eight to 15 years, depending in part on population density, the area is reoccupied and the cycle begins anew. This system is primarily one of subsistence farming; it never provides a very high standard of living and it produces little surplus for growing cities. Ordinarily it will support about 20 people per square mile when the soil is not too erosive. But if population pressure forces an increase in this ratio, the fallow period has to be shortened, the productivity of the soil can no longer be maintained, and yields soon decline to the point where people must move out or go hungry. Nevertheless, over 200 million people in the belt of tropics around the world are supporting themselves by this system.[1] In Mexico it is called the milpa system and is widely practiced in the more mountainous areas, as well as in Campeche and Yucatán. As yet modern science has contributed little to the improvement of traditional systems of shifting cultivation. Many of the areas thus farmed probably should be reforested or planted to some type of perennial tree crop. But the people who live by these systems are usually illiterate, highly independent, and, because of their isolation, suspicious of outsiders. The limited amount of research that has been done indicates that the existing difficulties—technical, economic, and educational—will make progress in these areas slow and costly. Mexico, like most countries, is inclined to invest her limited funds and to use her limited but growing supply of technical personnel where problems can be more easily solved, with larger and quicker returns to the national economy. The problem remains, however; it has only been deferred.

Soil-building rotations have not been extensively used in Mexico. Such rotations as the famous Norfolk one of roots, barley, clover, and wheat, which was introduced into England in the latter part of the eighteenth century, are credited with doubling the yield of wheat in England almost a hundred years before chemical fertilizers became

[1] P. H. Nye and D. J. Greenwood, *The Soil under Shifting Cultivation* (Horhenden, England: Commonwealth Agricultural Bureaux, 1960), Preface.

widely used. These systems owed their effectiveness primarily to two facts: one, that wheat, the principal grain crop, was preceded by clover, a legume which added considerable nitrogen to the soil in its stubble and roots; and two, that the root crop, turnips or beets, provided more and better winter feed for livestock and thus enabled the farmer to increase the size of his herds and flocks and consequently the amount of animal manure he had available for his cropland. Such rotations took various forms and were used particularly in Europe, the United States, Canada, Australia, and New Zealand. By their use a skilled farm manager could maintain the organic matter and nitrogen content of his soil at a fairly high level, even though it was producing a valuable crop each year. Much of modern Western scientific culture stems from these countries, and one wonders if they could have contributed so much if their people had not had the vigor which this system of farming provided in the form of a cheap, dependable supply of milk, meat, and eggs, all rich in high-quality proteins.

NITROGEN AND THE MEXICAN FARMER

The limited appeal of mixed farming rotations to the Mexican farmer is probably due to differences in traditions, climate, and the form taken by the livestock industry. Most of Mexico's beef cattle are produced on open ranges in the northern part of the country, whereas the dairy industry, which is of more recent origin and not highly developed, is clustered mainly around the larger cities. Alfalfa, the queen of forage crops and one of the most efficient nitrogen fixers (it will fix over 200 pounds of nitrogen per acre per year in the northern United States, where the growing season lasts only five months), is highly prized in Mexico, especially on dairy farms where it is often cut ten times a year when irrigated during the dry season. Because of the cost of establishment, it is not used in regular short rotations but is left down until reduced yields make it no longer profitable. As early as 1941 some dairy farmers in Mexico were reporting corn yields of over 100 bushels an acre on well-manured alfalfa sod. Such farmers are still rare, however, and the acreage of alfalfa still far too small.

Another approach to the nitrogen problem seems more attractive to the Mexican farmer. About 1912 the German chemist, Fritz Haber, discovered an economical industrial method for inducing the free nitrogen in the air to combine with hydrogen to form ammonia (NH_3). Few if any discoveries in history have had a greater impact upon agriculture. To date, this influence has been greatest in those countries with highly developed chemical industries. But with the development of larger and cheaper sources of hydrogen from natural gas and as a by-product of petroleum refining, large plants for making synthetic ammonia have been and are being constructed all over the world. Man has not yet learned how to fix nitrogen at ordinary temperatures and pressures as soil bacteria do, but he can now produce at a reasonable price all that is needed to meet the world's demands. He has learned to tap the inexhaustible supply of free nitrogen in the air.

Earlier in this chapter it was reported that hundreds of field experiments conducted in the major agricultural areas of Mexico showed that between 90 and 95 percent of these soils would produce higher yields of corn, wheat, beans, potatoes, and other crops if they were supplied with additional nitrogen in the form of chemical fertilizers. Many of these experiments were made on private farms, and neighboring farmers were often invited to see the results. Some were very dramatic, the increased value of the crop being three or four times as great as the cost of the fertilizer. It did not take long to convince the more alert farmers that they should buy some nitrogen fertilizer and try it out for themselves. At first, most of the nitrogen fertilizers had to be imported. But Mexico had plenty of nitrogen in her air and cheap sources of hydrogen from natural gas and her petroleum refineries. Four factories have now been constructed for combining nitrogen and hydrogen into ammonia and for processing the ammonia into fertilizers.

From 1950 to 1957 the amount of fertilizer used annually in Mexico increased from 61,400 to almost 370,000 metric tons. To produce the crops needed, Mexico will have to use much more. But before she can bring nitrogen and other fertilizer usage to the optimum level, there are other problems to be solved.

Time after time the soil science team found cases in which fertilizers would give a very profitable response one year and none the next. The farmer loved them the first year when he made a good profit, but his ardor cooled the next year when he had a loss. This led Laird to initiate several new series of experiments designed to find the reasons for this erratic behavior and ways of reducing it.

Utilizing the Water

DIRECT AND INDIRECT INFLUENCES OF WATER

Study of the accumulated experimental results showed that this annual variability in response to nitrogen fertilizers was much less when the crops were irrigated and so had an adequate and dependable supply of water. Responses to nitrogen also tended to be higher in wet years than in dry years. Both observations supported the theory that, when a response to nitrogen was not obtained, water, not nitrogen, was usually limiting the growth of the crops.

Shortage of water is an old story to farmers in much of Mexico. The Spaniards found numerous hydraulic projects already established when they came early in the sixteenth century. They were especially impressed by the *chinampas* found in the Valley of Mexico. Some of these still exist at Xochimilco, where as the "floating gardens" they attract many tourists. Recent anthropological studies indicate that in the pre-Hispanic period these installations were much more extensive, reaching along the margins of the lake as far as the site of the present city of Texcoco and the National School of Agriculture.

THE CHINAMPA SYSTEM OF OLD MEXICO

The individual garden or chinampa was 15 to 30 feet wide and about 300 feet long, giving it an area of between an eighth and a quarter of an acre. Each one was surrounded by narrow canals, just wide enough for the boats that brought in the workers and their supplies and took out the crops. These small canals connected with larger main canals, which carried most of the water from springs and runoff to the lake. The base of the chinampa was probably constructed out of mud from the bottom of the canals; then rafts of water vegetation were towed to the plots, dragged into place on top of one another until they were a few feet above the water, and covered with mud. As the vegetation decomposed, more was added, and each year the surface got a fresh dressing of mud and algae dipped up from the bottom of the canal.

All this took much hard work. Space on the chinampas was very valuable, and to maximize production on them all crops except maize were started in a nursery made by spreading a thick layer of mud over a bed of water weeds. After this had dried to the proper stage, it was cut into small blocks (*chapínes*); a small depression was made in the center of each; and the seeds were dropped in and covered with cattle manure. These beds could be protected from occasional light frosts by a thin layer of weeds. When the seedlings were of the proper size they were transplanted to the chinampa. In this way the Indians were able to grow two crops of corn a year and up to five crops of various vegetables—beans, tomatoes, lettuce, cabbage, chilis, onions, amaranthus, etc. Carp and other fish abounded in the canals.

There is evidence that some of the chinampas at Xochimilco were built about 2,000 years ago. According to Coe,[2] "It would probably be no exaggeration to state that the chinampas gave the ancient peoples of the Valley of Mexico intermittent sway over most of the country for 1500 years before the arrival of the Spaniards." In any case, the chinampas were a remarkable achievement. Their success was probably due largely to almost perfect water control at all times and the maintenance of a high fertility level through the annual dressing of mud from the bottom of the canals, enriched with nitrogen-fixing algae and supplemented by residues of crops and water vegetation.

It will be hard for the Mexicans of today to surpass the productivity of the chinampas. There are, however, several million acres of land that can be irrigated and on which reasonably good water control can be maintained throughout the year. Ever since the Revolution of 1910, the Mexican government has given high priority to the development of water resources. At the time of the Rockefeller Foundation Survey Commission's visit in 1941, the Irrigation Commission was one of the best supported and best organized arms of the national government. In recent years about two million acres have been put into irrigated crop production. Part of this area, like the Yaqui River development, consisted of virgin land of high natural fertility. When adequately watered and well managed, this land has become very productive and (as described in Chapter 5) has contributed much to Mexico's present self-sufficiency in wheat production.

[2] Michael D. Coe, "The Chinampas of Mexico," *Scientific American*, July, 1964, p. 90.

In other cases, water has been provided to supplement inadequate and highly variable supplies from natural rainfall. Both these uses of irrigation water have created new situations that call for research, because once adequate water becomes available, all soil and water management practices on farms must be adjusted if maximum benefit is to be derived. More intensive cropping patterns become possible; often new crops can be introduced; cultural practices must be adjusted, seeding rates increased, fertility levels raised, and weed control improved; new precautions must be taken to provide better drainage and prevent salt accumulation.

Because water is costly and scarce in the irrigated regions of Mexico, it was essential for farmers to learn how to use it efficiently —how to apply it uniformly, and at the best time and in the right amounts for all the different crops. Under Laird's leadership, the soil research team set up experiments to obtain the necessary information.

RAIN AND FERTILIZERS

Space is insufficient to describe the team's experiments in detail, but some proved to be of great general significance. Perhaps their most important contribution has been the overpowering evidence of the gains possible when the findings of specialists in different fields are brought together and synthesized into a single integrated package of management practices appropriate for a specific ecological situation. Probably much of the agricultural land of Mexico can never be irrigated because of the lack of water. What can be done to increase its productivity? Because there seem to be areas that regularly receive more rainfall than others, locations for experiments are now being selected systematically on the basis of long-term weather records in order to sample areas with different rainfall patterns and different drought susceptibilities. The corn experiments incorporate the suggestions of all the different specialists working on the crop: the breeders, entomologists, pathologists, and economists, as well as the agronomists. Results for 1963 are given in the table on page 142.

In the 12 experiments not seriously affected by drought, yields increased as the nitrogen supply was increased, and at 120 kilograms of nitrogen per hectare the average yield was 4.41 tons per hectare

—almost four times the yield of the check which received no nitrogen. Five experiments were heavily infected with the disease *Helminthosporium turcicum*, but in spite of this an average yield of 3.13 tons was obtained with the heaviest nitrogen application. Only three of the experiments were seriously affected by drought; these gave no increase in yield for the heavier applications of nitrogen.

Grain yields (ton/ha.) of unirrigated corn with different rates
of nitrogen fertilization in 22 experiments, Bajío, 1963.[a]

	Rate of nitrogen fertilization (kg./ha.)			
	0	40	80	120
Average for the 22 experiments	1.08	2.14	3.08	3.71
Average for 12 experiments not seriously affected by drought	1.16	2.47	3.65	4.41
Average for 3 experiments severely affected by drought	1.71	2.26	2.13	2.28
Average for 5 experiments affected by *Helminthosporium turcicum*	0.53	1.41	2.47	3.13
Average for 2 experiments severely affected by an excess of soil moisture	0.89	1.04	1.78	2.54

Source: The Rockefeller Foundation, *Program in the Agricultural Sciences, Annual Report 1963–1964*, p. 27.

[a] All experiments received 60 kg./ha. of P_2O_5.

In his 1963–64 report Wellhausen made the following significant comments on these experiments: "As an average of 22 experiments conducted along a transect of an area with total annual precipitation varying from 650 to 900 mm., an application of 120 kg./ha. of nitrogen increased yields by 2.63 ton/ha., or, more dramatically, each kg. of nitrogen applied increased grain production by 22 kg. This again points out the tremendous potential that might be realized through general application of the results of research in the higher-rainfall areas. By fertilizing all corn land in areas having above 700 mm. rainfall, and at the same time using good seed and better methods of weed control, Mexico could produce 25 million tons of corn, four times the present figure, and release for the production of sorghum 2.5 million hectares now utilized inefficiently in the drier areas."

FERTILIZERS WITH WATER CAN PAY BIG DIVIDENDS

The economics of this procedure also seem very attractive. In the 22 experiments, the average yield increase from the application of 120 kilograms of nitrogen was equivalent to 22 kilograms of corn for each kilogram of nitrogen. Corn is worth about one Mexican peso per kilogram, and nitrogen costs about four pesos per kilogram. At these prices the farmer would get a gross return of 22 pesos' worth of corn from four pesos' worth of nitrogen—550 percent—in less than a year. Investments of this type increase the prosperity of both farmers and the government. While this particular analysis is statistically sound, the averages quoted are calculated from highly variable yields on individual farms. As a result of this variability, some farmers will make a very large profit, others will suffer a loss. Small farmers have limited financial reserves and would rather have regular, consistent increases from year to year instead of occasional spectacular yields. Furthermore, very high yields often mean lower prices per unit, and so their attractiveness to farmers is reduced.

Because of such interactions, experiments like those cited above must be repeated over a period of years to find out the variation in yields at each location from season to season. When enough data have been accumulated, the probabilities for gains and losses can be calculated. Other experiments may indicate ways in which soil and crop can be managed to reduce the hazards of drought.

MORE EXPERIMENTATION NEEDED

All this calls for new experiments that involve more variables and are therefore more complex in design, requiring more work and more skill both to execute and to interpret. As a result, the total number of different experiments may decline. But there will be more relationships to observe, more interactions to interpret, and more lessons to be learned. Experience shows that the effect of each growth factor is influenced by every other. The optimum combination can seldom be predicted exactly from the simple, single experiments described at first. But once optimum combinations are found, the gains will be greater than would be expected from the total of the separate single gains. The whole is greater than the sum of its parts.

The reasons seem clear on reflection. Even though all the elements required for growth save one are present in quantities sufficient for a maximum yield, deficiency in this one will keep the yield below maximum and the surplus of the other elements will be wasted or at least not used efficiently. Once we know what element is lacking and supply the amount of it needed, we may get a very substantial increase in yield. Thus a very small investment in the deficient element may increase the returns on the much greater investment already made in all the other elements.

At times it is difficult to identify the limiting factor. For example, in 1957 in a corn experiment at La Cal Grande involving comparisons of plant densities and nitrogen levels, Laird found that the highest yield, about eight tons per hectare, was obtained with the combination of 200 kilograms of nitrogen and a plant population of 60,000. But only 200 meters away in the same field, in an experiment including these same variables and the same variety of corn but planted two weeks earlier, the maximum yield was 11.3 tons— a difference of 3.3 tons per hectare! This difference is about three times the average yield of corn in Mexico, yet the causes are still unknown.

Another interesting example may be mentioned. In a potato fertilizer experiment conducted by Niederhauser near León in 1957, the maximum yield obtained with heavy fertilization and following corn was only two thirds of the maximum following alfalfa. Why? The nitrogen supply was adequate in both cases. Did the alfalfa perhaps leave the soil in better physical condition than the corn did? The investigator must theorize, then test his theories by experimentation. There is no end to research; each experiment raises new questions that call for still more experiments. Perfection in agriculture, like heaven, is not reached in a single bound.

The early investigations indicated that while almost 95 percent of the soils of Mexico responded to nitrogen fertilization, only 25 to 30 percent responded to phosphorus and less than five percent to potassium. But as yields are doubled and quadrupled by nitrogen fertilization and irrigation, the soil's supplies of phosphorus and potassium will be subjected to greatly increased demand and eventually these too will have to be supplemented by fertilization.

All the research on soil and crop management indicates that if Mexico is to get maximum returns from the investment made in the various phases of agricultural research—in corn, wheat, potato, and vegetable breeding; in control of insects, diseases, and weeds; in forage crops, animal husbandry, and agricultural economics—she must continue to place high priority on the development of her water resources. She needs big dams and little dams to store surplus runoff water, and thousands of deep wells to tap her subterranean resources. Equally important, her farmers must learn to use water when and where it will yield greatest returns.

In the tropical zones Mexico has valuable land and water resources awaiting development. With intensive management, drainage and supplemental irrigation where and when needed, heavy fertilization, and multiple cropping with improved varieties developed for these regions, the agricultural potentialities seem enormous. Their development will give to large areas in Mexico many of the advantages that the chinampas gave to the Aztecs in their Golden Age.

Developing the Men

This chapter has been devoted largely to the story of the experiences of the soil scientists, Mexican and American, who have been working together on some of the soil and water problems of Mexico. Most of Mexico's soils were probably not very rich at the beginning, and when our story opened in 1941 even their modest reserves of fertility had been seriously depleted by several centuries of exploitative farming.

It is clear from the research already done that good yields of crops can still be obtained on much of the cultivated land of Mexico if the deficiencies of soil and water are supplied in some way. Much remains to be done, however—more research, more extension, and more use of chemicals, fertilizers, and water. Greater numbers of scientists, engineers, and educators, and millions of better-trained farmers will be needed. Without them, Mexico cannot develop the productive agriculture needed to improve the standard of living of her rapidly expanding population. If her experience to date is a reliable criterion, additional investments in research and education will be among the most profitable she can make.

Chapter 9

Crop Protection

Better Methods of Fighting Pests and Pathogens

Better control of the living enemies of crop plants was one of the Big Three that helped win the Mexican agricultural revolution: better varieties; better soil management; and better protection against destructive diseases, voracious insects, and noxious weeds. The improvement in men and measures to protect crops has been spectacular during the past twenty years. And it was sorely needed.

"Plant diseases and insect pests are a major factor in Mexican agriculture, and a better comprehension of their nature and more intelligent and widespread application of control measures are requisite to improvement of agriculture in general." Thus wrote the Foundation's Survey Commission in 1941. They wrote conservatively, for in many areas, weeds were choking crop plants and robbing them of food, and diseases and insects were destructive, periodically devastating, and prohibitive obstacles to the successful production of wheat and other important crops in some otherwise potentially productive regions.

Pests and pathogens annually destroyed a fourth of Mexico's actual and potential food supplies before the agricultural revolution. Although there are few accurate data for the Mexico of 20 years ago, the losses in the United States are still about 23 percent, and personal periodic observations indicated that losses in Mexico probably were greater. Indeed, they were far too great.

Twenty years ago wheat rusts often destroyed from 15 to 50 percent of the crop and sometimes ruined it completely in certain localities. Two of the three species of these rusts, stem rust and orange leaf rust, were destructive when the weather was warm and moist, and the other, yellow stripe rust, when it was cool and moist at the critical time. Although leaf rust alone frequently caused losses of 10 to 25 percent and yellow rust alone occasionally did, they seldom ruined the wheat completely. Stem rust, on the other hand, was a killer, likely to ruin fields alone or in combination with one of the others, especially orange leaf rust. One or more of these rusts often destroyed half the wheat in many areas and discouraged good farmers from growing it at all in some areas. Rusts were a major depressive factor in wheat production, and Mexico had no defense against them, because their nature is such that they cannot be controlled by seed treatment, the application of fungicides to the growing plants is not economically feasible, and Mexico had, at that time, no resistant varieties (as discussed in Chapter 5).

Although less devastating than the rusts, two kinds of smuts, the covered or stinking smut and the loose smut, commonly destroyed outright 10 percent of the wheat heads, and losses of 25 percent were not uncommon. Similar smuts of barley caused similar losses in that crop also. Less spectacular than the rusts and smuts was a group of debilitating root rots, leaf blights, and head blights that continually sapped the strength and reduced the health of grain plants. Complete health in wheat was rare.

Corn too bore a heavy burden of diseases in most areas of production. It had its own kinds of rusts and smuts, its own kinds of leaf blights and scorches that often caused obvious damage but relatively little concern. Seedling blights killed many plants in infancy and thinned the stands; root rots and stalk rots stunted the growth and weakened the stalks; and various fungi attacked the ears and destroyed many of the kernels. Mexican corn often looked healthier than it really was, partly because the damage was underground, inside the stalks, or inside the husks covering the ears, and therefore hidden from the casual observer. Moreover, the damage caused by fungi or bacteria was often attributed to insects, because often they and the pathogens were joint partners in crime and only the insects were visible to the unaided eye.

Frequently, insects and pathogens, principally fungi and possibly some bacteria, were so closely allied in their attack on corn that it was hard to assess the damage caused by each. Such insects as white grubs that chewed the roots enabled pathogens to enter and rot the roots and the base of the stalk. Of themselves, various borers damaged the plants by boring into the stalks and tunneling through them, but in their wake followed a number of fungi and bacteria, aggravating the damage by rotting the insides of the stalks and weakening them so that they produced nubbins for ears and were likely to break over under the slightest stress. Because in many instances pole beans were planted with corn, the cornstalks serving as poles to support the climbing vines, the stalks were so weakened by borers and rots that a young Mexican suggested that the farmers probably planted the beans so that the vines could support the cornstalks. Even if plants did produce good ears, earworms were likely to eat the kernels and pave the way for further destruction by rotting fungi. Thus, there were as many kinds of pests and pathogens of corn as there were types of corn, and it was evident that better control was essential.

Circumstantial evidence suggests that in different areas Mexican corns and Mexican corn diseases had reached a mutually livable biological balance in the long process of natural and human selection. Certain it is that, as an example, when some tropical varieties were grown in the Mesa Central near Mexico City, they were much more severely attacked by rust than they were in their native habitat, and vice versa. Then too, it later became evident that many native types were much more resistant to head smut (*Sphacelotheca reiliana*) than were certain improved types that had ten times as much smut as the native ones. And it has recently been shown that some native types are much more resistant to certain kinds of stalk rots than some improved lines.

There is always the danger of upsetting a biological balance by introducing for breeding purposes new varieties or parental materials into an area in which their resistance to diseases and insects has not been thoroughly tested; and there is the ever-present danger of bringing in foreign pathogens that were weak in their native home but highly virulent in their new home. Pathologists, entomologists, and breeders must be constantly on the alert to detect new pests and pathogens and to guard against upsetting the biological balance by producing otherwise superior varieties that may help elevate pathogens and pests of previously minor kinds to the status of major ones.

Diseases and insect pests were potent factors in depressing yields of beans (as we saw in Chapter 6). The damage caused by such insects as the Apion pod weevil and the bean beetle was always obvious and sometimes glaring; so also was that caused by such diseases as anthracnose, rust, and certain root rots. The white fly caused heavy losses in certain areas of the Bajío, but the damage was somewhat less conspicuous to the nonspecialist. Similarly, the losses resulting from certain kinds of root rots, bacterial blights, and viruses were sometimes severe without being as spectacular as those caused by better-known diseases, and in the early years it was not possible to study all diseases thoroughly because of lack of personnel. When John Niederhauser joined the program as plant pathologist in 1947, he immediately set out to study systematically the diseases of the principal crops. (The practical results of his intensive studies of potato diseases have already been discussed in Chapter 7.) William Yerkes, another pathologist, soon after his arrival in 1952, concentrated on bean diseases and then on bean improvement. His intensive studies revealed the importance of virus and bacterial diseases of beans, and he started trying to develop varieties with resistance to them as well as to other diseases (as described in Chapter 6). Thus it took several years to realize the full importance of diseases of beans, potatoes, and certain other crops.

To summarize the disease situation in Mexico twenty years ago: Wheat rusts often destroyed half the crop in many areas and discouraged good farmers from growing it at all in some areas where frequently they destroyed the crop completely. Smuts of wheat and barley commonly destroyed a fourth of the heads; rusts, root rots, and pod rots stunted, killed, or blemished the beans; smuts and rusts, and blights and rots sickened the corn or destroyed the grain; and the Sigatoka disease was ruining the banana plantations of tropical Mexico.

Insects too were taking a heavy toll. They were sucking the juices from corn and wheat and beans; they were chewing the roots of corn, weakening the leaves, boring into the stalks, and devouring the kernels on the ears; they were eating the leaves of beans, aborting the seeds within the pods; they were eating or spoiling huge quantities of stored grains and other foodstuffs or paving the way for molds to destroy what was left. Especially in the south, hordes of hungry grasshoppers occasionally devoured all the crops within sight and then swarmed on to new sites.

Rusts and rots, smuts and stunts, blasts and blights, sucking insects and devouring insects, always menacing the Mexican's food and sometimes destroying it before his very eyes while he stood helpless and hungry. One fourth or more of Mexico's cropland was feeding weeds, plant parasites, and hungry insects instead of hungry human beings.

Early Campaigns against Diseases and Insect Plagues

The Ministry of Agriculture, realizing the destructiveness of pests and diseases, established a special Departamento Fitosanitario —Plant Sanitary Department—to combat them. By 1941 the Department had organized 32 regional agencies, *delegaciones fitosanitarias,* to implement its purposes. Aims were praiseworthy, but accomplishments were somewhat erratic; four case histories show the increasing success as knowledge increased and organization improved.

THE CAMPAIGN AGAINST THE SIGATOKA DISEASE OF BANANAS

A devastating fungus disease, known as Sigatoka or *chamusco,* first appeared in Tabasco in 1936, and by 1941 it was terribly destructive in the states of Veracruz and Chiapas also. Prior to 1937, when this disease invaded Chiapas, good plantations produced about 800 bunches of bananas per hectare, of which 350 were exportable. In 1941 the best plantations yielded only half as much, and the poorer ones produced only a quarter of a crop of nonexportable bananas. Sigatoka had been a hard blow to the larger growers, who partially controlled the disease by available methods of sanitation and spraying; it had been a disaster to the smaller ones who had neither the knowledge nor the equipment to combat it.

In the early 1940's the Plant Sanitary Department strove to rescue the banana industry from death by Sigatoka, but the rescue operations failed and the disease continued on its destructive way. In 1958 Ing. Ricardo Coronado Padilla, a pioneer parasitologist, wrote: "The result was a resounding failure. . . . The banana industry suffered a collapse from which it has not yet been able to recover."[1]

Why was this campaign a "resounding failure"? Ing. Coronado considered that "this was an administrative failure and not a technical one, for by that time effective methods for controlling Sigatoka were well known, but it was indispensable to have enough spray machines, sufficient fungicides, and ample cooperation of the growers. . . ." Whatever the relative responsibility of administrative and technical deficiencies, it is fact that at a critical time and place

[1] Ricardo Coronado Padilla, "Como se formó la Especialidad de Parasitología Agrícola y cual ha sido su papel en el desenvolvimiento agrícola de México," *Chapingo,* Vol. XI, Nos. 67–69, January-June, 1958. (Translations by the authors.)

there were four sprayers that had never sprayed a drop, and the most expensive power machine had been dismounted and sat idly rusting in the rain. The larger growers in the area knew more about controlling Sigatoka than did the two *delegados* sent to help them, as the delegados themselves and everyone else realized. Nobody was fooled but everybody was frustrated. The delegados were fine men, but they were pathetically unprepared for their job, and they were far away from anyone who could help them with materials or advice.

Many similar campaigns against pests and diseases failed in other countries in their pioneer days of plant protection. Whatever all of the reasons, one common fault was that plans generally exceeded facilities for executing them—which is a very old and common fault.

THE CAMPAIGN AGAINST SMUTS OF WHEAT AND BARLEY

In 1941 crews of phytosanitarians—plant health experts—were waging a campaign against the stinking smut of wheat and the covered smut of barley by disinfecting farmers' seed grain in government-owned machines located at strategic centers. The campaign was well conceived and vigorously prosecuted, but the ammunition was poor, for many crews were treating the seed with antiquated copper dusts that had long since been replaced in many countries by newer and better organic mercury compounds. And some crews were treating seed corn, which was a waste of time and ammunition as far as smut was concerned, because seed disinfection does not prevent corn smut as it does the covered smuts of wheat and barley. There are many kinds of plant smuts, and each kind has its own kind of remedy. To some of the early phytosanitarians, however, smut was simply smut; and if seed disinfection prevented some smuts, it should prevent all smuts—which would be too good to be true. The antismut campaign did much good, but it could have done much more good if some of the campaigners had known more about the smuts against which they were campaigning.

THE CAMPAIGN TO ERADICATE FLAG SMUT OF WHEAT

Prompt and vigorous action protected Mexican wheat against the new and dangerous menace of flag smut in 1950. This seed-borne smut was known to be extremely destructive in Australia and certain other countries, but it had never been found in Mexico. Warned by competent pathologists of potential danger, Mexico had prohibited the importation of seed wheat from countries where the disease existed. Nevertheless, when wheat was imported from Australia in 1949 under a permit stipulating that it be used for milling purposes only, the seed was so attractively plump that some of it slipped from the mills into farmers' fields, with very unhappy results.

In 1950 Leonel Robles and several companions detected flag smut in a limited area of the State of Michoacán; there it killed from 15 to 40 percent of the wheat in many fields. Realizing the danger to other wheat areas, the Ministry immediately organized a campaign to eradicate the smut by burning all smutted fields and then enforcing a three-year quarantine on the affected area. Despite some violent opposition to this drastic action, campaigners led by Ing. Darío Arrieta succeeded in eradicating flag smut completely and thus eliminated a dangerous new menace to Mexican wheat production. This campaign was certainly both an administrative and a technical success.

THE CAMPAIGN AGAINST GRASSHOPPER INVASIONS

Mexico delivered a knockout blow to her "plagues of locusts" in 1947. According to Ing. Ricardo Coronado Padilla, grasshoppers had periodically devastated certain areas of southern Mexico, and campaigns against them had been relatively ineffectual. But knowledge became power when it was learned that most of the grasshoppers that fed on Mexican crops were not native Mexican grasshoppers at all but foreign invaders from south of the border. As the principal breeding grounds of the hoppers were located in several Central American countries, it was good strategy to fight them there, before they had time to overpopulate and swarm into Mexico. The Mexican Ministry therefore took the initiative in organizing an international alliance to combat locusts in Central America and Mexico. In 1949 a coordinating committee was established, with headquarters in Managua, Nicaragua, to fight the hoppers at their source. Since that time, grasshoppers have made no major invasions into Mexico.

Four campaigns: Of the two earliest, one was a failure, one a moderate success. Of the two later ones, one was a complete success, and the other has been a success for a decade or longer. This is at least a fair record of improvement. But Mexico wanted an even better record and had been learning how to make it.

The Need for Special Skills in Crop Protection

Mexican crop protectionists had learned much from the failures as well as from the successes in their crop-protection campaigns. They realized that often zeal for doing something had outstripped ability to do it, that organization had sometimes been good, but that sometimes there had not been enough good men to man the organization. Mexico urgently needed more specialists.

It was obvious that more special skills were needed to study and combat successfully the numerous and diverse enemies of Mexico's numerous and diverse crop plants. But there were so few specialists that the Plant Sanitary Department frequently had to use generalists in some jobs that would have taxed the abilities of the most experienced specialists. Naturally, the generalists often were bewildered when they were confronted by new and very diverse questions and problems and found themselves far from any source of information. Even at the source they got little help, for there were too few who could help. The Department had neither the men nor the facilities for experimentation and research to supply the control programs with essential information. During one period in the early 1940's it could afford the equivalent of only a half-time man for experimentation and research. Much more special knowledge and many special skills in obtaining and applying it were urgently needed, and some Mexicans had already anticipated the urgency.

The Evolution of Crop-Protection Specialists

THE ERA OF THE PARASITOLOGIST

A small group of professors and students at the National School of Agriculture were pioneers in recognizing the need for competent crop-protection specialists and in doing something to fill that need. Conspicuous among the faculty was Ing. Ignacio H. Olmedo, who taught both entomology and plant pathology; among the students was Ricardo Coronado Padilla, Olmedo's successor and now the "dean of agricultural entomology" in Mexico. When this maverick group proposed the establishment of a field of specialization in "parasitology," opponents ridiculed them, asserting that scarcity of subject matter would force the specializing students to roam around looking for something to learn; the proponents replied correctly that already there was too much rather than too little subject matter in the field and that it was increasing rapidly. The debate waxed stormy, but the mavericks were not blown off course by blasts from the opposition; they persisted, and in the spring of 1935 they attained their objective. In that year the first small group started to specialize, and in November, 1937, they received their diplomas as *pasantes,* with specialization in parasitology.

Parasitologists were educated at the undergraduate level only. During the last three years of a seven-year course (three at the college-preparatory level), students specializing in parasitology took courses in plant pathology, entomology, animal parasites, plant genetics, animal ecology, the use of insecticides and fungicides, and legislation affecting the health of plants and animals. On graduation, students received the title *pasante,* with the field of specialization indicated.

There was no provision for formal postgraduate study, but after the lapse of at least one year, all *pasantes* could earn the degree ingeniero agrónomo with field of specialization indicated, by presenting a thesis and passing an oral examination. The thesis did not require original research and was usually based on professional experience or on the study of scientific literature. Although many realized that more research was needed, the pioneer parasitologists had little opportunity for individual investigation and for obtaining practical experience in controlling pests and pathogens.

Naturally, most parasitologists were still in the bud when they emerged from college, proud of their school, usually, and grateful to some of their professors. Thanks to some exceptional teachers, the National School, the Antonio Narro School at Saltillo, Coahuila, and a private college at Ciudad Juárez in Chihuahua did start some top students on productive scientific careers. Later, the School of Agriculture of the Technological Institute at Monterrey contributed also. Among the pioneer parasitologists were some exceptional teachers whose direct scientific contributions were modest but whose indirect ones were beyond measure. They knew how to identify and encourage talent, even though they could not develop it fully.

Sometimes it is better to do nothing in plant protection than to do something wrong. The control of pests and pathogens by chemicals, as an example, is not a simple job. Whether applied to seeds or to growing plants, the wrong chemicals or the improper use of the right ones may cause serious injury. To cripple or kill crop plants while killing insects or preventing disease does a sad disservice to farmers and to the country. It is a large scientific job to prescribe properly for the control of hundreds of kinds of pests and diseases of scores of kinds of crop plants. And Mexico's job was constantly getting bigger.

The "patent-medicine" and "squirt-gun" days of plant protection were long gone by 1940. Time was when formaldehyde, bordeaux mixture, sulphur, and corrosive sublimate were the only important fungicides and when paris green, lead arsenate, tobacco juice, and soapsuds were the principal insecticides. But times had been changing fast when the first embryonic parasitologists began their special studies at Chapingo in 1935. Already there had been a succession of new fungicides and insecticides, each with its special virtues and defects; accordingly it became necessary to make special prescriptions for special purposes instead of general prescriptions for general purposes. Even for specialists in fungicides or insecticides, it was hard to keep abreast of the latest developments. Moreover, new areas of crop protection were demanding attention: nematodes (or eelworms) and nematocides to kill them; the chemical control of weeds, with various herbicides to kill the various kinds; a growing need for pathologists and entomologists to help develop resistant varieties of crop plants; new pests and pathogens or new races of old ones to combat. Parasitology had become too big a field; it had to be subdivided.

Because of the revolutionary developments in their field, some parasitologists in Mexico realized that they could contribute more to agriculture if they specialized more intensively. And so they began consciously to segregate into entomologists and plant pathologists. There had been some professional agricultural entomologists but no professional plant pathologists prior to 1943, when young José Rodríguez Vallejo started his career as an avowed plant pathologist in the Ministry of Agriculture.

Once under way, plant pathologists and agricultural entomologists developed fast. Some of the most promising of the young Mexicans who participated in the work of the Office of Special Studies chose to work under the guidance of such Rockefeller Foundation pathologists as Borlaug, Niederhauser, and Yerkes or under such entomologists as McKelvey and Dr. Douglas Barnes and Dr. William R. Young. Those who survived the most rigorous tests of intellectual ability and practical performance were given opportunity to expand their education, mostly in universities in the United States. From 1944 through 1963, The Rockefeller Foundation alone gave scholarships to 30 individuals in plant pathology and to 18 in entomology, while other agencies also provided some scholarships.

The number of individuals who earned advanced degrees is one measure of progress; another is what the individuals contributed to the improvement of Mexican agriculture. Judged by both criteria, the record is excellent.

In 1943 there were no Mexican plant pathologists or agricultural entomologists with advanced academic degrees; now there are close to 50.[2] Of the 26 Mexicans with the doctorate in agricultural sciences, 15 are in the field of plant protection. At least 30 plant pathologists now have advanced degrees: 10 have the doctorate, at least 20 have a master's degree, and more are on the way; five entomologists have the doctorate, about a dozen have the master's degree, and postgraduate students now in Mexico and the United States will soon bring welcome reinforcements. Although still too small for the needs of the country, this competent group of well-educated pathologists and entomologists are utilizing their education well in helping to improve Mexican agriculture. And some of the pioneers have already rendered yeoman service.

[2] As of November, 1963.

*Contributions of Plant Protectionists
to the Agricultural Revolution*

Mexican plant-protection scientists were a major force in the agricultural revolution. The contributions of the pathologists were especially conspicuous, because wheat rusts, potato blight, and certain bean diseases were primary barriers to improved production. Pathologists helped reduce the barriers by developing resistant varieties, thus raising yields quickly and permitting acreage expansion in certain highly productive areas where previously the disease risk had been prohibitive. Because the development of resistant varieties has become a standard method for controlling many diseases, but is not yet standard for controlling insects, pathologists have had a natural advantage over entomologists as contributors to varietal improvement.

Disease-resistant varieties were key factors in increasing acre yields of wheat and potatoes three-fold and those of beans by about 70 percent. And plant pathologists played key roles in each case, for they studied the complexities of *Puccinia graminis,* which causes stem rust of wheat; of *Phytophthora infestans,* which causes late blight of potato; of *Colletotrichum lindemuthianum,* which causes bean anthracnose. They studied many other disease-producing fungi, bacteria, and viruses as well and found that just as there are many varieties of wheat and potatoes and beans in Mexico, just so are there in Mexico many varieties or parasitic races of the fungi that cause stem rust, potato late blight, bean anthracnose, and many other diseases. To develop and maintain resistant varieties it was necessary to identify the numerous parasitic races of these pathogens, to determine their geographic distribution, the virulence of each one, and the changes in their relative prevalence, and to be constantly on guard against new races that might menace varieties that were resistant to the old races.

Plant pathologists made a key contribution to the wheat revolution by studying the numerous parasitic races of stem rust and then using plant-breeding methods to reduce their destructiveness. It is a continuing fight, however, for the rust continually menaces the resistant wheats of yesterday with the parasitic races of today and tomorrow (see Chapter 5). Fortunately, however, there now are Mexican pathologists who understand how to fight.

Blight-resistant varieties paved the way to increased potato production by relieving the large growers of an expenditure of 10 to 30 U.S. dollars an acre for controlling the disease by spraying with chemicals and by enabling small farmers who could not afford to invest money in spray machines and spray materials to grow their little patches of potatoes without fear of destruction by the blight. Here again, basic studies on parasitic races of the blight fungus (see Chapter 7) were essential to success. Young Mexican pathologists made the necessary researches, helped breed the resistant varieties, and helped Mexico produce her own seed potatoes instead of importing them at heavy expense from Europe. These men have significantly increased the potential of the potato in Mexican agriculture.

Mexican pathologists also helped increase the average yield of beans by 70 percent, largely by developing several new varieties with more resistance to diseases than the old ones.

The contributions of pathologists to corn improvement have thus far been mostly indirect. But researches on the smuts, the rusts, the leaf blights, the virus stunts, and the insidious and debilitating root rots and stalk rots are helping corn breeders to lay a foundation for the development of resistant varieties that may easily increase total corn production by 15 percent or more.

Entomologists have also made notable contributions to increasing and safeguarding Mexican food supplies. By means of basic researches and extensive experimentation, they have shown how to control many of the most destructive insects in the most effective and economical ways. Unfortunately, however, extension has not always kept pace with investigation, and practice sometimes lags behind knowledge.

Mexican entomologists have probably rendered their greatest single service by showing how to reduce the extensive insect damage to stored grains and their products. Entomologists and pathologists showed that insects and molds destroyed or spoiled an average of 15 percent of stored food products, and they have made extensive investigations on methods of control. Utilizing the results obtained, commercial and governmental agencies are reducing losses in the larger storage plants, and individual farmers are beginning to reduce them also by improved storage on the farm.

In addition the massive weed problem is being attacked by young

Mexican specialists who have learned the habits of Mexican weeds and modern methods of fighting each kind by means of appropriate chemicals and by cultural practices. This phase of crop protection is still in adolescence, but is rapidly becoming completely mature.

The evolution and the contributions of the several guilds of plant-protection specialists during the past two decades is an epic in the agricultural development of Mexico. Not only are there many good scientists, but they are also doing much good with their science: in research, in teaching, and in administration.[3]

The technical subdirector of the National Institute of Agricultural Research (INIA) has a doctorate in entomology; the projects for the improvement of wheat and other small grains, for beans, for sugar cane, and for potatoes are headed by four pathologists, all with the Ph.D. degree. The sections of entomology and plant pathology in INIA are manned entirely by Mexican personnel, and the head of each section has his doctorate. The director of the National School of Agriculture is still an outstanding entomologist, and the major professors of entomology and plant pathology in the School have the doctorate and are now educating students to the master's degree level.

The first and only director of the School of Agriculture of the Technological Institute of Monterrey, who has occupied his position for 16 years, was the second Mexican plant pathologist to earn an advanced degree in the United States, and on his staff there is an outstanding entomologist and an outstanding plant pathologist. The professors of entomology and plant pathology have long been among the most productive staff members of the Antonio Narro School at Saltillo, and a plant pathologist recently received a national award for his efficient management of a large irrigation district, with headquarters at Torreón. Some of these men are no longer in their original field of specialization, but they are serving Mexico well in their new fields.

Thus, "better control of the living enemies of crop plants" contributed significantly to the agricultural revolution, and the evolution of the plant-protection sciences themselves was a very significant phase of the revolution. The past record of crop protectionists is good; the future promises to be even better.

[3] The statements in the following two paragraphs are as of November, 1963.

Chapter 10

The Livestock Story

More and Better Feed to Produce
Milk, Eggs, and Meat

As we said in our first chapter, "Happily, there are indications of incipient revolution in animal production also, even though the animal program started 13 years later than the plant program." It was a late but promising start, and to discuss it, we should start at the beginning.

Livestock Were Introduced into Mexico by the Spanish

Domesticated animals were unknown in pre-Columbian Mexico. Lakes and streams and the canals connecting the "floating gardens" of the chinampa system (see Chapter 8) supplied the ancient peoples of the Valley of Mexico with many fish, and these, along with wild game, were the principal source of meat. In 1519 Cortez reported: "There are in this land all kinds of animals and birds . . . such as stags, roe deer, fallow deer, wolves, partridges, pigeons, doves of two or three kinds, quail, hares, and rabbits; in birds and wild animals there is no difference between this land and Spain."[1]

The early Spanish immigrants, accustomed to the important role of domesticated animals in their homeland, could not conceive of a permanent settlement without livestock. On his second voyage, in 1493, Columbus brought European livestock, poultry, and seeds to the New World for the first time. His fleet of 17 vessels, with 1,350

---

[1] Quoted in W. H. Dusenberry, *The Mexican Mesta* (Urbana: University of Illinois Press, 1963), pp. 28–29.

men aboard, carried some 20 stallions, 10 mares, and three mules, as well as an undetermined number of cattle, hogs, sheep, goats, and poultry—both male and female for breeding purposes (except for the mules). He also brought seeds of oranges, limes, melons, and all sorts of vegetables, plus a supply of tools and equipment—all that he felt necessary for founding the first European colony in the New World.[2]

The expedition landed on Española (Santo Domingo) on January 2, 1494. Ranches were created for producing both crops and livestock; because the Spaniards did not thrive on the Indian diet, they produced much of their own food. It became Spanish policy for each succeeding fleet to follow the example of Columbus in bringing livestock, seed, and tools, and soon present-day Cuba, Jamaica, and Puerto Rico were supplied. Livestock quickly multiplied on all four islands, some of them, especially the hogs, later becoming semiwild. It was from these sources that Cortez obtained breeding stock for starting livestock production in Mexico. In 1520 he ordered Gregorio de Villalobos to Veracruz to oversee imports of animals and supplies from the islands, and he sent Diego de Ordaz to settle south of Veracruz and to stock the settlement with livestock and chickens from Jamaica. Importations grew so extensive that the supplying islands had to place restrictions on exports to protect their thriving business. Once in Mexico, the livestock moved out in all directions to the new settlements.

The Spanish crown took an active interest in these developments. A royal decree of 1521 provided that in each new settlement "within a specified time, there must be from ten to thirty settlers, each with one horse, ten milch cows, four oxen, one brood mare, one sow, twenty ewes of Castile, six hens, and a cock. . . ."[3] It is reported that by the 1580's some 200,000 sheep, 100,000 cattle, and 10,000 horses were grazing on the ranges south of Querétaro. This expansion did not stop with Mexico but extended into South America and northward into what are now Texas, New Mexico, Arizona, and California. What was the livestock situation in Mexico three and a half centuries later?

[2] *Ibid.*, p. 25.
[3] *Ibid.*, p. 27.

Forages and Livestock in Mexico Today

WHAT THE SURVEY COMMISSION FOUND

To the Foundation's Survey Commission traveling in rural Mexico in 1941 it was obvious that the livestock introduced by the Spaniards in the sixteenth century had been thoroughly incorporated into Mexico's culture. Oxen were pulling plows; pigs and chickens were in evidence around many houses; herds of sheep and goats were grazing in the fields or ambling along the highways; large dairy herds were visible near most of the larger cities; herds of beef cattle roamed the range lands of the north and the open savannas of the tropics; burros had become beasts of burden; and the cowboy or *charro,* riding a prancing steed and wearing a broad-brimmed hat and classical costume, was a feature of most fiestas. Every type of livestock imported from Spain had found its place.

About a third of Mexico still is in native grasslands, and without livestock most of this large and important resource could not be used economically. In 1941 the quality of all forms of livestock was highly variable. Many closely resembled the descriptions of their European ancestors. More than three centuries in the New World had made but little change in them, although the same three centuries had witnessed dramatic improvement of the breeds of livestock in Europe. In the words of one experienced observer, "The Mexican ranchers take what nature provides without much assistance on their part." And his words applied to most of the pastures as well as to the livestock.

As might be expected, however, there were noteworthy exceptions. Near many of the larger cities, especially Mexico City and Querétaro, the Survey Commission saw several splendid herds of dairy cattle, mostly Holsteins and Jerseys, some of which came from the most distinguished blood lines to be found in the United States and Canada. These herds were well managed and very productive. And on the ranges of the north there were many excellent herds of Hereford beef cattle and some of the Aberdeen-Angus breed, produced largely for sale in the United States. A small amount of meat was exported also and some reached the Mexico City market, but most of the city's beef was lean and tough.

Much of Mexico's beef was produced on the tropical savannas, the greater part of which have pronounced wet and dry seasons. When there is plenty of rain there is plenty of grass, and the animals gain weight; but when the rains stop, the tall grasses soon become brown, woody, unpalatable, and indigestible, and cattle lose from a quarter to a half of what they have gained in the rainy season. As a result, in 1941 it took (and still takes today) from four to six years for a steer to reach marketable size under these conditions, instead of the two years required when the animal has the proper feed to keep it growing continuously.

To the Survey Commission, it seemed clear that Mexico needed cattle of improved types and that these cattle needed better feed than nature was providing in most cases. How could Mexico best accomplish the improvements needed? She had trained only a few competent scientists in either animal husbandry or forage-crop production. In addition, this situation was aggravated by the fact that workers in these two important and complementary fields were separated, in both educational and research institutions, so that close collaboration was difficult. Even more serious was the persistence of age-old rivalries and antagonisms between stockmen accustomed to pasturing their herds on native grassland and farmers producing crops by cultivating the soil. In northern Europe and in the humid sections of the United States, livestock production and crop production have been carefully blended, with a resulting improvement in the efficiency of both. Even today, however, there are few Mexican farmers who practice such systematic integration of feed and livestock production.

Traditionally in Mexico, all responsibility for research with livestock has been the exclusive preserve of the veterinarian. By tradition, also, the veterinarian has been primarily a specialist in animal diseases, to be called in only when an animal is sick. Most veterinary schools give little attention to animal breeding, animal feeding, or the practical management of healthy animals. In the colleges of agriculture, on the other hand, the primary emphasis has been on food crops, with but scant attention paid to forage crops. It is impossible, of course, to separate forage production from animal production at the practical level because each is of little value without the other. Until recently, all efforts to bring veterinarians and agronomists together in Mexico, and in Latin America as a whole, have met with small success. This schism, which according to Toynbee[4] goes back to Cain and Abel, is reflected in the Spanish terminology; *agricultura* deals only with plants, *ganadería* only with animals. As a result, Mexico's progress in the improvement of forage crops and animal production has been seriously impeded, and the Foundation's efforts to help have been delayed and complicated accordingly.

EARLY ATTEMPTS TO HELP

When The Rockefeller Foundation was planning its cooperative program with the Mexican government in 1943, the need for research on forage crops and livestock was discussed, but an existing emergency had to be given priority. At that time, stockmen in Mexico estimated that they had lost about 10,000 cattle as a result of a presumed virus disease called "derriengue," which was thought to be spread by the bite of a type of vampire bat. In response to a request, the Foundation arranged for Dr. Carl TenBroeck, of the Rockefeller Institute for Medical Research, to spend the month of August, 1943, in Mexico collecting samples of brain and salivary tissues of infected cattle. Studies of these tissues by TenBroeck in his laboratory and by Dr. Harald N. Johnson in the Rabies Laboratory of the Foundation's International Health Division in Montgomery, Alabama, demonstrated that derriengue was a type of pseudo-rabies, similar to that reported from other Latin American countries.

In the spring of 1944 Johnson spent two months in Mexico investigating this problem further in the field with members of the Instituto Pecuario (Animal Research Institute). They found a number of vampire bats in the infected areas, and these bats were shown to be the primary vectors of the disease. This discovery paved the way for control and possible eradication of derriengue by the destruction of the bats and the preparation of antirabies vaccines. Unfortunately, these early leads have not been followed up energetically, and the disease remains a serious problem in Mexico.

Initiation of research in the animal sciences was further delayed when in the late 1940's Mexico suffered a severe and widespread outbreak of foot-and-mouth disease. This was halted only after an

[4] A. J. Toynbee, *A Study of History* (London: Oxford University Press, 1934–1939), III, 13.

intensive and prolonged campaign, which was conducted jointly by the governments of Mexico and the United States at a cost of several hundred millions of dollars.

In the meantime, John Pitner, the cooperative program's soil expert and agronomist, started experiments with certain forage crops, especially alfalfa and hubam sweet clover (see Chapter 8). In 1954 Dr. Roderic E. Buller, a forage-crops specialist, joined the Office of Special Studies.

Buller started with a field survey of the principal grasslands and livestock-producing areas of Mexico.[5] This work was carried out in collaboration with two Mexican colleagues, Efraín Hernández Xolocotzi and Martín H. González. They divided the grasslands of Mexico into four large regions on the basis of climate, natural vegetation, type of cultivated forage production, characteristics of the animal population, and the main objectives of the livestock industry, as shown in the accompanying map and table.

Acres of grassland, livestock populations, and production of selected roughages by regions in Mexico[a]

	Regions			
	North	Central	Gulf Plains	Pacific Coast
Grasslands[b] (acres)	115,993,411	16,145,492	12,144,216	21,408,310
Total animal population (not including hogs)	10,671,628	5,807,023	2,357,477	2,786,219
Cattle	4,633,341	2,200,354	2,073,980	1,616,541
Horses	845,903	355,943	244,600	271,168
Mules	293,455	157,226	26,097	109,264
Donkeys	410,579	594,631	7,800	190,327
Sheep	1,458,170	1,196,140	2,000	166,839
Goats	3,030,180	1,302,729	3,000	432,080
Hogs	645,145	942,059	590,747	702,062
Alfalfa production (metric T)	533,840	1,139,311	nonreported	100,777
Corn stover (metric T)	982,356	1,968,445	424,900	860,181

Source: R. E. Buller, E. Hernández X., and Martín H. González, "Grasslands and Livestock Regions of Mexico," *Journal of Range Management*, 13 (1960), 1–6.

[a] Statistical data based on the 1950 census, Secretaría de Economía, Mexico, D.F., Mex.

[b] These figures include only the areas recognized as grasslands. From the point of view of livestock utilization, these should be augumented by the areas with browse plants.

[5] R. E. Buller, E. Hernández X., and Martín H. González, "Grasslands and Livestock Regions of Mexico," *Journal of Range Management*, 13 (1960), 1–6.

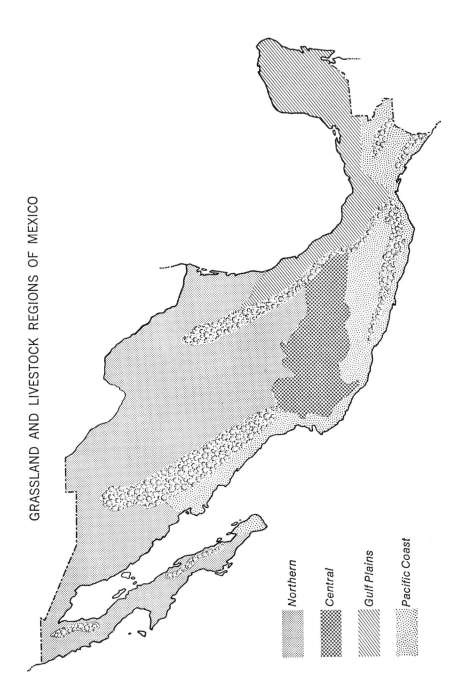

GRASSLAND AND LIVESTOCK REGIONS OF MEXICO

Northern

Central

Gulf Plains

Pacific Coast

THE FORAGE ZONES OF MEXICO AND THEIR LIVESTOCK PROBLEMS

The North Temperate Region comprises more than 100 million acres of native grassland and is one of the principal grazing areas of Mexico. It has long produced excellent beef animals, mainly of the Hereford breed, most of which are exported on the hoof to the United States. Although this region has not produced meat primarily for Mexican consumption, it has supplied a high percentage of the cattle that are exported annually to the United States and thus earn about 100 million U.S. dollars of badly needed foreign exchange.

Rainfall in the region occurs mostly in the summer months and varies widely, both from year to year (eight to 28 inches) and from place to place. As a result, the carrying capacity also varies widely; if a rancher has enough cattle to eat all the available grass in a wet year, he will be short of grass in a dry year. In 1960 it was estimated that the region had lost half its carrying capacity during the previous decade, chiefly because of overgrazing. In many of the drier areas 25 to 30 acres of range are required to support an animal unit (mature cow or equivalent).

Probably this huge area is close to the ceiling of its long-term capacity, but its importance to Mexico is such that steps must be taken to maintain and, if possible, increase its annual contribution to her meat output. Although a large investment for this purpose cannot be justified in view of the low income per acre, Buller and his colleagues expressed the opinion that research could lead to substantial improvements. They stated, for example, that from 3,000 to 4,000 head of cattle were lost each year as a result of eating poisonous plants. Destruction of these plants by airplane spraying with highly selective herbicides would prevent such losses. In addition, proper grazing rates should be determined for the different sectors, supplemental feeding should be tried in those with more favorable conditions, better water-supply systems for livestock should be devised, and the possibility of reseeding with superior species of grass plants should be studied. Researches along most of these lines are already under way, and some have yielded valuable results.

The Central Temperate Region has two distinct types of forage land: about 16 million acres of natural grassland and about 90,000 acres of alfalfa. Annual rainfall averages from 12 to 32 inches, most of it occurring between June and October. Many of the problems involving the natural grasslands are similar to those in the northern region. Because of generally more favorable rainfall, however, there is more cropping in the lower-lying areas, many of which are irrigated; consequently, supplemental feeding is more often feasible than in the north. Most of the open grazing land is communal property; mixed herds of sheep, goats, and cattle move out from the villages to the pastures in the morning and return at night. During years of extreme drought, overgrazing weakens and sometimes even kills the grass. If drought is followed by torrential rains, erosion gets a start and, unless checked, seriously damages large areas.

During the dry season, the irrigated alfalfa in the valleys provides a sharp contrast to the brown grasslands. When properly managed, alfalfa thrives luxuriantly on these lime-rich soils and is the principal feed for the large dairy herds surrounding Mexico City, Querétaro, and other cities. It is grazed or cut, often by hand, and fed to the cattle each day. It is a wonderful feed and grows most of the year, although growth is retarded by low temperatures during the winter months, especially at the higher elevations. Because some interesting research has been done on alfalfa, further discussion of its potential will be reserved until later.

The Tropical Areas on the Gulf and Pacific Coasts, which together comprise 33 million acres, supply much of the beef consumed in Mexico. Annual rainfall varies from 32 to 120 inches in the Gulf area and from 20 to 60 inches in the Pacific area, most of this being concentrated in the summer rainy season. The total in each case is well above that for the two temperate regions. Because of the heavier rainfall and the higher winter temperatures, the animal and forage production potential of these tropical areas is enormous, especially under intensive management, including fertilization and supplemental irrigation during the winter. The cattle are mostly native and of Spanish origin, with the majority showing also pronounced Zebu characteristics. There are also some Santa Gertrudis and Brown Swiss crosses. Zebu blood has been introduced from India, Brazil, and the United States to improve the tolerance of the native cattle to the high temperatures and humidities and the attendant insects and internal parasites. In the past, improved pastures have been seeded primarily to paragrass and guineagrass, both tall-growing species that become very woody, unpalatable, and low in protein as they approach maturity. Their carrying capacity is about one animal unit per 2.5 acres throughout the year. Because of the more favorable rainfall, however, these areas seem to have the greatest potential for expansion, and a modest program of research has therefore been started in the Gulf region.

FORAGE RESEARCH BEGINS AND YIELDS VALUABLE RESULTS

Research is more complicated with forage crops than with a single crop like corn or wheat. A wide range of species of both grasses and legumes are used for forage in different parts of the world, but for the most part these are perennials, some of them difficult and costly to propagate. Their relative value is not easily determined because it may vary widely with the way they are managed; consequently final judgment on a forage crop must be rendered by the animals that eat it. It may yield well and have the proper chemical analysis, but if cattle or sheep do not relish it enough to consume large quantities and to make satisfactory gains in weight as a result, it will not be acceptable as a forage crop.

For these reasons forage research is usually started by establishing an introduction garden or, as it is sometimes called, a forage-crop nursery. Seeds and cuttings of species judged to be worthy of trial are assembled and planted under uniform conditions and their relative performance systematically observed over a period of three to five years. After one to three years certain types will obviously be inferior to others and can be eliminated; others will appear superior and hence worthy of further trial under a wider and more practical range of conditions.

Under the cooperative program, nurseries of this type were established in the northern and central temperate regions and in the Gulf Coast tropics. In the central region attention was focused primarily on forages for the dairy herds around the larger cities. Alfalfa is the principal forage used for this purpose. A large number of improved strains of alfalfa and other legumes were introduced, as well as a wide range of forage grasses, and the legumes and grasses were also grown in mixtures, as is commonly done in Europe and the United States. Results came fast and were clear-cut. Alfalfa proved to be by far the best legume. But at very high altitudes—8,800 feet or above —Kenland red clover was often equal to it and sometimes superior. Furthermore, this clover behaved like a perennial and could be cut as many as 22 times during a four-year period, whereas in the United

States it behaves like a biennial and can seldom be cut more than twice a year—further evidence of the advantages of Mexico's longer growing season.

Variety trials with alfalfa showed that the highly prized winter-hardy varieties from the United States were inferior to many Mexican varieties, demonstrating again the danger of importing improved varieties without first testing them in comparison with the best native ones. Valencia, a variety from Spain, topped the list for a few years until a selection was made from a variety grown near Tanhuato, Michoacán. This selection, now known as Tanverde, is currently preferred because of its consistently high yields of 20 to 28 tons of hay per hectare per year and its above-average growth during the winter months, the period when the forage supply is shortest.

Ordinarily, Mexico imports much of her alfalfa seed (in 1957, for example, 2,500 tons of it). The normal purchase price is about 1,000 U.S. dollars per ton. But the area around Torreón, Coahuila, where alfalfa seed yields of from 300 to 800 kilograms per hectare are commonly obtained, seems to be ideally suited for production of alfalfa seed. Here, then, is a golden opportunity for alert Mexican farmers to retain for their country this $2.5 million in foreign exchange, to develop a very profitable business for themselves, and to provide other farmers with a reliable source of seed of the varieties that grow best in Mexico.

Less research has been done on forage crops for the tropics than for the temperate regions, but several promising leads have been obtained at the Cotaxtla Experiment Station near the city of Veracruz. Pangolagrass, a recumbent type, has proved outstanding for grazing under favorable moisture conditions. Live weight gains of over 400 kilograms per hectare have been achieved with beef cattle pasturing on this grass for the period from July 1 through January 15; this is more than three times the gain obtained with the more common guineagrass under the same conditions. For cutting, Merkeron, a tall-growing grass (*Pennisetum purpureum*) developed by G. W. Burton in the United States, has given phenomenal annual yields of over 200 tons green weight per hectare—equivalent to about 42 tons dry weight—when irrigated and adequately fertilized with nitrogen. It shows promise either for feeding when freshly cut or for silage. Several types of tropical forage legumes also appear promising.

To produce milk or meat economically, animals must eat regularly. Probably the most difficult practical forage-production problem is the development of a system that will provide for these regular requirements in an area having a four-to-six-months dry season. In some places the answer may be irrigation, in others silage or some other preserved supplementary feed. There is still much to learn, and men are being trained to learn it.

Work with Livestock Gets under Way

ANIMAL SCIENTISTS JOIN THE PROGRAM

Partly because of advantages inherent in the nature of poultry, the science and art of poultry production usually makes more rapid progress in a country than any of the other animal industries. Such was the case in the United States, and the spectacular advances achieved there by the early 1950's stimulated the same pattern in Mexico. When progressive Mexican poultrymen tried out the new methods, however, they frequently encountered problems for which they were unprepared, and so they appealed to their government for assistance. The Mexican government relayed these requests to The Rockefeller Foundation, which in 1955 responded by appointing to the Office of Special Studies Dr. John A. Pino, who had already earned an enviable reputation among poultrymen in the United States, where he was associate professor of poultry science at Rutgers University. In Mexico, Pino quickly initiated a broad research program, first with chickens and then with turkeys. His competence and personality soon won the respect and confidence of both practical poultrymen and professional animal scientists.

In 1960 Pino was joined by Dr. Daniel D. Hagen, an animal pathologist, and the next year the Foundation appointed Dr. Ned S. Raun to assist primarily with nutrition problems of ruminants. These three men are the only full-time Foundation staff members associated with the animal science program in Mexico as this is being written.[6]

[6] Late 1964.

Because livestock problems in Mexico are both numerous and difficult, special emphasis was given from the start to the selection and further education of promising young Mexican scientists. Pino, Hagen, and Raun take more pride in the progress of the men selected than in any other aspect of their work.

PIONEERING WITH POULTRY

Unlike cattle, sheep, and goats, poultry does not have a rumen in which to store and partially digest large volumes of coarse forages; to grow quickly and economically, poultry must have concentrated feeds like cereal grains, oil meal cake, and fish meal. Human beings, pigs, and poultry are similar in this respect and often are competitors for grain when the supply is short. For this reason, even in the more developed countries poultry was long considered a luxury food, one which the masses of the people could usually afford only on holidays, Sundays, and other special occasions. But in the past twenty years this has been changed. In many countries poultry is now much cheaper than beef, largely because research on breeding, feeding, disease control, management, and marketing has brought about increases in the efficiency of poultry as converters of grain into meat or eggs.

The chicken offers several obvious advantages over the cow as an experimental animal; not only is it much smaller and hence less costly per unit, but also its reproductive cycle is much shorter and hence economical of time. Experiments involving hundreds, even thousands of chicks can be carried out more easily and at less expense than experiments with ten to a hundred cattle. In addition, chickens are normally raised in confinement where the environment is less variable and therefore simpler to control. Furthermore, poultry research conducted in one country is more likely to prove applicable in another than is the case with many of the larger animals. Most of the basic research on poultry nutrition carried out in the United States applies in Mexico, and many of the highly developed breeding strains can be imported into Mexico and used directly. As a result, Mexico has been able to achieve striking improvements in her poultry industry in a short time and with but little expense.

Many problems, however, can be solved only in the local environment. Because of differences in climate, Mexico's problems concerning sources of feed for poultry, housing, diseases, insect control, and sanitation are different from those in the United States. Mexican poultrymen must also contend with rapid changes in market demand and prices, to which they must adjust quickly or else face financial ruin. In the past few years Pino and his Mexican colleagues have been besieged for advice on poultry management problems. Because feed represents the most costly item in the poultryman's budget, they have been exploring every local product that shows promise as a satisfactory and cheap substitute for an imported one.

The *garbanzo* or chickpea (*Cicer arietinum*), which is widely grown in Mexico, has been found to be an excellent feed for poultry and is a very good source of high-quality protein that can be substituted for more expensive imported sources to a considerable extent without any reduction in productivity. Grain sorghum has been found equal to corn in poultry rations. Molasses, available in Mexico in large quantities because of increased sugar production, can supply up to 25 percent of the energy requirements of broilers and can also be used for feeding layers. Dried blood, a by-product from the slaughterhouses, has been found to be a good local source of lysine. And the petals of the Aztec marigold have proved to be a rich as well as highly economical source of xanthophyll for improving the yellow pigmentation of egg yolks and the visceral fat, skin, and shanks. These local sources of feed, properly developed and utilized, will be worth much more to Mexico than the ancient stores of Aztec gold.

With profit margins per egg or per broiler decreasing as a result of competition in a limited market, Mexican producers have begun to realize that high chick mortality, poor feed conversion, and mediocre production cannot be tolerated. In the modern poultry industry profit margins on the individual bird are extremely small. Overall profits depend on raising very large numbers, in limited space, on carefully balanced rations, under the most sanitary conditions, and with all operations mechanized as completely as possible. All this requires a level of management, an attention to details, unknown to the older type of poultryman accustomed to letting his small flock fend for itself. Some of these smaller producers have made the necessary adjustments to modern methods and stayed in business; others have not and may soon cease to be poultrymen. But they now have available the resources of the rapidly moving poultry research program that Pino initiated only nine years ago.

A New Livestock Center Is Established

In 1962 Mexico took a major step forward in improvement of her livestock when the Minister of Agriculture, Ing. Julián Rodríguez Adame, established the National Center for Livestock Research, with headquarters at Palo Alto on the outskirts of Mexico City. All research in the animal sciences was consolidated in this new unit, including the animal sciences program initiated in the Office of Special Studies and temporarily attached to INIA. Pino, Hagen, and Raun, the three Foundation staff members working in this program, were transferred to the new unit, and Pino was named director of the Center.

In recognition of the Center's importance, the Mexican government has sharply increased its support for research in the animal sciences. Existing buildings have been renovated and repaired, and other facilities added; the number of research personnel is steadily expanding; and new departments concerned with range management, forage utilization, and animal genetics have recently been created. In addition to furnishing three staff members for the Center, the Foundation has appointed scientists on a short-term basis to collaborate on special projects and has helped with the purchase of equipment and supplies and with other operating expenses.

Most important of all, perhaps, in the long run, the Foundation has assisted in the training of many promising young Mexican scientists for service in the animal science field. Because for various reasons research and higher education in the animal sciences have been seriously neglected in Mexico, the supply of well-trained men in the various specialized disciplines has always been woefully short, and the creation of the new animal research center, with wider responsibilities and an expanded budget, inevitably aggravated this shortage. Beginning in 1960, however, in-service training was stepped up and the Foundation provided increased numbers of fellowships and scholarships for training abroad. Under its sponsorship, 17 men have now obtained graduate degrees at institutions in the United States; six have either earned the Ph.D. degree or will soon complete the requirements, and the others have earned the M.S. degree. These men have studied in a wide range of special fields, and many of them have already demonstrated unusual qualities of leadership.

Since animal foods—milk, eggs, and meat—are expensive, although of high nutritional quality, one school of thought maintains that countries with large numbers of underfed people should concentrate primarily on increasing the production of edible plant products like cereals, vegetables, and fruits. Those who hold such views often overlook two very important facts. First, many such countries have large areas of semiarid land that cannot be used for cultivated crops but can, as we have seen, produce enough grass to carry millions of cattle. Second, only about half the calories in most food plants are in a form readily digestible in the human stomach; the rest, which often would be useful as animal feed, are commonly wasted.

In addition, many crops grown for processing leave residues that are extremely valuable as animal feeds. The cake left after the extraction of oil from cottonseed, soybeans, sesame, peanuts, coconuts, and many other oil seeds constitutes an excellent feed for livestock—and even for human beings if properly processed. Molasses, a by-product of the sugar industry, is one of the cheapest and highest-quality sources of energy for a wide range of animals, from chickens to cattle, if not used in excess of 20 to 30 percent of the animal's energy requirements. These factors are all of great significance in Mexico now, and they will grow in significance as her population increases. According to the 1960 census, over eight million of her 34 million people (more than 23 percent) were not eating eggs, milk, meat, or fish. Before many years, however, it is possible—even probable—that Mexico will be producing more wheat and corn than her people can consume and that some of the surplus grain can then be used to produce more pork and poultry products, as is now true of 90 percent of her sorghum production.

Viewed as a whole, these developments in forage-crop production, in livestock production, and in the animal sciences, although relatively new, are already making important contributions, and the foundations have been laid for even greater achievements. To secure these gains, further steps must be taken to bridge the ancient chasm between the livestock men and the producers of crops. To the extent that both feed and animals are produced on the same farm by the same man, this bridging may become increasingly feasible.

It is to be hoped that a quarter of a century hence, some clever agricultural economist will calculate the returns that Mexico has received from her increased investment in education and research in the animal sciences. Only then will the true significance of Minister Rodríguez Adame's action in setting up the National Center for Livestock Research be fully appreciated. It would also be interesting for Mexico and other countries to speculate, on the basis of such studies, about how much she and they have lost by not starting such research half a century sooner.

Chapter 11

Education

*The Evolution of Agricultural
Scientists and Educators*

The development of a competent corps of Mexican agricultural scientists and scholars was the most valuable permanent contribution of the revolution in agriculture. Indeed, most of the present generation were the direct products of the revolution because they helped win it while serving in the ranks, and now they are insuring its continuing success by their leadership in research and education.

From the very first, the Survey Commission recognized that the primary obligation clearly was to help improve agricultural materials and methods through research, but they also were insistent on capitalizing on the educational values of that research. How far the primary obligation was discharged has been told in preceding chapters. And the ways in which young Mexicans became productive scientists have also been discussed. These general sketches and incidental allusions cannot, however, do justice to the tremendous significance of the intellectual revolution that transformed Mexico from a dependent to an independent country scientifically. No number of words can do it entire justice. But let some Mexicans speak for themselves, for there is truth and wisdom in their words.

Two decades ago, Mexico "urgently needed technical assistance in order to initiate a revolution in agriculture properly." But twenty years later: "Thanks to individual training, including the sending of Mexicans to study at the best agricultural institutions in the United States, we now have a technical corps that can compete at the highest professional level with agricultural technologists anywhere in the world. For us in Mexico this is the meaning of international cooperation, in this case between The Rockefeller Foundation and the Federal Government of Mexico." Both statements were made in connection with the film *Harvest,* a portrayal of some phases of the Mexican agricultural revolution. And both were made by two extraordinary Ministers of Agriculture: the first by Don Marte Gómez, who had the wisdom to initiate the revolution, and the second by Ing. Julián Rodríguez Adame, who had the skill to capitalize its values.

To make Mexico's native resources most fruitful required making her native scientific intelligence more functional. This is easily said but harder done. The accomplishment required not only the conceptual wisdom of Gómez and Rodríguez Adame but also the persistent efforts of many other dedicated and resourceful men. Although the intervening ministries of Nazario Ortíz Garza and Ignacio Flores Muñoz made some contributions also, the alpha and the omega, 1943 and 1963, are the administrations of Gómez and Rodríguez Adame, because the hopes that were sown in the first have produced abundant fruits in the second.

There may be a little pardonable pride in the statement that "we now have a technical corps that can compete at the highest professional level with agricultural technologists anywhere in the world." But there is no boastfulness in it, for Mexico is indeed rapidly approaching the upper echelons in the world's family of nations. As President López Mateos said in speaking to 300 members of the Mexican Union of Associations of Engineers, "We are no longer an underdeveloped country, but a nation in course of full development, which requires the professional competence and human qualities of all its sons."[1]

To maintain the pace that she has set in developing scientists and technologists, Mexico is striving to strengthen her base of general education for the masses. On May 17, 1963, a significant editorial appeared in *Excelsior,* commenting on the "Teacher's Day" speech of Dr. Jaime Torres Bodet, Minister of Public Education. In the preceding 53 months the government had constructed 20,105 new classrooms for public schools. Enrollment had increased 67 percent in primary schools, 95 percent in intermediate schools, and 120 percent in technological institutes or trade schools. During the same period appropriations for universities had increased almost 177

[1] Quoted in the Educational Edition of *Excelsior,* May 15, 1963, in an article by Regino Díaz Redondo.

percent. Mexico is indeed striving to educate her people, for she realizes that the success of a democracy depends on the fullest possible education of all its members.

Our primary present concern, however, is with the evolution of higher education in agriculture. To appreciate the course and significance of this evolution it is necessary to leave the relatively bright days of the present and start again with the grayer days of the past.

More Scientists Needed, 1943

The statement of Gómez that "to initiate a revolution in agriculture properly, we urgently needed technical assistance" was literally true in 1943. As José Merino Millán wrote: "To be honest, we must admit that for many years the general panorama of agriculture in the economic development of the Republic was based more on theories, words, and on sporadic efforts feebly guided by the government, rather than on definite programs and concrete facts of immediate practical value."[2] He also points out that the interest of the administrations of the past twenty years in the development and progress of agricultural investigation and education was a fact of "surpassing importance." And that was really the way it was.

In 1943 most Mexican agrónomos were generalists and few were specialists. Relatively few had the confidence born of personal experience in successfully applying available knowledge to the solution of practical problems, and still fewer had the confidence and technical skills to obtain the new knowledge that was so urgently needed. Some were too timid about doing things and some were too bold. The scientifically timid made few mistakes but did little good; the bold took chances but made many mistakes because they did not know how to calculate the chances. And so between the two of them they left a wide gap. How could it be filled?

Realizing the need for regional experimentation, the Ministry had established a number of outlying experiment stations. Not unnaturally, however, the idea had developed that thinking and planning had to be concentrated in Mexico City and that all directions had to emanate from there. Many station directors therefore

[2] In "Panorama General del Desarrollo Agrícola en México," *Revista Hoy*, No. 1320, September, 1962, pp. 35–50. (Translation by the authors.)

functioned only as straw bosses in executing the detailed plans that the City sent them. They did not know the names of the varieties in varietal tests because the prepackaged seed for planting came to them under code numbers. They did not know which fertilizers gave the best results because they did not know what fertilizers they had applied. Naturally, they could not tell the farmers how to profit from the experiments when they themselves did not know what profit was in them. Experiment stations were urgently needed, but they urgently needed experienced men to operate them. Mexico simply did not have enough scientific manpower, and the colleges were not developing it fast enough.

The situation in Mexico in 1943 was not unlike that in the United States in 1883. Following the enactment of the Morrill Act in the United States, which became federal law in 1863, the various states established colleges of agriculture and mechanic arts. Then they groped around for almost a quarter of a century trying to find out how to be useful, because there was no coherent body of scientific knowledge for professors to teach and for students to learn.

After trying this and that without conspicuous success, a few leaders in the United States realized that the colleges had to learn something useful through experimentation and research if their teaching was to be of any help. Therefore they urged the establishment of agricultural experiment stations to serve as living sources of progress in agriculture and agricultural education. The federal Congress responded by enacting the Hatch Act in 1887, providing for the establishment of state experiment stations, and from that time onward the colleges began to evolve into useful institutions of higher learning. Instead of merely retailing old information, they began to produce new information. Being creative, they became progressive and thus contributed largely to scientific and social progress.

In Mexico, too, research catalyzed the revolution in agricultural education. Like many other countries, Mexico had tried to improve her research and educational institutions by changing the patterns of organization, but this mechanistic approach had been relatively futile and probably explains why so many patterns had been tried. The Survey Commission had written: "But the schools can hardly be improved until the teachers are improved; extension work cannot be improved until extension men are improved; and investigational work cannot be made more productive until investigators acquire greater competence." The question in 1943 was how and when the improvement could be made; the problem in 1963 is to measure the improvement and evaluate the factors that contributed to it.

The New Education Begins Officially, 1944

THE THREE PHASES OF THE NEW EDUCATION

The best educational programs are those that work best in the conditions under which they must operate. There were special conditions in Mexico when the cooperative program started. The immediate need was for speed in producing more food; the ultimate need was for Mexican scientists and scientific institutions that could guarantee continuity of effort in producing it. Efforts to meet the immediate need therefore took priority over those to satisfy the ultimate one; investigation had priority over education. Although Harrar and his group naturally had to do first things first, from the very first they tried to combine their experimentation with education. Because there were several reasons why it was not feasible to engage in formal education, they engaged in informal education and thus built the basis for the improvement of formal education.

Three interrelated and interacting educational phases were incorporated into the Mexican Agricultural Program: (1) the internship phase, whereby young Mexican agrónomos learned how to do useful scientific work by helping to do it; (2) the fellowship phase, which enabled the best interns to amplify their formal education in foreign universities; (3) the institutional phase, which helped in the development of Mexican schools of higher learning in agriculture. Research was a vital force in all phases, and resourcefulness in capitalizing its direct and indirect values was the keystone that bound the phases together.

THE INTERNSHIP PHASE: INFORMAL IN-SERVICE EDUCATION

Education is wherever one can find it. It is most fruitful when students and teachers foregather with zeal where there is much for both to learn and little prescription regarding the time and manner of learning it. Thus young Mexican agrónomos and Foundation scientists worked and learned together in fields and laboratories that were workshops of productive enterprises. This educational procedure is age-old because it is natural. Whether called the pedagogical, apprenticeship, or internship system, or in-service training, it worked well in ancient Greece and it worked well in modern Mexico.

"There is the best blankety-blank teacher that ever trod the ground of this campus," said a picturesque dean in the Virginia Polytechnic Institute, where George Harrar was teaching plant pathology and several other biological subjects, sometimes as many as 23 credit-hours a week. He also found time to supervise the pruning of the campus trees, to determine the bacterial content of water and milk supplies of nearby Roanoke, to act as assistant coach of the track team, and to participate in campus activities generally.

"Doctor Harrar, you sure did make yonder tree look pretty; I'm not sure I can make this one to match but I sure am trying," a student helper observed solemnly from the top of a lofty tree that he was trying to beautify. And a member of the track team, who had placed second instead of first in the decisive race of a dual meet, said lugubriously, "Doctor Harrar, sir, I could have won that race if I'd run it like you showed me in practice and if I hadn't eaten those cold potatoes for lunch like you told me not to. But if you give me another chance I sure will try hard to come in first next time." The general student verdict: "He helps us a lot, and he funs a lot with us, but there's nothing funny about what he expects of us."

Mexico needed a man like Harrar in 1943, and he wasted no time in starting to teach young Mexicans. In a progress report dated June, 1944, he wrote: "It was mutually agreed by the Secretaría de Agricultura y Fomento and the Rockefeller Foundation that the staff members of the Foundation should be available for educational service when so desired by the Secretaría de Agricultura y Fomento. The first service of this nature is being rendered through the commissioning of young Mexican scientists to the Rockefeller Foundation resident staff and designating the group as the Oficina de Estudios Especiales de la Secretaría de Agricultura y Fomento. These young men participate actively in the field and laboratory phases of research projects in force, have an opportunity to become familiar with research techniques, and help plan and direct research activities and evaluate research data. Subsequently by mutual consent a number of these young scientists will be given Rockefeller Foundation scholarships for advanced study in the United States or elsewhere. The first of these men, Ing. José Rodríguez Vallejo, has recently departed for a year of study at the University of Minnesota. . . ." Thus the Mexican Ministry and the Foundation established an organic union between research and education, and the Ministry, to enable the organism to function effectively, created within itself, under Harrar's direction, the Office of Special Studies about which we have had so much to say.

José (Pepe) Rodríguez Vallejo, the first of about 550 Mexican agrónomos who were commissioned to the Office, was originally self-commissioned, for he invited himself to help even before the commissioning system had been established. In the spring of 1943 a member of the Foundation's agricultural advisory committee was in a laboratory of the Department of Agriculture in Mexico City, taking notes on harvested samples of wheat. A dapper young man appeared in the doorway and asked politely, "May I come in?"

"Sure, the door's open."

After a short exchange of polite banalities, young Rodríguez said, "Will it bother you if I watch what you're doing?"

"No, I'll just have to be more careful not to make mistakes."

After watching for a short time, Rodríguez remarked, "Maybe I could help instead of just watching."

"You could, but I don't want to interfere with your regular duties."

"I'll make this one of my regular duties."

"But will it be all right with your immediate superior? Who is he?"

"Ing. Darío Arrieta, the Director General of Agriculture."

"Well, would you mind asking his permission?"

"It's not necessary, but I will if you want me to."

Soon Pepe came back. "It's okay."

"Arrieta consented?"

"No, he commanded; he told me to go to work, to help all I can, and to learn all I can."

A few days later "Dynamo Darío" stopped by and asked, "Is Pepe helping?"

"Yes."

"Is he learning?"

The answer had to be: "I couldn't keep that young fellow from learning if I tried."

Pepe Rodríguez was soon followed by other outstanding young Mexicans. By December 1, 1945, less than two years after the program began, 24 had participated, and three had already prepared and eight were preparing theses for their professional ingeniero degree based on their own researches and educational experiences. Within 10 years 192 young men had received specialized training and education; by 1954 the number had increased to 250; and in 1956 there were "86 young Mexican scientists in various stages of training," according to E. J. Wellhausen, then in charge of the Office. Some 550 were schooled in the Office of Special Studies during its lifetime from 1944 to January 1, 1961.

What did these young men learn? The first thing they learned was how to work; the second was how to work effectively; the third was how to work independently. At first it was mostly physical work, for a successful agricultural experimentalist cannot avoid some drudgery. Field experimentation cannot be done in an air-conditioned ivory tower; it must be done in the open, where the sun can burn and the wind can sting. And yet it must be done.

Field work came as a shock to some young interns who had expected their agricultural education to emancipate them from the hardships of the fields. "Are we then to be *peones*, working the fields with our own hands?" Some sputtered and some spat, and a few decided to forget the whole thing. But most of them stuck with it. They were shocked again when they saw Harrar and Wellhausen and Borlaug change from city clothes into field clothes and calmly go to work in the field. As one of them said later: "We knew that those fellows were bigger shots scientifically than we were. So when we saw them working in the field as if they were used to it, we took another look. And look where we are now!"

When it became apparent that Harrar and company could and would run anything from a hand cultivator to an electric calculating machine, the boys began to realize that probably this was one reason for their success. And so they learned to do likewise. As they began to see the results of the experimentation, the fields acquired new attractions and field garb became a badge of distinction. And when they were given higher responsibilities as they developed higher abilities, they began to see that the purpose of field work had not been to haze them but to help them learn methods of improving agriculture from the ground up in order that they might help others up from the ground. They learned that success was compounded of industry and intelligence.

Neither action without knowledge nor knowledge without action is particularly productive. Accordingly, the Office aimed to combine technical training with scientific education. As there was no post-graduate college at Chapingo, the Office itself assumed some of the functions of a graduate school. As soon as the various research projects got under way, the Mexican boys were assigned to project leaders—Wellhausen, Borlaug, Colwell, Pitner, Laird, Niederhauser, McKelvey, Barnes, and others, with Harrar acting as coordinator of the entire enterprise. Each project leader then became professional supervisor and educational adviser of the interns in his project. There were no orthodox classroom exercises, but there was much learning where the sources of learning were—the experimental fields, the laboratories, the library, and the seminar room.

The seminar room and the newly created library soon became the common intellectual center for all members of the Office. The seminars, held every Saturday forenoon, were mutual-benefit meetings for exchanging facts and experiences, for expressing and defending ideas, for developing concepts, and for developing perspective on aims, procedures, and relative values. They were seminars in the true sense of the word *seminarium,* a place where seeds are sown. Many intellectual seeds were sown in these *seminarios* and many young men reaped a rich intellectual harvest, for Harrar and others breathed real life into all seminars and made them vital factors in the education of the participants.

The best that any educational institution can do is to do the best it can for its students. Naturally, there were differences in the degree of educability of the 550 young interns, but the Office tried to help each one develop his capacities fully and to guide him according to his aptitudes and interests. Accordingly, those interns who functioned best in practical ways were guided into practical fields; those with special intellectual interests and abilities were granted fellowships for study in universities abroad. The fellowship system early became an integral part of the educational program.

THE FELLOWSHIP PHASE

"1944. This date is memorable in the history of higher education in agriculture, because a beginning was made in sending professional agronomists abroad to perfect their studies. . . ." This statement appears in a report of the Mexican Ministry of Agriculture on its activities from September 1, 1960, to August 31, 1961. The year 1944 was indeed the beginning of a new era, because it marked the beginning of systematized efforts in selecting and sending good men abroad to amplify their education.

The Foundation appointed as the first fellow, not surprisingly, Pepe Rodríguez; this was done officially in April, 1944. The next year it gave fellowships to Leonel Robles Gutiérrez, now director of the School of Agriculture of the Technological Institute of Monterrey; Joaquín Loredo Goytortua, the present director general of agriculture in the Ministry of Agriculture and Animal Husbandry; and Benjamín Ortega Cantero, now in charge of an important irrigation district in northern Mexico.

As the number of men assigned to the Office of Special Studies increased, the number of fellowships increased also, to an average of about 15 a year. The Foundation granted 252 fellowships to 155 individuals during the 20 years under consideration. Of this number, 52 individuals obtained both the M.S. and Ph.D. degrees, 91 received the M.S. alone, and only 12 returned without a degree.

The degrees were obtained in almost all fields of plant science related to agriculture and in a few fields of animal science, from 32 universities and colleges in the United States extending from Maine to Washington State, from California to Florida, and from North Dakota, Minnesota, Wisconsin, and Michigan to Mississippi, Louisiana, and Texas, with numerous intermediate locations. Germany contributed one Ph.D. degree. The fellows, therefore, were certainly not molded into a single pattern, but brought back to Mexico a wide diversity of experience and abilities.

THE INSTITUTIONAL PHASE

How did the graduates of the Office of Special Studies use their education? A random sample in 1958–1959 showed the following distribution of major activities: teaching, 30; investigation, 25; administration, 10; technical services, five; extension, five; private or commercial, five. It is noteworthy that the director of the National Institute of Agricultural Research and the two assistant directors are "graduates" of the Office of Special Studies and that five of their six advanced degrees were obtained on Rockefeller Foundation fellowships. All the principal project leaders in the Institute also graduated from the Office of Special Studies. The cooperative educational efforts centered in this Office have furnished Mexico with a high percentage of its principal investigators and educators in agriculture.

The Survey Commission had written: "But the schools can hardly be improved until the teachers are improved." The Office of Special Studies did not set out to train teachers; it set out to help young Mexicans to become educated scientists, naturally hoping that some would want to use their education in helping others to get an education. And so it proved to be, for close to half of the former Rockefeller Foundation fellows are now doing at least some teaching. They have been vital factors in elevating the level of higher education in Mexico.

The Agricultural Colleges, Old and New, 1943–1963

THE NUMBER OF COLLEGES INCREASES

Progress can be measured by comparing the number and the quality of agricultural colleges in 1943 and 1963. It is easy to show the increase in numbers by simple figures, but it is harder to demonstrate the improvement in quality by simple words. Taking the simpler job first, there were three schools then, and now there are seven. Pertinent data regarding them are given in the table on page 188.

Of the three older schools, the National School is still under the direction of the federal Ministry of Agriculture. The two others, originally privately supported, have been affiliated with or incorporated into state universities. The Hermanos Escobar was established in 1906 by the father of the present Escobar brothers as the Private School of Agriculture of Ciudad Juárez. It remained under the sole management of his sons until recently, when a supervisory board was established, comprising representatives of the federal Ministry of Agriculture, the government of the State of Chihuahua, the director of the School, the University of Chihuahua, the faculty of the School, the student body, the alumni organization, and a representative of Escobar Brothers and Company. The federal Ministries of Agriculture and of Public Education and the State of Chihuahua now contribute to the financial support of the School. The Antonio Narro was born of the philanthropy of Don Antonio Narro Rodríguez, who left for the purpose his entire fortune, comprising prin-

Name, location, date of establishment, and number
of students in colleges of agriculture.

Name	Location	Date established	Number of students, 1963	
			Total	Percent
Escuela Nacional de Agricultura	Chapingo, Mexico	1854	658	29
Escuela Superior de Agricultura "Hermanos Escobar," Universidad de Chihuahua	Ciudad Juárez, Chihuahua	1906	445	20
Escuela Superior de Agricultura "Antonio Narro," Universidad de Coahuila	Saltillo, Coahuila	1923	314	14
Escuela de Agricultura y Ganadería, Instituto Tecnológico y de Estudios Superiores de Monterrey	Monterrey, Nuevo León	1948	281	12
Escuela de Agricultura y Ganadería, Universidad de Sonora	Hermosillo, Sonora	1953	250	11
Facultad de Agronomía, Universidad de Nuevo León	Monterrey, Nuevo León	1956	123	5
Escuela Superior de Agricultura, Universidad de Sinaloa	Culiacán, Sinaloa	1960	200	9
			2,271	100

Source: From a report by the Asociación Nacional de Directores de las Escuelas Superiores de Agricultura, entitled "Educación, Investigación y Extensión Agrícolas en México," January, 1964.

cipally his Hacienda de Buenavista, some 12,000 acres of land near Saltillo in the State of Coahuila. This school was privately operated during its early years, but the State of Coahuila assumed responsibility for it in 1938 and adopted it as part of the State University in 1957.

The four new colleges were established as schools within universities or the equivalent. The Technological Institute of Monterrey, a private institution, was founded in 1943 and now comprises six professional schools, including the School of Agriculture and Animal Husbandry, which was created September 1, 1948. The other three are schools within state universities—Sonora, Nuevo León, and

Sinaloa. At present, therefore, there is one federal institution, four are within state universities, one has university connections, and one is privately supported and managed but fully and officially accredited in Mexico and by the International Association of Universities and several other accrediting agencies.

The three pre-1943 schools still enrolled 63 percent of the 2,271 agricultural students in the country in 1963. Of the 37 percent in the new schools, 20 percent are in the Pacific Coast area where there were no schools prior to 1953, and 17 percent are in the new schools in Monterrey.

The cost of schooling differs considerably in the different schools. In the National School 99 percent of the students have full-expense scholarships. In the Instituto Tecnológico at Monterrey, on the other hand, 80 percent pay their own way; because 21 percent are non-Mexicans, many with scholarships from their own countries, it appears that almost all of the Mexican students pay for their schooling. In contrast, 88 percent of the agricultural students at the State University in Monterrey have some financial help, and those from the State of Nuevo León usually are excused from paying even the nominal tuition fees if they present evidence that they cannot afford them. "We needed a poor boys' university in Nuevo León" is the reason usually given for the establishment of the University Faculty of Agronomy after the nearby Instituto Tecnológico was already in operation. The universities of Sonora and Sinaloa also reflect the principle that higher education should be within the reach of people of modest means, as upwards of 95 percent of the students have scholarships of some kind. Whatever the virtues and defects of the present scholarship systems, the need for financial aid to worthy students will continue as long as the average per capita income in Mexico is only about 10 percent of that in the United States.

THE QUALITY OF TEACHERS AND TEACHING IMPROVES

Not only are there more schools of agriculture, but there is higher quality in the schools now than in 1943. There are more competent teachers, many students are better prepared, libraries and laboratories are better, teaching and research are closer together, two schools now offer postgraduate work, and educational leaders are cooperatively trying to improve existing schools and to help develop an adequate system of agricultural schools for the future.

More teachers have good academic preparation and they spend more time in teaching now than 20 years ago. In 1943 the number of professors with advanced degrees was negligible; now about a third have them. Of the 249 professors in the seven schools, 18 have the doctorate and 52 have a master's degree. Of course, advanced degrees do not guarantee proficiency in teaching, but they are a reasonable guarantee of proficiency in subject matter to be taught. And mastery of subject matter is still an important requisite for effective teaching at the higher levels in science. Some of the most skillful teachers of the past could give their students only limited help, either because of limited knowledge or because of limited time to spend with them. One of the most obvious defects in the old days was the lack of full-time teachers.

Two decades ago less than 10 percent of those who taught were full-time teachers. There was a general shortage of scientific manpower, and several other fields of activity were more attractive and lucrative than teaching. Some professionals were willing to enhance their prestige and amplify their income by giving some college lectures, but their teaching was incidental and sometimes perfunctory. Those who were willing to dedicate themselves primarily to teaching usually had to supplement their meager salaries by gainful extracurricular occupations. Whatever all the reasons for the part-time system, the results were bad. Most college students needed more guidance than they got because many of them were poorly prepared for independent learning. The faculty-student ratio appeared to be fairly high, but it was really low when calculated on the basis of full-time faculty.

Recognizing the problem, the schools have been making persistent efforts, and about 50 percent of the professors are now on full time. About two thirds of those at the Monterrey Instituto Tecnológico and at the University of Coahuila (Antonio Narro) are on full time. At the other schools the actual numbers of full-time and part-time as given for 1963 were: the National School, 39 and 74; Hermanos Escobar, 12 and 8; University of Nuevo León, 8 and 10; University of Sonora, 12 and 10; and University of Sinaloa, 5 and 6. Thus more than half were on full time in all but three schools, which is indeed gratifying progress.

There has been gradual improvement in the preparation of students for the agricultural colleges as standards of public education improved and expanded beyond the large cities. In 1943 many students still had to prepare for college at the college itself—in *preparatorio;* now, the general requirement for admission is the *bachillerato* or equivalent, which in the past has implied 11 years of schooling in elementary and secondary schools and soon will imply 12 years, as in the United States. Special entrance examinations also are required in some cases. It is well to remember, of course, that what a student knows when he enters college is not so important as what he learns in college and what he can do after he graduates from it. In those colleges that now require the bachillerato or equivalent, the course takes five years, thus requiring a total of 16 years of study for a college degree. The requirements in Hermanos Escobar and the University of Sinaloa are somewhat lower.

Mexico is making commendable progress in strengthening her entire educational system. Thanks to the "New Education" most students now know considerably more and certainly can do much more on graduation from agricultural college than in the old days. From the verbalism of the "Old Education" to the sense realism of the "New Education" is a long distance conceptually, but Mexico has covered it in record time.

The contrast between the worst of the Old Education and the best of the New is the difference between dusk and dawn. In 1941 Ing. Jesús Patiño Navarrete, a distinguished alumnus of the National School of Agriculture and Subsecretary of Agriculture, 1958–1964, said about the Old: "We had to be taught much about agrarian reform and agricultural theory; but some of us wanted to look through a microscope to find out for ourselves whether the chromosomes which our professors talked about were mere words or real things, but there were almost no microscopes. We applied for permission to make experiments on small pieces of the school land to find out whether we could learn how to make useful plants grow better, to get some much-needed money, or to show nearby farmers the advantages of progressive agriculture, but we were branded sometimes as troublemakers."[3] Now, all advanced students know chromosomes. In Patino's day (late 1920's) the 800 acres of school land at the National School really were covered with weeds, some beauti-

[3] Quoted by permission.

ful but all noxious; now they are covered with useful crops and beautifully designed experiments. Then the library was a miscellaneous collection of books and pamphlets, mostly old and dusty; now there is a well-kept library containing 20,000 books, more than 17,000 scientific bulletins, and about 350 collections of scientific journals. And students and staff use the library more now than then.

It was about 15 years ago that The Rockefeller Foundation made a grant to help Chapingo develop a modern library. On a visit to the School, one of us asked the Secretary, "How is the new library?" "Beautiful," came the quick reply. But there was nothing quick about a proposed visit to see it; indeed there was strong evidence of a skillful delaying action. After several muffled telephone conversations, the last of which ended with the semiaudible admonition, "Tell them to hurry up and get over there," the walk to the new library started—by a circuitous route. On arrival, there were two students in the big reading room, one obviously panting for breath and fumbling with some papers, the other deeply absorbed in reading a magazine. A discreet peek over the reader's shoulder to see what was so absorbing revealed the *Saturday Evening Post* held upside down. The episode provoked a good laugh between good friends and also the reflection that good facilities are not good for much unless they are well used. But that was then; it is different now. The most recent visit was really unannounced, and there were 40 students studying in the reading room. All of them may not have been panting for knowledge, but there was no evidence that any of them were panting for breath.

Also symptomatic of the New Education is the attitude toward experimentation and research. In the old days there were no good experimental fields at any of the schools until the Office of Special Studies established one next to the National School at Chapingo. Even then, staff and students seldom went to this living treasure-house of interesting and important information. And when they did go, they went like tourists on an "it's the thing to be done" trip. Of course, there were always some professors who did a little research if they could find time and facilities. But now the best schools expect professors to do research and to help students learn how to do it. It is part of their job.

The Instituto Tecnológico at Monterrey illustrates the aims and procedures of the New Education for undergraduates. Founded in

1943, the Instituto added the School of Agriculture in 1948, and Ing. Leonel Robles has been its first and only director. One of the earliest "graduates" of the Office of Special Studies, Robles had made a brilliant academic record at Chapingo, learned how to do experimental work during his internship in the Office, then made a fine record in course work and research while earning his M.S. at the University of Minnesota. He is one of the early pioneers who sacrificed the doctorate in order to help promote the New Education in Mexico.

The School of Agriculture of the Instituto Tecnológico is dedicated to teaching, research, and extension. The ratio of full-time teachers to students is about one to 13, with 22 teachers and 281 students. Most of the 22 professors have done postgraduate work on Rockefeller Foundation scholarships; six have the doctorate and 11 have a master's degree. The School operates a fine experiment station, and faculty members devote about 40 percent of their time to investigation, 55 percent to teaching, and 5 percent to extension. Students too must do research, because a thesis based on original investigation is a prerequisite for the ingeniero degree, along with the completion of a well-designed program of course work. The faculty, not the students, run the School. Discipline is strict but reasonable, and there has never been a student strike, which is noteworthy in Latin America, where students tend to think that they own a school by virtue of their attending it. Instead of being paid to go to school, most students at Monterrey pay for the privilege, and they get their money's worth.

Postgraduate Work Begins, 1959

The establishment of the Colegio de Postgraduados, the Postgraduate College of the National School of Agriculture at Chapingo, in 1959 is a conspicuous landmark of Mexico's evolution toward independence in agricultural education and research. It is a living monument to the vision and courage of the few men who created it, despite some active and much passive opposition, and who sustained it during a precarious infancy. The reasons why it was unwanted and unloved by some people are less important than the fact that it is alive and thriving, thanks to the educational statesmanship of Minister of Agriculture Ing. Julián Rodríguez Adame and the dynamic leadership of Ing. Jesús Muñóz Vázquez, director of the National School, and a small group of faithful supporters. These men deserve the everlasting gratitude of their countrymen for pioneering the way to higher education in agriculture for Mexican youth, in Mexico, and for Mexico. And in simple historical justice it should be recorded that Dr. Gabriel Baldovinos, the first director of the College, and two major professors, Dr. Marcos Ramírez Genel and Dr. Alfredo Campos Tierrafría, helped keep the institution alive during the darkest days of its infancy, when some men of lesser faith said, "It was born prematurely, it will not live anyhow, so we may as well let it die now." The College owes much to these professors who had a faith born of dedication to a worthy cause and made the sacrifices necessary to keep the cause alive. These men had families to keep alive also, and for almost half a year they had to do so on faith and borrowed money because the College had no money to pay their salaries.

Despite its early struggles, the College has grown into a vigorous and productive institution. At the beginning, in 1959, there were only a dozen students and five full-time professors, with five additional ones on a part-time basis. Now there are close to 70 students and 15 full-time faculty members, with about an equal number of temporary or part-time teachers. Students have come from 13 foreign countries: Brazil, Colombia, Costa Rica, the Dominican Republic, Ecuador, Guatemala, Haiti, Nicaragua, Panama, Peru, El Salvador, the United States, and Venezuela.

Admission requirement is the ingeniero agrónomo degree or its equivalent—roughly the Bachelor of Science degree in the United States. So far the College offers work to the Master of Science level only, and the program requires 18 months of course work and thesis research. The fields of specialization originally were plant breeding and genetics, soils and plant nutrition, entomology, and plant pathology, but other fields are being added. To earn the degree, students must present a thesis based on original research and pass an oral examination given by a committee of three. As the examination is often attended by other graduate students and staff members and usually lasts two hours or longer, it is a test of fortitude as well as of attainments. The Mexican M.S. is not a cheap degree; if anything, the requirements are too exacting rather than too lax.

The College also gives some intensive service courses during the summer, primarily for the benefit of persons who are professionally engaged and want to amplify their knowledge in special fields. In addition to teaching, all professors are expected to do some research and probably will do more as a more adequate staff can be built. So far it has had to depend largely on relatively young Mexicans and short-term visiting professors. There is need for a permanent staff of full-time professors with talent and zeal for teaching, supported by special services from Mexican and foreign scientists who have something special to contribute. In education, even the best is hardly good enough.

Since February, 1960, the Instituto Tecnológico at Monterrey has offered graduate work in the field of parasitology, which includes entomology and plant pathology. The other schools are not yet ready for graduate work, but the march is on. Mexico can be as independent as she wants to be in agricultural education within another decade; and she can be pre-eminent in graduate education if she develops and utilizes wisely her best teaching talents.

Roots and Sprouts of the New Education

The roots of the New Education were in postrevolutionary Mexico itself. The slogans *"Paz y Pan"* and *"Tierra y Libros,"* "Peace and Bread" and "Land and Books," epitomized the aspiration of the Mexican people for bread and the land to produce it and for an education that would enable them to retain their lands and husband them in such a way as to produce food more abundantly and easily. (Mexico's early attempts to make education function effectively in the improvement of agriculture and rural life are discussed in Chapter 2.) The yearning for bread, land, and education was the soil that nourished the roots of the New Education.

The sprouts of the New Education are the men and the institutions that it produced. The cooperative program of the Mexican Ministry of Agriculture and The Rockefeller Foundation began by helping educate a corps of Mexican agricultural scientists. The formation of the Asociación de Directores de las Escuelas Superiores de Agricultura in February, 1959, and its subsequent studies and recommendations have promoted notably the standards of the colleges. We have seen other steps taken that were of great importance: the affiliation of two existing colleges with state universities and the creation of the four new colleges; the establishment of the all-Mexican National Institute of Agricultural Research (INIA); and the foundation of the Postgraduate College. But most significant for the future of the New Education is the "Plan Chapingo": the establishment of a national center for agricultural education, research, and extension at Chapingo.

The plan is to build a physical plant on the campus of the National School of Agriculture at Chapingo to house the National School, the National Institute of Agricultural Research, and the Dirección General de Agricultura, which has charge of extension and certain service activities. Although these three entities are dependencies of the federal Ministry of Agriculture and Animal Husbandry, they are separated physically—the School at Chapingo, about 20 miles from Mexico City, and the other two at different places in the City. The objective is to bring them together in order to promote cooperation and coordination of effort.

Funds from the Mexican government, The Rockefeller Foundation, the Ford Foundation, the United Nations, the Inter-American Bank, and the Agency for International Development assure the development of buildings for the Center. The building plans provide for contiguity of research, teaching, and extension units in the same scientific fields, to facilitate easy communication and common use of expensive equipment. Administratively, the present plan contemplates federation of the three principal components rather than complete consolidation. Although the entities will be semiautonomous, an administrative mechanism to assure cooperation and coordinated effort is envisaged. It is the way of democracy.

Thus the cooperative program has helped to produce scientists and technologists, and Mexico now is on the way to producing them independently in her own educational institutions. She is utilizing their services in her own independently managed research and educational institutions, public and private. The graduates of the New Education are assuming more and more responsibilities and can contribute more and more if they themselves become wiser as they become more scientific and if institutional management is wise enough to enable them to function freely. Mexico's scientific potential, if soundly developed and utilized, can keep her on the road of "tremendous progress" and on the way to a satisfying indigenous culture. May there be no roadblocks on the way!

Chapter 12

Extension

Getting Farmers to Use the Results of Research

Extension must be an equal partner with research in agricultural improvement, for unless the better materials and methods that have been developed are put to use by farmers, the time and money spent in developing them will have been largely wasted. Accordingly, a specialized organization, commonly known as the extension service or advisory service, is needed to act as intermediary between research scientists and farmers. This service therefore helps to guarantee that investments in agricultural research yield substantial dividends. And these can be very high. In the United States, for example, by 1955 the return on the total investment for research on hybrid corn over a period of 40 years was about 700 percent a year.[1] The increased production of the principal food crops in Mexico, demonstrated by the statistics in previous chapters, suggests potential returns of comparable magnitude. That Mexico actually did realize a handsome profit is indicated by the fact that agricultural production doubled between 1945 and 1957. Although industrial production increased 130 percent from 1939 to 1957, the record of agriculture is even more impressive.

Few countries in the world can match the economic development of Mexico during the past 20 years. Like agricultural production, the gross national product has doubled between 1945 and 1957, while the population, one of the most rapidly growing in the world, increased 40 percent. All sectors of Mexico's economy have grown at more uniform rates than those in any other Latin American country, and agricultural improvement contributed largely to this

[1] Hirsh Zvi Griliches, "Research Costs and Social Returns: Hybrid Corn and Related Innovations," *Journal of Political Economy*, 66 (1958), 419–431.

growth. As the potential returns on agricultural research are so great, it is of the utmost importance to the national economy and to the populace generally to get all farmers to use results of such research as quickly as possible. Just as research and development are linked in industry, so also should research and extension be linked in agriculture; both are necessary to complete the job.

In agriculture, as in industry, development based on research costs more than the research itself. It costs more, for example, to teach thousands of farmers how to use the results than it does to do the research in the first place, and the efficiency of an extension service is often rated by the length of time elapsing between the announcement of a scientific discovery and its use by a high percentage of the farmers whom it can help. In countries with competent and well-integrated teams of research and extension workers, a profitable new practice is frequently adopted by the majority of farmers in from one to three years; in developing countries, on the other hand, many years may be required to achieve widespread adoption of the same practice. Some of the Mexican experience with this problem to date[2] has been thrilling and some has been disappointing. But there are lessons to be learned both from the thrills and from the disappointments.

Experimentation as the Living Source of Extension

WHY RESEARCH HAD TO PRECEDE EXTENSION IN MEXICO

When in 1941 the Survey Commission made its recommendations about the proposed cooperative program, they suggested a small team of carefully selected, well-trained, and experienced men— a plant breeder, an agronomist and soils expert, a crop protection specialist, and an animal husbandman—keenly interested in using and having others use their research for improving the agriculture of the country. Some may ask, why start with research? Research takes time, is expensive, and has been conducted in many countries for many years. Why not recruit someone familiar with practices that have improved agriculture in the advanced countries—an experienced extension worker, for example—and let him use his

[2] Late 1964.

knowledge in the new environment? Too often overlooked are the facts that in his home country such an extension worker could draw upon a backlog of years of research and proven extension techniques and that his program was probably developed in cooperation with the investigators at his experiment station, men who were as close to him as his telephone when unexpected emergencies arose that he did not know how to handle.

Experienced agricultural scientists know that small, subtle differences in environments can have very great effects on crop yields. These differences must be recognized and cultural practices adjusted accordingly. Because unreliable advice is worse than none, the scientist needs to be reasonably sure he is right before he gives advice, and the best way for him to acquire this confidence and trustworthiness is to test his ideas in well-designed experiments carried out in the particular area. Ordinarily, within three to five years he will have learned enough to justify encouraging and teaching a few innovating farmers to try out some of his recommendations.

Why a team of research specialists? Why not a well-trained generalist who knew a little bit about each of the sciences represented on the original team? The answer is that while a generalist might have been useful, the research needed was of such a nature that it could be done only by specialists. Although it was expected that each specialist would learn how to increase yields by the application of his science alone, experience had already shown quite clearly that he would seldom get maximum returns unless he worked closely with his colleagues in the other sciences. For example, a plant breeder may develop a new hybrid corn that is slightly better than a native variety if grown in the traditional way, and a soil scientist may improve yields in some degree by fertilizing the native variety of corn. But it is only when they combine their findings and use the optimum fertilization on the corn with the greater genetic potential that they obtain much higher yields.

This combination may seem to result in a peculiar new type of mathematics in which the whole is greater than the sum of its parts, but the interaction of optimum combinations of the different environmental factors in increasing crop production can produce some surprising kinds of additions and multiplications. To employ the best known combination of all the separate factors in the environment obviously takes teamwork. The results, however, are usually astounding, especially to the farmers in a developing country. As research continues, better combinations can be attained, with larger interactions and larger yields. We do not know what the maximum possible yields really are, but they are certainly five to 20 times higher than those commonly obtained in most developing countries and three to five times the average yields in the more advanced ones. In this chapter, however, our problem is to get the results to the farmer.

EXPERIMENTATION DOUBLES AS DEMONSTRATION

Some scientists so pride themselves on being "pure" that they disdain to help get their findings to farmers and only publish them in scientific journals for their scientific colleagues to read. There are few places for such scientists in developing countries; the time lags and the losses in efficiency are too great. Each member of the Foundation's team in Mexico was willing and eager to have his findings used on farms as soon as possible. Consequently, no sharp line indicated where research left off and its application or "extension" began. Nor did this interest in the practical values of science preclude important contributions to basic science, some of which, as we have seen, attracted worldwide attention.

The Foundation scientists in Mexico took pride in their experiments and were eager to show them to visitors. Exhibits were set up and field trips arranged. One corn farmer near Texcoco, not far from the experiment station at Chapingo, was interested in obtaining seed of one of the strains under test. The supply was very limited, but Wellhausen agreed to provide him with some seed if he would plant it, fertilize it, and manage it throughout the season as directed. The farmer, in turn, agreed to permit the use of this planting as a demonstration of what could be done on his farm when the best management practices known at that time were combined. He carried through splendidly and was rewarded with a fabulous crop. A field day was arranged, and the President of the Republic, Miguel Alemán, attended with many of his high officials. The press naturally was on hand. Farmers had never seen such corn! When harvested, it yielded over 125 bushels an acre—one of the highest yields ever reported in the Valley of Mexico. The Office of Special Studies was soon deluged with inquiries from farmers who had read newspaper accounts and wanted more information about how they too could grow such bumper crops.

In the spring of 1948 Sr. Aureliano Campoy, a large wheat farmer from Sonora who had been cooperating with Borlaug in his wheat experiments in the Yaqui Valley, came to Mexico City to visit a nephew who was editor of *El Universal,* one of the city's leading daily papers. After describing Borlaug's work and what it had meant to him personally as well as to the other farmers in Sonora, Sr. Campoy urged his nephew to visit nearby Chapingo to see the experiments in progress. A field trip was arranged for the editor and several members of his staff. Young Mexican scientists were on hand to explain the different experiments with the various crops. The visit lasted almost all day; feature writers asked hundreds of questions, staff photographers took scores of pictures. The feature article in *El Universal* the next morning was devoted to what the staff had seen and learned at Chapingo. And because this paper was widely read throughout Mexico, editors of dozens of local papers saw the article and republished selections from it.

These are only a few examples of the reaction of prominent leaders to the field days arranged at appropriate times at the various experiment stations. It is important for leaders, as well as farmers, to know what is being done to improve agriculture in their country, and these field demonstrations opened many eyes to undreamed-of possibilities for improving the agriculture of Mexico.

DEMONSTRATION CREATES DEMAND FOR MORE EXTENSION

These field days and other events increased the numbers of visitors and letters to the Office of Special Studies to such an extent that they interfered with the research. This in turn increased the demand for an extension specialist on the staff to assist with these responsibilities. The first step taken was the temporary appointment in the spring of 1947 of Dr. Mortier F. Barrus as an extension specialist. A retired extension professor from Cornell University, he had had considerable experience in Puerto Rico and Costa Rica. In addition to looking after visitors, answering inquiries, and arranging meetings, Dr. Barrus and his Mexican associates set up about 40 simple field trials to compare the best local varieties of corn with the best-adapted improved strains available at that time. Each type of corn was grown with and without appropriate applications of chemical fertilizer.

These plantings were made in different sections of the country and were used both for experimental purposes and for local demonstrations. Over the years the soils men—Colwell, Chandler, Miller, Pitner, Laird, and their Mexican colleagues—carried out hundreds of similar field trials involving a wide range of fertilizer combinations. (See Chapter 8.) Besides yielding information regarding the types of fertilizer needed on these diverse soils, many of these trials brought some of the early fruits of research to the attention of hundreds of communities and thousands of farmers in most of the important agricultural regions. As a whole they served their purpose well; they helped people to realize the need and value of experimentation.

Probably the most effective demonstrations were those in which specialists in the various sciences collaborated to find out the combinations of practices that would give the highest yields, sometimes amounting to increases of 200 to 300 percent. A demonstration showing a rise of 20 to 30 percent resulting from a single practice had much less impact, because farmers had often seen variations of this magnitude occur from year to year as a result of natural causes. But increases of 200 to 300 percent had never before been seen—nor even dreamed of in Mexico. More important still, the combination of practices was usually much more profitable financially. Such demonstrations are more likely to stimulate alert farmers than any other extension device. Gains of this order are worth striving for.

As these experiments revealed the rich potentials of certain sectors of Mexican agriculture under scientific management, many of the country's influential men were motivated to initiate and support efforts to expand research and, perhaps even more significant, to intensify efforts to get more farmers to use the new methods. Pressure for stepping up extension activities therefore continued to mount; it came from many sources and took many forms, but the goal was always the same—a more productive agriculture for Mexico. Because The Rockefeller Foundation had stimulated much of this interest, it was natural for Mexican leaders to turn to the Foundation for help in the next phase of Mexico's agricultural development: the expansion and strengthening of the federal extension service.

Direct Aid to Mexico's Extension Service

A request for help in developing an effective extension service in Mexico had long been anticipated and discussed by the officers of the Foundation. Although the Ministry of Agriculture included an extension section at the time of the Survey Commission's visit in 1941, Mexico had not made much progress in this field because there was so little research to extend; now research had produced abundant new information and the more progressive farmers were clamoring for it.

AN AGRICULTURAL INFORMATION SERVICE

The obvious first step was to make this new information readily available to everyone interested in it. By the early 1950's the volume of such material made it difficult for the regular staff to put it into popular form, and, in addition, many of the technical publications needed to be reworked into a series of simplified, well-illustrated Spanish editions for widespread distribution. These problems called for a specialist who could devote full time to them and to related activities. Dr. Delbert T. Myren, who had earned his Ph.D. in agricultural journalism at the University of Wisconsin, was therefore brought to Mexico in 1955 and given the responsibility for organizing and heading a new information service. Besides relieving some of the research men of this work, Myren soon found ways to enlarge the use of the available information.

An excellent photographic service had already been created under Neil B. MacLellan, who had a special talent for getting pictures of field experiments that told the story "better than ten thousand words." This systematic pictorial record has been invaluable for many purposes (including the illustrating of this book). In addition to their use in the publications of the Office, the photographs have been available for exhibits, as illustrations for stories supplied to newspapers and farm journals, and for the preparation of lantern slides to accompany extension talks. Requests for pictures, both old and new, continue to come in from all over the world.

In recent years, 16 short, inexpensive motion picture films dealing with various agricultural subjects have also been made and widely distributed, both in Mexico and in other Latin American countries.

The federal extension service currently maintains three mobile movie projection units that use these and other films.

Among its other functions the information service has assisted in making arrangements for the field days that have become an important part of the activities of each of the regional research stations. It handles the publicity for these meetings and distributes publications to farmers attending them. By interviewing the participating farmers, the staff of the information service has learned a good deal about their interests and background. Other kinds of research are under way, designed to obtain a better understanding of the response of various types of Mexican farmers to information disseminated in different ways and of the effectiveness of different methods for inducing farmers to change their practices. Such information will be of value in the further development of the extension service. Farmers seldom become completely convinced of the advisability of changing the practices of a lifetime until they have been exposed to the same idea repeatedly, through different media and in a variety of forms so that it becomes personally meaningful and relevant. Impressions thus accumulate and stimulate farmers to discuss their problems with the extension agent, who often can convince them that they should try the new methods.

AIDING THE PILOT-PLANT OPERATION IN MEXICO STATE

An exceptional opportunity to set up a pilot-plant extension operation arose in 1951 when Ing. Salvador Sanchez Colín, an experienced agricultural scientist, was appointed governor of the State of Mexico. While working in the Ministry of Agriculture, Sanchez Colín had become well acquainted with Harrar and the research program of the Office of Special Studies, and in his new position he asked the Foundation to help establish an extension service covering important agricultural sections of his State. On Harrar's strong recommendation such assistance was provided, and in January of 1952 one of the best extension experiments in Mexico was started.

The State was divided into eight agricultural regions, ranging in size from about 2,000 to 5,000 square kilometers of tillable land, according to the crops grown, communications, topography, and climate. An agronomist, supplied with a pick-up truck and operating funds, was placed in charge of the extension work in each region.

Field trials with improved crop varieties, fertilizers, and new cultural practices were set up, and at appropriate times field days were organized. The governor attended these whenever possible; farmer interest was high; and early reports on the project were optimistic. In 1952 Wellhausen wrote that "next to the basic research which had to come first, it is one of the most far-reaching and significant projects yet undertaken in Mexico and should be encouraged to the fullest extent possible." Foundation support was continued for a period of six years.

Indications are, however, that this project, which started out with so much enthusiasm and promise, instead of gaining in strength and influence is actually losing in both. Why? The answer is not yet clear, but one view is that the project expanded faster than the supply of qualified extension workers. The experienced men became supervisors who spent more and more time in their offices, while the newly recruited workers handled most of the contacts with the farmers in the field. The quality of the demonstrations declined, farmers found them less convincing, and so enthusiasm and influence waned.

THE RESULTS OF TWENTY YEARS

The federal extension service was a problem in 1941. Twenty years later it had changed much, but many problems were still unsolved. In 1961 there were over 220 employees, about 40 percent of whom held the ingeniero agrónomo degree. The present director, Ing. Joaquín Loredo, like many others in high positions in the agricultural establishment of Mexico, once worked in the Office of Special Studies. He was a member of the first soil research team organized by Colwell in 1945 to study the effect of fertilizers on corn. Even at that time he displayed unusual skill and aptitude for dealing with farmers and therefore was usually assigned the responsibility for negotiating arrangements for field trials with the farmers. One visitor, after watching Loredo approach a few farmers, commented: "That boy would make a good extension worker."

When he returned to Mexico after graduate work at Cornell, Loredo joined the federal extension service and within a few years became its head. He is now trying to improve its efficiency, but there are still many obstacles to be overcome. Because the extension service is in a different branch of the Ministry of Agriculture from the research work, contacts with the research men are not so easy or so frequent as they should be. Under the new Chapingo Plan, these services will be located close together in the new National Agricultural Center, and communication and coordination at the top administrative level and at the various regional centers will be facilitated.

A shortage of competent and dedicated extension men and investigators is one of the most serious problems that confront Mexico and all developing countries. In Mexico, men with experience in the Office of Special Studies are preferred, but they are so few in number and competition for their services is so keen that the best men are lured from one service to another and still another. Until there are enough trained men to go around, this inefficient practice of trying to strengthen one service by weakening another will probably continue. Mexico urgently needs to educate more men to do the various kinds of jobs that need to be done, including extension work.

Lessons Learned

The above story of extension in Mexico is far from complete, but it shows clearly that there have been thrilling successes and disappointing failures. Let us now try to get a better understanding of both, because there is good reason for thinking that principles valid in Mexico are valid in other countries also, even though wide variation may exist in minor details.

Every agriculturist knows that certain supplies, services, and incentives—good seed, fertilizers, roads, credit, markets, etc.—must be available to the farmer on favorable terms before he can or will make important changes in his practices. Assuming that all these prerequisites for success are adequately met, the most troublesome problems often are those involving people; and the more people involved, the more complicated these problems become. In agricultural extension we are concerned largely with three groups: scientific investigators, who produce and test scientific information about the factors that influence production; farmers, who produce crops and animals; and extension workers, who function as intermediaries between the other two groups. In Mexico, as in most countries, there is a wide range of abilities within each of these groups, the range being probably widest among the farmers.

FARMERS DIFFER IN ATTITUDES TOWARD CHANGE

At one extreme is a rather small class of relatively affluent farmers, usually well educated, well read, well traveled, and well informed about what is going on in the world. They are interested in new ideas and eager to try them out, especially if they promise to increase the yields of crops or animals. Often they are innovators who like to experiment; therefore, they visit experiment stations, get acquainted with the scientists who are investigating problems of interest to them, and frequently offer space and facilities on their farms for experimental purposes. Because such farmers often deal directly with the research scientists, many of them have little need of an intermediary. Their farms are usually large, highly mechanized, and with good land, probably much of it irrigated. The scientific investigators try to locate their field experiments on such farms because the owners understand the purpose of the experiments and give them intelligent care. Most of the early progress in Mexico resulted from direct contacts between research men and interested farmers. Developing countries, endeavoring to improve their agriculture as rapidly as possible, should make maximum use of the talents of these sophisticated farmers.

At the other extreme is the great majority of the farmers—impoverished, illiterate, isolated, suspicious of strangers. Their farms generally are small, the soil poor and often worn out by centuries of mismanagement, the farming methods laborious, primitive, and traditional. These farmers seldom travel any distance away from home, so extension workers have to go to them. Because their resources are so limited, they cannot afford to experiment with new methods; failure of the experiment could mean no food at all. They and their families usually consume most of the crops produced, selling only a small surplus, should there be one, in order to buy the few necessities they cannot produce themselves.

Extension work with these farmers is much more expensive than with the prosperous ones because it must be intensive and thus requires more extension agents per unit of farm area. Because most of these farmers cannot read, an agent must visit them. Because they do not travel far, demonstrations must be made in their own neighborhoods; that is, there must be many demonstrations for relatively small groups. Because they have had little or no schooling and are firmly bound by tradition, it may take a long time to persuade them to try new methods and materials. Because their resources are limited and they usually live in the more isolated communities, supplying them with the goods and services required by new practices tends to be both difficult and expensive. And because each farm is small and produces but little, the net increase to the national agricultural product will likewise be small even after all the above conditions have been met. In a country with limited resources, therefore, efforts to improve agriculture should not begin with this class of farmers, but neither should they cease until these farmers have been serviced effectively. The record shows that many individual small farmers have been helped by skilled extension agents to make notable improvements. Such work can and should be done, but it takes both time and money.

Between these extremes is a class of farmers intermediate in numbers, education, farm resources, and attitude toward change. With national improvement in agriculture, this group tends to expand as more and more of the poorer farmers adopt better methods and join its ranks. In the advanced countries this middle group is usually the largest and accounts for most of the agricultural production. Obviously the extension job can be greatly simplified by increasing the proportion of farmers in the two higher groups, but this must be a long-term objective; its achievement will take time. In the United States, where farmers constitute less than eight percent of the population, those corresponding to the lowest group in Mexico have almost disappeared in most sections; either they have become better farmers and joined a higher group or they have given up farming and moved to the city. Economic pressures and opportunities have encouraged these shifts.

Mexico, as we have seen, has a wide range of soils and climates as well as of farmers. Any country aspiring to a well-balanced, sustained development needs to take inventory of its resources, natural as well as human, before launching ambitious schemes. In emerging countries, resources seldom are sufficient for starting to work on all needed improvements at once, so priorities must be established. The question is how, and on what basis? To get agreement is difficult, for the decisions involve the welfare of many people over a long period, at least a generation or two.

The question of priorities arose in 1941 even before the Survey Commission reached Mexico City from Laredo, Texas. The Commission members passed many large, level farms obviously operated by relatively prosperous farmers; but on nearby mountain slopes, often just across the road, were small farms cultivated exclusively by traditional and laborious hand methods. Census figures for Mexico in 1950 indicated that about 34 percent of all private holdings of less than 12.5 acres were still being farmed by the ancient pre-Hispanic hoe culture without benefit of plow or oxen. Even today these farmers clearly need help more than do their prosperous neighbors in the valley. But can they use efficiently the limited amount of help that the government of a developing country can afford to give them? Governments are interested in increasing the commercial production of food in order to feed the people in their rapidly growing industrial cities. How to get the needed food most quickly and cheaply is the problem that has to be given priority. The experience of Mexico during the past twenty years provides a clear-cut answer to the above question, and one that is probably generally valid.

SOME FARMERS NEED BUT LITTLE EXTENSION WORK

The dramatic story of the increase in wheat production in Sonora (already told in Chapter 5) is a good example of the returns that can be obtained when a relatively small investment is made in a potentially favorable environment. Wheat yields in Sonora were low twenty years ago. There were extensive areas of level, deep, relatively fertile soils; farm units were fairly large, and the farmers themselves were progressive and had means well above the national average; water was available for irrigation from the recently completed dam on the Yaqui River. But stem rust of wheat was a limiting factor in the area, and the varieties being grown were susceptible to the existing rust races. For a relatively small investment in research, Borlaug and his colleagues developed a wheat resistant to this rust. Cooperative experiments with Laird, the soils specialist, showed that very profitable increases in yields could be obtained by the use of nitrogenous fertilizers when rust was controlled. The earlier varieties lodged, however, if the nitrogen applications were too heavy. So the wheat team produced varieties in which the necessary rust resistance was combined with short, stiff straw that conferred lodging resistance under heavier nitrogenous fertilization and irrigation. Yields comparable to those in the better wheat-growing areas of the world were now obtained easily, and the results of the demonstrations made by Borlaug and his colleagues were so striking that the farmers of Sonora needed no persuasion to adopt the new varieties.

Equally dramatic were the results of experiments with corn. But while hundreds of progressive farmers have increased their corn yields from 20 to 70 bushels or more per acre on good, well-watered soils by using the results of research by Wellhausen and Laird, so far this research has had little impact upon the practices of the hundreds of thousands of small, poorly educated corn farmers who eke out their living from the poorer soils with undependable sources of water. The improvement of wheat farming was almost spontaneous; farmers were looking for something better and when they saw it they quickly adopted it. In the case of the small corn farmers, a different approach must be used. Eventually they too will adopt new materials and methods, but several years of work by hundreds of well-trained, experienced extension agents will probably be required to convert them, unless far more effective extension techniques than any now known are developed.

It seems clear that Mexico's extension service will have to be greatly improved and expanded in order to obtain the full benefits from agricultural research. More good extension men are needed— men with the ability to win and hold the confidence of the farmer. To be successful, an extension man must be technically competent, understanding of the farmer and his problems, and able to talk to the farmer clearly and convincingly. Experience shows that men who have assisted in the research program for two to three years make the best extension workers. There seems to be an inverse relationship between the effectiveness of the extension man and the distance in time, space, and mental attitude between him and the scientific investigator. Because the first "demonstrations" in a new environment are really experiments to test the applicability of the results of experiments made elsewhere, the reasons must be found if the results obtained differ from those anticipated. This calls for more research on the spot, preferably by the local extension worker in collaboration with the research worker at the central station. In a very real sense then, the pioneering extension worker must often extend and modify research findings before he can safely and confidently recommend them to local farmers. Some experience with research and close ties with research workers are therefore important for him.

The research program at the National School of Agriculture at Chapingo has proved to be a good training center, but it would have difficulty in training the necessary numbers and kinds of extension workers for all parts of the country because of limitations in the types of agriculture and field research that are possible near Chapingo. Mexico has a system of research centers representing all of her important agricultural regions, however, and it is hoped that each of these can be developed into a center for all aspects of agricultural development in the region, agricultural education and extension as well as research, so as to achieve effective coordination of these activities. In time, these centers should win considerable local support and autonomy. If each would train 10 to 15 extension men a year, within five to 10 years Mexico would have enough men familiar with the research program in each region to staff her extension service adequately. Then, probably, expansion should proceed mainly by increasing the radius of the area served by each center. This seems to be the pattern that Mexico is evolving for extending the benefits of modern science to all her farmers.

Cost-of-Production Studies Are Basic to Extension Programs

Evidence is overwhelming that one of the strongest forces motivating farmers in all countries, developed and underdeveloped, communist and capitalist, is profit.[3] Profit is also a principal concern of government planners intent on investing from their inadequate revenues in projects that will yield maximum returns to the national welfare. In spite of the importance of farm economics, little reliable information on the subject has been available in Mexico or Latin America as a whole. Agricultural economists on The Rockefeller Foundation's Board of Trustees and Board of Consultants for Agriculture strongly advocated the addition of an agricultural economist to the Office of Special Studies even in its early years. Although a

[3] Theodore Schultz, *Transforming Traditional Agriculture* (New Haven: Yale University Press, 1964), pp. 162–168.

few short-term studies were made, it was not until 1957 that Dr. Donald K. Freebairn was appointed as the first agricultural economist, a capacity in which he served until 1964.

In this book the increased production of basic food crops has been especially emphasized. Obviously, however, increased production alone is not necessarily an adequate measure of progress, for the cost of increasing the production must also be considered. On many farms greater production results in greater profits, but on others the cost of producing more may exceed the value of the increased production, in which case both the farmer and the country in which he lives may be poorer than they were. In Mexico it seemed desirable to study the cost of production on farms in different regions and under different systems of management, and Freebairn therefore gave special attention to this question.

Mexico provides a fruitful field for such studies because of the revolutionary changes in her social and economic structure during the past 40 years. For the agricultural economist the structure of her agriculture is of interest because it is in a transitional stage: while much of the traditional remains, much that is modern is being developed. The agrarian reform programs carried out principally in the 1920's and 1930's formed the two present classes of farmers —the small proprietor and the *ejidatario*. The principal agrarian goal of the Revolution of 1910 was the redistribution of land, and by 1943 allotments had been made to more than 1.7 million landless individuals, in parcels averaging about 11.5 acres of "cropland" per person. Originally, individuals were not given title to this land; it was communally held, much as in the pre-Columbian days, and the unit allotments were known by the ancient name, *ejido*. In some places the ejidos operated communally, in others each farmer was assigned an ejidal allotment to farm as he pleased. This ejidal pattern provides a great diversity of experiences in farm management, and even though the business records of the various units are incomplete, many significant trends are discernible.

Freebairn and his young Mexican associates studied three types of farm tenure classes in the highly productive Yaqui Valley of Sonora in northwestern Mexico. As indicators of comparative productive efficiencies they used: (1) crop yields, (2) labor requirements per unit of production, (3) land use intensity, (4) residual income, and (5) product per unit of input. Although differences in crop yields proved to be slight or nonexistent, very significant differences were found in the intensity with which cropland was utilized. Where water is available, three crops can be grown in two calendar years in this area. At the time of the studies, private farmers were beginning this practice, but the ejidal units still tended to plant only one crop a year, either cotton or wheat.

The private farmers achieved considerably more product per dollar of input than did the individual ejidal farmers. Labor requirements were higher on the collective ejidal farms, apparently because many members of the collective were given easy and relatively nonproductive supervisory jobs. But although private farmers earned a greater income than the other two groups, they too had substantial management problems, demonstrated by the frequency of negative labor incomes. While their standard of living was generally high, their investment in both farm machinery and labor seemed to be excessive. The ejidos in this area are reputed to be among the most prosperous in Mexico, but these studies indicated that their average incomes are still too low to provide a reasonable standard of living for their members. As many Mexican leaders realize, ways must be found to help both ejidal groups if the goals of The Revolution are to be fully attained.

Freebairn and his group have also investigated the marketing of farm products and the economics of farm production on different types of land in the densely populated Bajío region. These studies will be of value in the further development of the program. Like all other Foundation staff members in Mexico, Freebairn believes, however, that the education of young Mexican scientists represents the greatest value of all. Summarizing the record of the agricultural economics program in 1963, he wrote: "By far its most important accomplishment has been its contribution to the development of a small group of young agricultural economists competent to undertake systematic study of urgent national and regional problems."

Wider Distribution of Benefits—A Continuing Problem

It is already apparent to some of Mexico's far-sighted leaders that a further, very important objective must be achieved if all the efforts described in the preceding chapters are to be of lasting benefit to the country. The increased income resulting from agricultural development must be so distributed that further growth and development will be encouraged and sustained. The farmers responsible for the increased production, the government that supported the research and encouraged its application, and the general public that paid the taxes to support the government's activities are all entitled to share in the gains. Farmers should share, for unless they find these new practices more profitable than the old, they will drop them and the whole new growth process will stop. The public must share if it is to continue its support of the government's research and extension programs. In the United States, the consumer group has gained more than any other from improvements in agriculture; food costs have been lowered so much that the average factory worker, for example, can now feed his family on less than 20 percent of his wages, in contrast to the 40 to 50 percent required in most countries, leaving more to be spent for education, housing, clothing, recreation, and the other items needed to raise his standard of living. The Mexican government must also share if it is to continue and increase its expenditures for agricultural research and extension. We have seen that the great majority of Mexico's small farmers have not yet gained much from agricultural research because they have not yet applied it. A substantial fraction of the increased gains received by the government should be reinvested in further improvement and expansion of the extension service so that all Mexican farmers, large and small, rich and poor, educated and uneducated, can profit by the investment in research.

Mexico as a whole cannot reach the level to which it aspires until the people in the impoverished rural areas are given the opportunity of bettering their lot. In addition to a more intensive extension service as a means of improving the small farmer's output and income, there must be better schools for his children. All countries find, sooner or later, that the principal limiting factor in agricultural or industrial development is the supply of educated people. In spite of the enlarged investment that Mexico is now making in education, she is depriving herself of the service of about 50 percent of her potential trained manpower because in earlier years she did not invest more in the education of her rural youth. Education in rural areas is costly, but in the long run it is less expensive than ignorance.

Such data as are available in Mexico indicate that the increased wealth produced by the improvement of agriculture in the past

20 years has gone largely to the upper income groups. Even though the minimum wage was legally increased by about 30 percent between 1952 and 1958, the level of real wages (corrected for inflation) for the country as a whole is still below that of 1939, and wages on farms are usually lower than in cities.[4] Ramón Beteta, once Minister of Hacienda (or Secretary of the Treasury), later director general of a leading Mexico City newspaper, and one of the foremost students of Mexico's economic development, states: "We industrialists are treating farmers as an underdeveloped nation. We sell high to them and buy cheap from them and the inevitable result is that, in the long run, they cannot acquire the products turned out by industry."[5]

President Ruíz Cortines was greatly concerned about this problem and in his annual report to the nation in September, 1956, spoke as follows: "Yes, we have made progress, but the progress obtained by the country as a whole enables us to see with greater clarity those who have still not benefited by this progress, or at least have not benefited as much as we fervently hoped for. . . . I think, with much emotion, of the great masses who are still suffering ignorance, illness and poverty. . . . So long as these masses do not progress at the same pace as the rest of the country, we will have to say to those who are satisfied with the present situation, 'We have done very little indeed, the essential promise has yet to be fulfilled.' "[6]

The fact that these and other Mexican leaders are speaking out strongly about extending the benefits to all gives reason to hope that ways will be found for distributing the wealth created by research more equitably among all concerned. The agricultural sciences cannot make their maximum contribution to the economic development of Mexico until all of her farmers, small as well as large, have learned to apply their teachings and found it profitable to do so. Research and extension have contributed much to Mexico, but they still have a big job to do, contributing still more to many more Mexicans.

[4] Oscar Lewis, "Mexico since Cárdenas," in *Social Change in Latin America Today* (New York: Vintage Books, 1961).

[5] Ramón Beteta, Mexico City *News*, November 16, 1964, p. 25A.

[6] In Lewis, "Mexico since Cárdenas."

Chapter 13

Extending the Mexican Pattern

Action Programs in Colombia, Ecuador, and Chile

The programs in Colombia and Ecuador and in Chile were evolutionary extensions of the Mexican Agricultural Program. Men schooled in that program moved southward in successive stages, carrying with them materials, concepts, ideas, and wisdom that they had acquired in helping to solve problems of agricultural production and of human relations in Mexico. These men had become proficient in Spanish and had learned much about the ways of utilizing science efficiently in improving agriculture and educating people in Latin America.

Worthy of emphasis is the fact that Harrar, in his various, increasingly responsible capacities, linked these national programs into an organic international system. Consequently the programs were mutually stimulating and helpful, and their cooperative efforts produced far greater values than if they had been operated as unrelated entities. They functioned as a family of autonomous members dedicated to the cause of doing as much good as possible wherever they could, and by so doing they did far more good than appeared on the surface. Many and subtle are the ways in which men and institutions may do good.

Colombia

THE BEGINNING OF FOUNDATION HELP

The establishment of the cooperative operating program in 1950 was not the Foundation's first effort to help improve Colombian agriculture. On the recommendation of Dr. Harry M. Miller, Jr., of its

Division of Natural Sciences, it had been making financial grants to three faculties of the National University since 1942: the Faculty of Veterinary Medicine and Animal Husbandry, located at University City in Bogotá; the Faculty (or College) of Agriculture at Medellín; and the College of Agriculture at Cali, which affiliated with the National University in 1946 and soon thereafter moved to Palmira, about 25 miles distant from Cali. These institutions had received liberal grants for equipment and apparatus, for the construction of student dormitories at Medellín and Cali, and for foreign travel and study by selected faculty members and outstanding students. A special grant had enabled the two colleges of agriculture to send one or two of their best students in each year's graduating class for a period of intensive study in the Office of Special Studies in Mexico.

The renown of the Mexican program had created a desire in other Latin American countries for similar programs, and in 1948 the President of Colombia officially requested Foundation help in establishing one in his country. An agreement was made in 1949, and work began the next year.

The Mexican program was ready in 1950 to send experienced and zealous men to carry the gospel of scientific agriculture to Colombia. Dr. Lewis M. Roberts and Dr. Joseph A. Rupert, both with five years' experience in Mexico, started the Colombian program in May, 1950, Roberts as director and corn breeder and Rupert as wheat breeder. It was another big undertaking, for Colombia was a very diverse country with a diverse population and a great diversity of problems.

THE LAND, PEOPLE, AND INSTITUTIONS

Colombia, embracing about 450,000 square miles, is entirely within the tropics but three north-south ranges of the Andes Mountains divide the country into several distinct climatic zones. At elevations of less than 3,500 feet the climate is hot, with a mean annual temperature of 75° to 80°F. and a range of 65° to 100°; between 3,500 and 6,500 feet the climate is temperate, with an average annual mean of 65°; between 6,500 and 10,000 feet the temperature averages about 55°; and above 10,000 feet it is chilly to cold. The elevation of Bogotá, the capital, is 8,660 feet and the average mean temperature is 58°; it can be hot in the sun and chilly in the shade. Annual rainfall in the country ranges from a few inches to 350 or more. A diverse climate indeed! And the people are as diverse as the climate.

The population was about 11 million in 1950; at present it is probably between 15 and 16 million, and the rate of increase is about 2.2 percent a year. About 20 percent of the people are of European ancestry; five percent are Indians; five percent are Negroes; and the remaining 70 percent are of mixed blood, so-called *mestizos*. About two thirds of the people are classed as rural, with 40 percent living in the hot areas, 35 percent in the temperate zones, and 25 percent in the cold areas. Figuratively, it is a long way from the steaming tropics, where cooking bananas are the staff of life, to the bleak and chilly paramos, where the potato is a basic food. And it is a long way from the primitive living conditions in the tropical jungles and on the paramos to those in the pleasant and fertile temperate-zone valleys and in the modern cities such as Bogotá, Medellín, and Cali; Colombia is as diverse culturally as it is topographically.

The Colombia of 1950 was a land of great riches and of abject poverty, of munificence and of squalor, of culture and of ignorance. Education was not compulsory and was not even available in many areas. Although about three fourths of the urban population was literate, three fourths of the rural people could neither read nor write. Sunk in peasantry, they looked to political rather than scientific remedies to improve their lot.

What Colombia really needed to improve agriculture and rural life was more science. As Miller wrote after his first trip to South America in 1941, "But the great need in South American countries is for trained investigators." And in 1962, after nine years in Colombia, Roberts wrote: "Twelve years ago the faculties of agronomy were giving only textbook instruction to students who came almost entirely from urban centers. The graduates were not really prepared to make contributions to the practical solutions of problems confronting the country's agriculture. As a result the agronomy profession had no prestige, the services of the agronomists were not in demand, their salaries were pitifully low and very few youngsters were attracted to the study of agriculture." The simple fact was that in 1950 the agricultural sciences were contributing very little to Colombia, so Roberts and Rupert undertook to increase their contributions.

In 1943 weeds, insects, and diseases were taking a heavy toll of Mexico's crop plants (Chapter 9). Rust was killing the wheat and smuts were destroying the heads of wheat and corn.

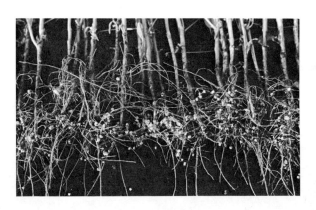

Root rots were damaging beans, and insects were boring into the stalks of corn.

Weeds often choked the fields; but weed experts learned how to control them by means of chemicals (here applied in strips to help corn get started) and better cultivation.

Insects and molds destroyed much grain in storage, even in the
better farm granaries such as this.

Using experimental "granaries," entomologists and pathologists studied storage problems and showed how to preserve grain better.

Plant pathologists contributed to better crop protection by helping to produce resistant varieties. Susceptible varieties on the left, resistant ones on the right.

The use of certified seed potatoes has reduced the destructiveness of virus diseases. Healthy plant in center, flanked by diseased plants.

Seed treatment with appropriate fungicides to control seed-borne diseases has contributed to the better health and productivity of Mexican crop plants.

Mexico needed more milk and eggs and meat (Chapter 10). Mexican farm animals had to scrabble for their food, although there were some excellent dairy cattle near the cities.

Because most cattle needed better feed, extensive tests were made of forage grasses at the Cotaxtla Experiment Station in Veracruz. Merkeron and others converted scrubby pastures into rich forage lands.

The development of a superior variety, Tanverde, helped increase the production of alfalfa, "the queen of forage crops."

There are vast areas of range lands in northwestern Mexico.

Range management studies, with the cooperation of animals such as these, have given promise of more and better beef.

Research has helped Mexico maintain the efficiency of her modern poultry plants.

Better education helped Mexico revolutionize her agriculture (Chapter 11). Mexico has built good rural schools, and many boys and girls evidently want to learn.

New agricultural colleges have been built
and old ones improved. The Technological Institute of Monterrey established a
School of Agriculture and Animal Husbandry in 1948. Ing. Leonel Robles, M.S.
(right), the first and only director of the
School, has persistently promoted the
"New Education" in agriculture.

The Hermanos Escobar at Ciudad Juárez, established in 1906, is Mexico's oldest college of agriculture except for Chapingo. Laboratory facilities always have been limited, but generally the spirit of learning has been good. The College is now affiliated with the University of Chihuahua.

The recently established School of Animal Husbandry of the University of Chihuahua not only teaches but also participates in programs of research and demonstration.

"Getting farmers to use the results of research" is not always easy (Chapter 12). The Office of Special Studies tried to do its part by means of field demonstrations and special exhibits.

Potentially, the most significant event of Mexico's revolution in agriculture is the federation of research, educational, and extension agencies in the new Chapingo Center.

THE OPERATING PROGRAM BEGINS TO PRODUCE RESULTS

Operations in the Colombian Agricultural Program began officially on May 15, 1950, when Roberts and Rupert started work in the specially created Oficina de Investigaciones Especiales, the Office of Special Investigations, similar to the Office of Special Studies in Mexico. As in Mexico, the objectives were to increase the production of basic foods, especially corn and wheat; to help educate young scientists; and to promote the development of educational and research institutions.

Headquarters were established at Medellín, as the College (or Faculty) of Agriculture at that place seemed particularly promising, the Tulio Ospina Experiment Station was nearby, and climatic conditions were favorable for corn improvement work. Accordingly Roberts stationed himself at Medellín, but Rupert went to Bogotá, 8,660 feet high, where the climate was more suitable for wheat and other small grains and where the La Picota Experiment Station was located. A small group of Colombian agrónomos who had been trained in the Mexican program under the Miller-recommended grants welcomed the newcomers, who then went to work and soon produced results that led to requests for more work of the same kind.

Roberts began by testing lines of corn, while Rupert worked with wheats, from Mexico and other countries in comparison with Colombian varieties, and by the end of 1951 several superior selections already were being multiplied for distribution. Among these was Eto, a synthetic variety of corn produced by Ing. Eduardo Chavarriaga, a Colombian agrónomo who had spent half a year or more in the Mexican program. Among the 7,000 lines of wheat tested, mostly from Mexico, one of Mexican origin was so outstanding in yield that seed was quickly multiplied for distribution as the variety Menkemen. Funza barley was the third of the first trio of superior crop varieties.

It did not take influential Colombians long to see what science was doing for Colombian agriculture, and they set out to get more of it. The Ministry of Agriculture quickly increased its financial contribution, increased the number of interns, and urged that the program be expanded to include varietal improvement of beans, potatoes, and rice, and researches on soils, insect pests, and plant diseases. The Foundation responded by increasing its own financial contribution and by furnishing a soils expert, a potato specialist, an entomologist, and a plant pathologist, all of whom began work during 1952–1953. Headquarters of the Office of Special Investigations were moved to Bogotá in May, 1953, where physical facilities for experimental work already were being rapidly expanded.

TIBAITATÁ AND OTHER EXPERIMENT STATIONS

Because the old La Picota Experiment Station, on the edge of Bogotá, was being squeezed by the expanding city and had become too small and outmoded for the needs of the rapidly growing experimental projects, the Ministry bought 550 hectares of land about 12 miles from the city and appropriated money for the construction of buildings for a new station. The Foundation brought experts from the United States and Wellhausen, Harrar's successor in Mexico, to help in the planning and designing. The new station, Tibaitatá, was occupied gradually during 1952–1953 and was officially dedicated in February, 1954. Tibaitatá is an experiment station of which any country could be proud. Better still, every country could be proud of the results obtained there.

But this central station could not meet all the needs of the very diverse Colombian agriculture; accordingly, the Ministry undertook to establish a good system of regional stations also. In 1952 the Ministry had created the Department of Agricultural Research (DIA) and requested Roberts to act as director, pending the availability of a sufficiently experienced Colombian scientist. Roberts continued as director for three years, during which time the experiment station system evolved, the quality of researches improved, and the program expanded into new spheres.

NEW PROJECTS AND MORE SCIENTISTS

In 1955 projects in animal sciences and forages were added to the program. A meat-production specialist was appointed early in the year, and a dairy specialist and a veterinarian soon followed. Colombia had a comprehensive program of research at the end of the first five years of cooperative effort.

The program had started with two Foundation scientists and three Colombian agrónomos in 1950. Five years later there were 11

Foundation staff members and 40 Colombian agrónomos in the Office of Special Investigations, and by 1960 there were 144 scientists in the cooperative program, comprising 128 Colombians and 16 Foundation staff members. All had at least the equivalent of a B.S. degree; 14 Colombians and one American had the M.S.; and one Colombian and 14 Americans had the doctorate. The organization comprised 14 sections: six for crops; three for animals; and one each for soils, plant pathology, entomology, and biometry. Finally, there was a section of "experiment station administration," comprising one Foundation staff member and six Colombians, of whom two had degrees in civil engineering and four the degree ingeniero agrónomo. This section had responsibility for the mechanical and engineering phases of establishing and operating the various experiment stations. The activities of the Office extended to 13 strategically located experiment stations.

Such was the situation when Roberts left Colombia. After having directed the Office for nine years, during which he served under ten ministers of agriculture and survived two major political upheavals, Roberts went to New York as associate director for agricultural sciences at Foundation headquarters. He was succeeded by Dr. U. J. Grant, who had been a corn breeder in the Colombian program from 1951 to 1957 and in charge of corn and sorghum improvement in the Foundation's program in India from 1957 to 1959.

PROGRESS IN CROP PRODUCTION

In Colombia special attention was given to improvement of corn because it occupies a larger acreage than any other crop except coffee and plantains and is grown from the hot lowlands to the cool highlands by all kinds of farmers, rich and poor.

Thirty-six improved varieties, variety-hybrids, and double-cross hybrids have been produced and released for distribution during the past 14 years, and they are making their way to good farmers' fields. In 1953–1954 the Caja Agraria (the Government Agricultural Credit Bank), which had the responsibility for seed multiplication and distribution, sold 115 tons of improved seed and 10 years later is selling close to 1,200 tons a year; moreover private seed companies are selling as much as or more than the Caja.

About 85 percent of the corn acreage in the fertile, well-farmed Cauca Valley is planted to improved varieties or hybrids, and they produce an average yield of around 55 bushels an acre as contrasted with a little more than 30 bushels for unimproved varieties. Many of the best farmers produce 75 to 90 bushels an acre from improved seed, some have produced 100 or more, and some of the latest hybrids have yielded 160 bushels in experimental trials. Yet the average for the entire country is only 16 bushels an acre, because only about 10 percent of the total acreage is planted to improved varieties and in many areas cultural methods are, according to Roberts, "much the same as at the time of the Spanish Conquest." It would be easy to double this average if the results of the research program were used fully. But they are not, for education has not kept pace with research.

As in Mexico, improved wheat made its way faster than corn. Acre yields have doubled since 1950, from about 12 bushels to 24 bushels, and the most progressive farmers are producing upwards of 50 bushels an acre. Menkemen, Bonza, and Nariño started a procession of continually higher-yielding varieties, but the six most recently produced—Miramar, a composite variety, Crespo 63, Napo 63, Tiba 63, Tota 63, and Bonza 63—can yield twice as much as the early group and four times as much as the old Colombian varieties Bola Picota and No. 150. It sounds easy, but it was not. As in Mexico, progress resulted from hard, intelligent work and great resourcefulness in overcoming obstacles.

Yellow rust (*Puccinia glumarum*), usually a minor disease in Mexico, proved to be a major menace to wheat in the cool, moist highlands of Colombia, as was shown by Dr. Juan Orjuela, the first Colombian agrónomo to obtain a Ph.D. in the United States. The problem was most acute in the very high sierras of southern Colombia and Ecuador, as well as in Guatemala and Peru. After the usual vicissitudes in attempting to produce and maintain resistant varieties, the variety Nariño seemed to have solved the problem, because it was almost immune from rust and yielded exceptionally well. But in the spring of 1962 a previously unknown race of yellow rust attacked it so suddenly and severely as to knell its doom as a commercial variety. Fortunately, other varieties soon were ready to fill the breach and still others are in process of formation. Resistance to yellow rust has become a special virtue of Colombian wheats, and many of them have therefore become cosmopolitan.

Although grown on virtually the total domestic wheat acreage, Colombia-bred wheats now occupy a far larger acreage outside the country than within it. Because of their exceptionally good resistance to yellow rust, wide adaptability, plump kernels, and other valuable characters, there has been increasing demand for them, both for immediate commercial use and for use in breeding programs. During 1963, seed of some 19,500 varieties and lines was sent to almost a dozen countries: Argentina, Bolivia, Brazil, Chile, Ecuador, Guatemala, Israel, Kenya, Mexico, Peru, and Yugoslavia.

Although started later than the wheat project, projects on barley and rice have also been very productive. In 1950 Colombia imported 70 to 80 percent of her barley; thanks to such improved varieties as Funza and better cultural practices, she now satisfies her own requirements. Superior malting varieties that yield 25 percent more than Funza are being multiplied and will improve quantity and quality of production still more. Although varietal improvement of rice was not begun until 1958, the production of this very important food crop is being improved, and resistant varieties are insuring the production against several destructive diseases, including the virus *hoja blanca* (white leaf) disease that caused great apprehension a few years ago.

Potatoes have long been important in the diet of Colombia, ranking fourth among the country's food crops. The crop is grown mostly in the cool highlands and yields an average of only 75 to 100 bushels an acre despite the expenditure of many man-hours of labor and the expense of spraying 13 to 21 times to control late blight. But this need no longer be so, for the potato group have produced blight-resistant varieties that do not have to be sprayed. Experiments have shown that acre yields can easily be increased three-fold in general and up to 10- or 12-fold on good land. Research has done its part; extension still needs to do its part.

Beans too have been improved greatly. Disease-resistant varieties help safeguard the crop against some of the most dangerous diseases, and early varieties make it possible to grow two crops a year where only one grew before.

Soil science has contributed significantly to better tillage and fertilizer practices. Phosphate fertilizers have given spectacular results in some areas; proper management and fertilization of grasslands have doubled their animal-carrying capacity; and the addition of small amounts of the microelement boron to deficient soils in the

Cauca Valley and near Popayán has made it possible to grow alfalfa profitably where previously it could not grow at all.

Crop protection also has made its contribution. Studies of pathogens, including those that cause cereal rusts, late blight of potato, virus diseases of several crops, and bacterial diseases of certain important food crops and forages, furnished the key to the development and maintenance of resistant varieties. Entomology, too, has contributed to the protection of crops against insect depredations in the field and in storage. Indeed, every major measurable increase in crop production has been based on special knowledge obtained by the research and experimentation in genetics, soil science, plant pathology, entomology, and related fields. And, of course, increased plant production, especially of forages, has contributed to animal production also.

PROGRESS IN MEAT PRODUCTION

Colombia has begun to develop her vast potential for meat production, thanks largely to the animal research program that began in 1955 and now embraces beef and dairy cattle, hogs, sheep, and poultry.

There are almost 70 million acres of grasslands and some 13 or 14 million cattle. The number of cattle about equals the number of people; hence, there should be plenty of meat. But there is not, because too many of the grasslands and the cattle that feed on them are relatively unproductive. It takes as much as five acres of native grassland to support one beef animal, and it takes the animal four years or longer to get himself ready for market. But the animal scientists already have shown how the carrying capacity of the land can be doubled or even trebled by introducing better forage plants and by better fertilization and pasture management. And they have shaved a year from the four previously needed for an animal to mature for market. Colombia is potentially a beef-exporting country, and the organization of a national cattlemen's association in 1963 gives promise that private enterprise will help realize the potential.

Biologically, Colombia could advance rapidly in dairying, poultry production, swine production, and the production of wool. Dairy herd improvement by means of artificial insemination, better nutrition, good management, and disease control can increase milk production greatly. Pork and poultry production can be similarly increased, but certain economic factors prevent the full realization of the biological potential. An unfavorable and relatively unstable ratio between the price of concentrated feeds and that of milk and pork and eggs has been a deterrent in the past. If a dairyman pays as much for a ton of feed as he gets for a ton of milk, he either goes out of business or resorts to cheap feed, cheap labor, and primitive and sometimes unsanitary methods of production. Colombia still needs more corn, oats, sorghums, or other feedstuffs and a more stable and balanced price structure to ensure the most efficient animal production.

CLOSING THE GAPS BETWEEN RESEARCH, EDUCATION, AND EXTENSION

More than 200 young Colombian agronomists have participated as interns in the Office of Special Investigations, and about 80 have earned advanced degrees in the United States on Foundation fellowships. Several important administrative positions and the projects on bean improvement, entomology, soils, and forages already are in the charge of new-generation Colombian scientists.

But the results of research must be carried to farmers if farming is to be improved. And research must become a part of the educational process if good scientists are to be developed within the country. Colombia has learned and is putting into practice what she learned; she has established the Instituto Colombiano Agropecuario (ICA) on the foundation of the Tibaitatá Experiment Station, ten years after Tibaitatá was founded.

THE NEW COLOMBIAN INSTITUTE OF AGRICULTURE— A LANDMARK OF PROGRESS

The federation of research, extension, and postgraduate education in agriculture and animal husbandry is one of the most significant events in the agricultural history of Colombia. "On December 23, 1963, Their Excellencies, President Guillermo León Valencia and Minister of Agriculture Virgilio Barco, presided over a ceremony at Tibaitatá in which the newly constituted Colombian Institute of

Agriculture (Instituto Colombiano Agropecuario, ICA) received jurisdiction over the federal government's experiment station system and responsibility for nationwide agricultural research and extension. All the assets of the former Division of Agricultural Research (DIA), including 140 technical workers, approximately 1,200 other employees, and 13 experiment stations with an estimated value of $50 million, have now passed to the new institute."

Grant's 1963–1964 report continues with this statement: "Before the institute began to function officially, the Minister of Agriculture, the Minister of Education, and the Rector of the National University reached full agreement on the agricultural education program to be followed by ICA. Subsequently they signed an agreement stipulating that ICA would assume responsibility for the postgraduate school of agriculture to be established at Tibaitatá. The National University will participate in the academic activities of the school under a contract with ICA."

The board of trustees of the Institute is made up of the Ministers of Agriculture and of Education, the director general of the National Institute of Agrarian Reform (INCORA), the director general of the Bank of the Republic, a representative of the Colombian Association of Universities, the rector of the National University of Colombia, the director general of ICA, and two private citizens. This broad representation among the trustees should insure ICA against undue political or bureaucratic domination.

Dr. Alberto Lleras Camargo, President of Colombia from 1958 to 1962, deserves much credit for the establishment of ICA, for it was conceived and baptized during his administration. Lleras knew something about education as well as statecraft. He had been rector of the University of the Andes and had the vision to see that the program of agrarian reform on which Colombia had embarked should include not only problems of land tenure but also those of land productivity. And he had the educational statesmanship to capitalize on the educational and extension potential of Tibaitatá, one of the best agricultural experiment stations in Latin America. He had the cooperation of some of the most intelligent and public-spirited citizens of his own country and the help of the Rockefeller, Ford, and Kellogg Foundations. But some traditionalism, inertia, ineptitude, and vested interests had to be overcome. The creation of ICA was not easy, but it was a magnificent creation.

IN COLOMBIA AND BEYOND

Clearly, there has been a conceptual revolution regarding agriculture in Colombia, and in some areas, like the Cauca Valley, there has been a revolution in agriculture itself. This alone is reason for pride, but Colombia has reason for additional pride because of her contributions to other countries, near and far. Many professional visitors from Latin America and some from distant lands have come for varying periods of time to get facts, ideas, and materials. Seed has been sent from the Andean corn germ plasm bank (which had more than 3,600 specimens as early as 1954) to dozens of countries for experimental purposes (see Chapter 15). And seed of improved corn, wheat, barley, beans, potatoes, and certain forages has been sent to all continents of the world.

But Colombia's near neighbors in Central America, in Venezuela, Ecuador, and Peru have benefited most directly. Relations were closest with Ecuador, which became closely associated with the Colombian program, informally at first and finally by formal agreement.

Ecuador

DIVERSITY AND ITS PROBLEMS

During the past two decades, Ecuador has modernized her agricultural institutions. Several international agencies, including the technical assistance organizations of the United States, the Food and Agriculture Organization of the United Nations, and The Rockefeller Foundation, have contributed in various ways and with varying degrees of success. Although The Rockefeller Foundation established an independent advisory service in the country only recently, it had helped effectively for more than twenty years by making liberal grants for educational and investigational purposes.

Whatever all of the contributing factors, the establishment of a National Institute of Agricultural Research by the Ecuadorian government in 1961 was a significant event and a monument to the patriotic enterprise of some of its citizens. It seems that the establishment of the Institute should have been easy because it was sensible. But common sense alone seldom determines the course of events, because rarely is there complete agreement as to what is most sensible, especially in a country like Ecuador where geography tended to create sharp sectional differences.

Although it is a small country, comprising about 106 thousand square miles of territory lying astride the equator, there really have been several Ecuadors, ecologically, ethnologically, and culturally. From the Pacific Coast to Quito, the capital, is only about 125 miles horizontally, but it is some nine thousand feet vertically, and nearby snow-capped peaks rise up to about 20 thousand feet. It is a beautiful country, but it has been a difficult one, for two parallel ranges of the Andes divide it into three major parts. They were relatively discrete until a few years ago when improved communication and transportation lines began to tie them closer together. Nevertheless, there still are three natural zones, and it is natural that each should have its special interests and ambitions.

The low-lying tropical coastal area, *Costa,* with Guayaquil as its principal city, has recently become the world's leading exporter of bananas; in 1947 they accounted for four percent of the total value of Ecuador's exports and by 1958 the percentage had risen to 55 percent. Because of extensive areas of rich soil and a favorable climate, high-quality cacao, pineapples, rice, sugarcane, and other tropical crops also are grown, and a considerable cattle industry has developed.

High above the Costa is the *Sierra,* with Quito as the principal and capital city, beautifully situated at 9,300 feet elevation. Temperate-zone agriculture is carried on in a series of high mountain valleys in and between two parallel ranges of the Andes. Potatoes, corn, wheat, barley, beans, and various forages for livestock are the principal crops. Although some valleys at intermediate elevations produce coffee, citrus, and other subtropical products, the two most distinctive regions are the Costa and the high Sierra. East of the mountains is an underdeveloped tropical jungle area.

Of Ecuador's approximately 4.6 million people, more than half are classed as rural. About 10 percent are white, 40 percent Indian, 40 percent mestizo (mixed blood), five percent Negro, and five percent belong to other ethnic groups. The percentage of illiteracy still is high, and, although education is free and legally compulsory, many children in the remoter rural districts either do not go to school at all or get only a third- or fourth-grade education. Yet the country has made notable progress during the past decade and can greatly accelerate future progress if present plans are carried out.

MODERNIZING RESEARCH AND EDUCATION

Twenty-five years ago, in 1940, there was virtually no experimentation and research in Ecuador. There were several practical schools of agriculture whose graduates, *peritos* or "experts," had been trained to do practical things but had not been educated to do research. Higher education in agriculture was provided by the Central University in Quito and the State University at Guayaquil, but neither was equipped to do research or to capacitate students for it.

The responsibility for research, extension, and regulatory work resided in the Ministerio de Fomento (Ministry for Development), but its efforts were relatively ineffective. In the hope of increasing production, a number of commodity commissions had been established: the Wheat Commission, the Rice Commission, and half a dozen others that were essentially promotional rather than research organizations. Ecuadorian leaders had long been seeking ways to modernize their agriculture and, recognizing the need for research, they asked for Rockefeller Foundation help and the Foundation responded with limited help that had far-reaching implications.

In 1956 the Ministry of Agriculture established a wheat improvement program, and the Foundation agreed to provide the advisory services of Dr. John Gibler, the leader of the wheat work in Colombia, thus implementing the general policy of regionalizing its efforts. An experimental field was established near Quito and the National University, and soon it was covered with thousands of varieties and lines of wheat, a beautiful sight to anyone interested in bread and ways of getting more of it. This really professional job of crop improvement and similar experiments with oats, barley, and potatoes helped fortify the resolve of Ecuador to strengthen her agricultural services, and in 1958 the Ministry of Agriculture solicited the Foundation's advice in organizational planning.

SYNTHESIS: THE NATIONAL INSTITUTE OF AGRICULTURAL RESEARCH

In the spring of 1958, Gibler, highly regarded in Ecuador because of his contributions to the wheat program, and Stakman spent three activity-packed weeks in various parts of the country and were joined during the last week by Roberts, director of the Colombian program. After extensive personal observations and consultations with Ecuadorian leaders and representatives of the United States and other technical assistance programs, they suggested the basis for federation of agricultural improvement agencies. It seemed simple justice to write: "Although there may be differences in judgment [among Ecuadorians] as to what is best for the country, the ambition to learn and do what is best deserves high tribute. As long as this attitude of service to the country prevails it seems certain that the best ways can be found." And Ecuador did find at least a good way.

In 1961 the government established a National Institute of Agricultural Research (INIAP), concerned with both plants and animals. There are two principal research centers, one in the highlands near Quito and the other in the coastal area near Guayaquil, and they collaborate closely with the respective universities. A few years ago it was necessary to write, "Ecuador needs more money for agricultural research and education, but she also needs to learn how to get her money's worth from what she already has." She has more money now: the budget for INIAP in 1963 was eight times that in 1961, and the Foundation has made liberal grants both for education and for research. Still better, there is evidence that the moneys are paying dividends; agricultural research and education are on the road of progress in Ecuador. Leaving Ecuador reluctantly, it is time to go to Chile.

Chile

A FOOD PROBLEM CREEPS UP ON CHILE

About twenty years ago Chile suddenly realized that she had a food problem. Before that she had produced enough for her own needs; she imported only some tropical fruits and some animal feeds, which she could pay for easily by exporting nitrates and copper and wines. But human reproduction began to outstrip food production, for the population was increasing about 2.5 percent a year, per capita food consumption was increasing more than 0.5 percent a year, and agricultural production was not keeping pace. Then the demand for nitrates decreased, the price of copper dropped, and Chile was in trouble.

Shortly after World War II several agencies extended helping hands to Chile, although at times there were more hands than help. The United States technical assistance agencies operated in the country under various names and in various ways; the Food and Agriculture Organization of the United Nations and miscellaneous missions gave advice and possibly some help. The country was booming with zeal and activity, but agriculture went on its weary way, brightened periodically by mirages but not by miracles of production. Most of the foreign agencies had not yet learned the nature of their job, underestimated its magnitude, and went at it wrong. Because of financial uncertainties and official restrictions they could not commit themselves to long-time research, but they welcomed an agency that could.

The Rockefeller Foundation was favorably known in Chile because its International Health Division had maintained a cooperative program there for a number of years and because the success of the Mexican and Colombian agricultural programs had attracted wide attention. So Chile asked the Foundation for help, and the Foundation continued its southward march in 1955.

A LONG, NARROW STRIP OF LAND

The Foundation was now well south of the equator, for Chile, with an area of 286 thousand square miles, extends southward 2,600 miles from latitude 17.5° south to almost 56°, a distance about equal to that from Mexico City to Hudson Bay. The average width of the country is 109 miles and the maximum is 221 miles, and it would be hard to widen it, for it is bounded by the ocean on the west and by the 15-thousand-foot wall of the Andes on the east, with several peaks higher than 20 thousand feet. A low coastal range divides part of the country into a coastal area and the principal central agricultural valley, about 600 miles long and 45 miles wide or less. Northern Chile is a mineral-rich desert, one of the driest areas of the world, with no measurable precipitation. The middle portion has a Mediterranean-type climate, with mild, moist winters (minimum 37°F.) and a long, hot summer (average temperature 84°F.). Rainfall ranges from 10 to 45 inches in most of this area, but is about 200 inches in the cold, wet, windy South. The population is somewhat more than eight million, about 30 percent of European racial stock, 68 percent mestizo, and two percent pure Indian.

Crops in approximate order of importance are wheat, potatoes, oats, onions, corn, barley, rice, beans, and sunflowers. Citrus and temperate-zone fruits, wine grapes (about a quarter of a million acres), sugar beets, and several other crops are important in some areas. Livestock and large-scale dairying are among the important agricultural industries. Close to 90 percent of the farm lands are concentrated in relatively few large holdings.

THE FOUNDATION LENDS A HELPFUL HAND

The basic agreement between Chile and the Foundation was signed in April, 1955. In May Dr. Joseph A. Rupert, who had won his spurs in the Mexican and Colombian programs, established headquarters at Santiago and was ready to go to work but was delayed until the Chilean Congress authorized importation of the necessary equipment. Chile particularly wanted help in increasing the production of wheat, meat, and milk; accordingly Rupert started the wheat' program as soon as possible, followed by a forage project in 1957 and one on pasture and range management in early 1958. A section of experiment station development and management was added in 1959. The pattern of operations was similar to that in Mexico and Colombia. An Office of Special Studies was established in the Ministry of Agriculture and effort was made to combine research with training and education and the development of an adequate experiment station system.

The wheat improvement project was the first to yield concrete results. Of approximately 18,000 lines from Mexico and Colombia that Rupert started testing in the spring of 1955 (later helped by Dr. Robert Romig), several superior ones were reselected and multiplied. Two were named and distributed in 1958 as the spring-wheat varieties Orofén and Rulofén. Several other varieties followed three years later, among them Orofén 60 and Chifén, each especially well adapted to particular wheat zones. Worthy of re-emphasis is the fact that Orofén and Orofén 60 were selected from a joint product of the Mexican and Colombian programs, [(Newthatch × Marroquí) × (Kenya × Mentana)] × Frontana (as is described in

Chapter 16). They were the product of a triple play: Mexico to Colombia; Colombia to Mexico; Mexico to Chile. These new wheats yield 60 to 75 bushels an acre on good soil in their area of adaptation. Winter wheats, which are more productive than spring wheats in some localities, have also been improved. The movement toward short, stiff-straw spring wheats that can stand up when given fertilizers, which are badly needed in certain areas of Chile, is progressing. Chile is well on the way to more and better bread.

Chile is also on the way to more meat production, especially through the improvement of forages and better pasture management. More than 50 percent of the agricultural land is in pasture or ranges, and it has already been shown that there need be no shortage of animal products if materials and facts now available are widely used. Better varieties of alfalfa, red clover, and certain grasses can produce more and better feed. On good pasturage alone animals have produced more than 2,600 pounds of beef per hectare during the grazing season, September through May, as shown by experiments at Chillán in cooperation with the University of Concepción. As Rupert wrote in his 1961–1962 report: "If a yield of only 50% of that obtained in these experimental trials were attained commercially on 500,000 hectares with adequate moisture, the national meat deficit could be eliminated. This goal does not seem unreasonable when it is considered that an estimated 15,000,000 hectares, mostly dryland and mountain range, are in permanent use for the production of livestock."

Thus Chile is verging on a new era of bread and meat production.

FORMING AN ALLIANCE BETWEEN RESEARCH AND EDUCATION

The Chilean Office of Special Studies was early entrusted with the responsibility of helping develop an adequate experiment station system, which now comprises three principal stations: the Central Station near Santiago; the South Central Station at Chillán; and the Southern Station at Temuco. So located as to serve directly about 80 percent of the agricultural area, these stations also are strategically located with respect to educational institutions.

Since the Central Station at Santiago started operating about four years ago, some 100 agricultural students from the National and the Catholic Universities have obtained practical experience in field research, either as trainees during their three-month vacation or in doing thesis work. The station at Chillán is operated by the University of Concepción, whose students of agriculture spend their final years of study at Chillán; and the station at Temuco has a working agreement with Austral University at Valdivia, about 125 miles distant. Research and education are growing together in Chile. Concrete evidence for this statement is the recent creation of the "Agricultural Research Institute."

In 1961, the Ministry of Agriculture, the Chilean Development Corporation, the University of Chile, the Catholic University, and the University of Concepción established the autonomous Agricultural Research Institute, with a board of directors comprising representatives of each constituent agency. In order to facilitate closer cooperation between research and extension, the three-man executive committee includes the director of extension of the Ministry. Thus research, education, and extension are united in a common purpose, and in this unity there is hope for future progress.

Research—The Key to Progress in Latin America

Research was "the living source of progress" in all of the Foundation's operating programs in Latin America. From research came better materials and methods that made the land more productive wherever they were used. Participation in research was the principal device for selecting and helping to educate potentially productive national scientists. And research paved the way for the more effective organization and coordination of investigational, educational, and extension agencies. True, the researches did not contribute much to an understanding of the origin and nature of life, but they did contribute a great deal to the lives of millions of human beings. Admittedly, education has not yet carried the results of the researches to millions of humble farmers who urgently need them, for extension has not kept pace with research. But all education is an evolutionary process; the evolution is already in progress and is progressing at an accelerating rate. Research and education already have made the present brighter than the past and can make the future much brighter than the present.

Chapter 14

India
Modifying a Pattern to Suit Special Conditions

India in 1957 was a country trying to subsist close to two and a half times as many people as there are in all of Latin America on a land area about one fifteenth as great. Since gaining independence in 1947 and becoming a republic in the British Commonwealth of Nations, India has been confronted with an awesome complexity of problems of human subsistence and human relations. Wealth and poverty have long existed side by side. Tales of the fabulous wealth of the Indies reached Europe several centuries before the birth of Christ and, as every school child learns, even Columbus was looking for a shorter route to this wealth when he accidentally discovered America.

The Rockefeller Foundation obviously knew much about both the wealth of the few and the poverty of many and was much more concerned about the many. Could the Foundation help some 400 million people in India as it had helped some 50 million in Latin America? Encouraged by success in Mexico and Colombia, and urged by some influential Indians, the Foundation decided to examine the possibilities.

In 1952 it had sent Warren Weaver, then head of its Division of Natural Sciences and Agriculture, J. G. Harrar, and Paul C. Mangelsdorf to India to study the situation, talk with agricultural leaders there, and visit agricultural colleges and experiment stations. After a second trip by Weaver and Harrar the following year, the advisability of extending agricultural activities to India was taken up with the Board of Consultants for Agriculture and with the Trustees. Both groups gave enthusiastic approval to the idea, although the Consultants added one qualification: the Latin American programs already in progress should not be weakened in order to start new ones in India.

In the spring of 1955 opportunities for helping India were canvassed further by Richard Bradfield, newly appointed as the Foundation's temporary regional director for agriculture in the Far East, and Robert F. Chandler, Jr., who had recently joined the New York staff as assistant director for agriculture. Like their predecessors, Bradfield and Chandler visited many of the major agricultural colleges and experiment stations and talked with state and national agricultural officers. They met many scientists who were well informed about modern developments in agriculture, but as they traveled hundreds of miles through the countryside they were impressed anew by the poverty and hard lives of the masses of the people. Much to their surprise, however, they also saw numerous indications that India was endowed with many natural resources that could supply her people with a more abundant life. India's situation began to look less hopeless; obviously there was something to work with. But just as obviously something was missing; one sensed this in the atmosphere. There seemed to be so much to do and so many people doing so little.

Why had agriculture not thrived in this ancient land supplied with so many talented citizens? Why was it that India, known throughout the world for its contributions to art, religion, and philosophy for over 2,000 years, had made so little progress in applying modern science to improve her agriculture? Bradfield and Chandler asked themselves these questions. The answers require an understanding of India's agricultural resources—her land and climate, and her people.

The Foundation Explores India

A UNIQUE LAND AND CLIMATE

The Indian subcontinent, which is about half the size of the United States, is shaped like a triangle standing upon its apex, with the broad base in the north extending into the foothills of the Himalayas, the roof of the world. This is of great significance to India, for these massive peaks, many towering 25,000 feet or higher above sea level, serve as a barrier that deflects the cold winds from the interior of

Asia away from India and toward China and other countries to the east. India therefore has a much milder winter climate than would otherwise be the case, and crops like sugarcane can be grown up to the foothills of the mountains at about 30° north latitude. From here the country extends to 8° north latitude at the southern tip. As a glance at a map will show, the Himalayas have another significance for India in that their snowfields are the origin of many of her great river systems. Three of these—the Indus in the west, the Ganges in the great central plain, and the Brahmaputra in the east—cross the country on their way to the sea and are important sources of irrigation water, as well as the cause of destructive floods.

The Ganges Valley, extending for over a thousand miles across northern India, is one of the most densely populated areas in the world and its soils produce much of the country's food. The Deccan Plateau, sloping eastward, forms the central core of the lower part of the Indian triangle. The coastal plains, rather narrow on the west and much wider on the east, are climatically alike and both are heavily populated.

Because frosts are rare in most of India, crops can be grown throughout the year if other conditions are favorable. Temperatures reach their maximum, 110° to 115°F., toward the end of the dry season in May or early June.

Rainfall is the climatic factor of greatest importance to India's agriculture. The average annual precipitation is often cited as about 42 inches, but during this century it has varied between 31 and 50 inches. Regional rainfall differs widely—from five inches a year in the Rajputana Delta in the northwest to 430 inches in Cherripungi in the northeast, the wettest place in the world. It has been calculated that India's rivers carry enough water to the sea each year to cover the entire country to a depth of 20 inches. The pattern of distribution of rainfall, however, makes it difficult to use the water efficiently, because India has a monsoon climate.

The southwest monsoons, which break in late May or June, bring rains that often are torrential, amounting to 10 to 20 inches or more a month—sometimes even 10 inches a day. During this period rivers are likely to flood and inundate large areas of land. The monsoons usually reach their peak in July and August, decline in September, and end in October. Then, except for the regions that receive additional rain from the northeast monsoon, the country receives little or no rain until the next May or June. During the dry period skies are generally clear, radiant energy is abundant, and, where water is available for irrigation and soils are suitable, large areas have much of the agricultural potential of the Imperial Valley of California, the so-called Greenhouse of America.

The soils of India are as diverse as the climate, some being incredibly good and some incredibly poor. If they were all well used they might support India's rapidly increasing population. But they are not, and this fact, together with the uncertainty of rainfall, has created one of India's most serious problems—too little food and too much hunger.[1]

POPULATION OUTSTRIPS FOOD PRODUCTION

India probably has more hungry people than any other country in the world, and this situation is becoming worse because her enormous population, now more than 450 million, is increasing faster than the already inadequate food supply. During the past 400 years the country has suffered 45 famines, averaging one every nine years, and the frequency seems to be increasing. In the Bengal famine of 1943, between one and three million people died. And each year there now are about 10 million additional people to feed. Clearly, India must either reduce the rate of human reproduction or increase her food production, or both, if she is to maintain even her present low level of subsistence.

The government of India is giving high priority to population control. Thousands of birth control clinics have been established, and the more intelligent people are making progress in family planning. But progress in this respect is likely to be slow among the three fourths of the population who are still illiterate. The present rate of population increase is about two percent a year and the total population will be more than 490 million by the year 1966—10 million more mouths to feed each year. India is in danger. Either she must produce more food or fewer people. But she already has too many people clamoring for the food that she now produces.

Food production must be increased, but there is no quick and easy way to increase it. Like other food-deficient countries, India must either bring more acres into cultivation or make each cultivated acre produce more, unless she can afford to buy food from other

[1] Unless otherwise indicated, the viewpoints in this chapter are as of 1963–1964.

countries. The amount of usable land per capita already is small, however; it was only two acres in 1921 and 1.4 acres 30 years later. At present there is only three fourths of an acre or less of cultivated land per capita, and current prospects for raising the ratio are not promising in view of the tremendous annual increase in population. This puts a heavy responsibility on the land now under cultivation.

The efficiency of food production is generally low. Acre yields of such basic crops as rice and wheat are only half or a third as high as those in most advanced countries. Like much of the land, the productivity of labor too is low. Whereas in the United States less than 10 percent of the population produce more food than the country uses, in India 70 percent of the population are engaged in producing less than that country needs. About 80 percent of India's people live in 558,000 villages, many of which are almost as isolated now as they were a century ago.

There are many reasons, both natural and man-made, for the low productivity of land and labor and the consequent shortage of food. Uncertain and variable rainfall, insufficient irrigation water, droughts or floods, some naturally poor or impoverished soils, and pests and diseases of important food crops are some of nature's obstacles to abundance and certainty of food production. And there are human faults and failures also. Traditionalism, lack of education among the masses, fatalism and mysticism, disruptions following independence and disunion, lack of cohesion because of differences in language and customs among the numerous linguistic and ethnic groups, the lingering effects of the caste system, imperfections in systems of communication and transportation—all these have had a depressive effect on food production and distribution and have contributed to a rigidity in the social structure that impedes progress generally.

Confronted with these huge problems, India has been making strenuous efforts to help herself.

Operation Bootstrap: The Five-Year Plans

Soon after independence, the new government of India called some of its most able citizens to serve on a National Planning Commission authorized to study national needs and to formulate definite plans for achieving them. The first Five Year Plan (1951–1956) established agricultural targets, which, on the whole, were met. The

Second Plan placed more emphasis on industrial development. The Third Plan, now in progress, gives top priority again to agriculture, with funds allocated for improving agricultural production aggregating 2,703 million U.S. dollars—an increase of 92 percent over the corresponding amount in the Second Plan.

The objective of the Third Plan is to double the rate of increase in agricultural production, from 3.01 to 6.4 percent a year. In the case of food grains, the goal is a total increase of 30 percent, or approximately six percent each year. Most of this increase is expected to result from efforts to raise acre yields, by expanding, for example, the area under irrigation from 80 million to 90 million acres and by a five-fold increase in the use of chemical fertilizers.

India has depended heavily on her Community Development Program and on her extension workers in trying to attain her food production goals. With liberal support from the Ford Foundation, a nationwide effort was made to improve agriculture and rural life. A revised experimental model, the "Package Program," was organized in 1960. Although subsequently modified somewhat, this plan originally contemplated integrated improvement programs in some 10,000 of India's 558,000 villages, including some five million people and embracing close to six million acres of land in the various states of the entire country. This is an experiment on the grand scale in which attempt is made to help provide whatever is needed to improve agriculture—information, materials, methods, and credits.

Recognizing the magnitude of the problem, the Indian government has sought and obtained advice and help from teams of foreign specialists and various aid programs, national and international. Although there seems to be consensus that food production goals can eventually be attained, it is evident that there must be a long, hard pull before that happy day arrives. In spite of such strenuous efforts as those here mentioned, the gap between human reproduction and food production seems to be widening. During the first year of the Third Five Year Plan there was only a 1.6 percent increase in agricultural production over the previous year instead of the projected six percent—hardly closing a gap. An integrated effort will be needed to close it, and many Indian leaders have realized that more experimentation and better education must be strong factors in the integration. They therefore solicited the help of The Rockefeller Foundation in this phase of their efforts.

The Foundation's Program: Aims and Accomplishments

In April, 1956, The Rockefeller Foundation and the Indian government entered into a formal agreement to cooperate in the improvement of maize, sorghum, and millet production and in the development of a modern postgraduate school of agriculture at the Indian Agricultural Research Institute (IARI, formerly known as the Pusa Institute) at New Delhi. The specific objectives were limited to these two projects, for the conditions in India were quite different from those that the Foundation had encountered in Mexico, Colombia, Ecuador, and Chile. Indeed they were almost unique.

The problem in Latin America had been to introduce agricultural sciences into the various countries; the problem in India was to help agricultural scientists to function. Whereas there had been almost no scientists with advanced degrees in the Latin countries, there were many in India who had doctorates from English or American universities. But most of the Indians were engaged in academic pursuits, because they could hardly do anything else. India, independent for less than a decade in 1956, was still struggling with the political and economic problems that independence usually brings and had begun to realize that some were almost too big for her to handle all alone. Food was one of the biggest. She had her own potential hunger fighters, but she also had her own special bureaucracy that kept many of them from effective work. Indian leaders knew that the efficiency of her corps of agricultural scientists was low and were striving to free them from their bondage and give them the incentives and facilities for efficient operation. But time would be needed and time was pressing. So the Foundation went to work, and it expanded its work as it went along.

Because the original objectives of the Indian program included not only projects on crop improvement but also the conversion of a research institute to a national postgraduate agricultural university, it was clear that a successful director would need a very special combination of qualities. The Foundation therefore selected Dr. Ralph W. Cummings—scientist, educator, administrator, and a human being of strong moral purpose. Born in North Carolina in 1911, Cummings was graduated from North Carolina State College in 1933, obtained the Ph.D. degree in soil science at Ohio State University in 1938, and then taught at Cornell University for five years, after which he returned to his alma mater as professor of agronomy and head of the department. He became successively assistant director and associate director of the Agricultural Experiment Station and then director of research. From 1954 onward Cummings was associated with the University of North Carolina Agricultural Research Mission in Peru and was chief of mission in that country for several years.

Since assuming his duties as director of the Indian Agricultural Program, Cummings has become a living tribute to the wisdom of the Foundation in choosing him, as should become apparent in subsequent pages of this chapter.

THE MAIZE IMPROVEMENT PROGRAM

In 1956 maize was not a major crop in India; only about 11 million acres were planted to it and the average yield was extremely low, only about 700 pounds an acre. But the chances of improving yields, with consequent expansion of acreage, seemed distinctly promising. In 1954, after an extensive survey made at the Indian government's request, E. J. Wellhausen and U. J. Grant of the Foundation's Mexican and Colombian programs had reported that the average yield could be increased three- or four-fold by varietal improvement and better cultural practices and that large areas of land were well suited to maize production. Following his appointment as head of the cooperative maize program, Grant returned to India in the summer of 1956 for preliminary planning, and work began officially in the succeeding January.

Of all people in foreign aid activities, agricultural scientists actively engaged in research in their specialized fields seem to be among the happiest and the most effective. They adjust more quickly to the new environment and are less likely to get frustrated. Even though the land and people are strange and at times difficult to understand, when the agricultural scientist gets into the field with his corn, wheat, soils, insects, or pathogens, he is among old friends, or at least close relatives of old friends. This was true of the Foundation's staff members in Mexico and Colombia and it proved true in India. Grant brought with him from Colombia methods and materials tested in that country and in Mexico. He had only to train new assistants, and in one respect even this was easier than it had beéñ in Latin America because these Indian colleagues and assistants spoke fluent English. On Grant's departure in 1959 to become director of the Foundation's Colombian Agricultural Program, his associate, Dr. Ernest W. Sprague, took over the maize program in India and is still in charge.

The program moved rapidly from the beginning. In 1957, the first year of operation, 14 yield trials were established in different sections of the country, and 11 of them were harvested. The 10 top yielders, mostly imported hybrids, yielded, as an average of the 11 locations, between 3,718 and 4,196 pounds per acre. The local varieties, which were used as checks and were given the same fertilizer and cultural treatments as the hybrids, yielded an average of 2,862 pounds, almost four times the average national yield. These results were most encouraging, because they showed that yields of native varieties could be increased quickly by cultivating and fertilizing the soil properly and that varietal improvement could help push yields even higher. Another encouraging result was that the breeding materials from both North and South America seemed to be usable in India. At the end of the year, a three-day conference of maize breeders was held, and all who had participated in this new venture were involved. The experiences of the first year were discussed and plans for the next year were made; these included plans for crosses between dent and flint types. Indians like the harder flint types of corn, which ordinarily do not yield so well as the improved dents that are commonly grown in the United States. These two types were therefore crossed, with the hope that satisfactory grain quality could be combined with better yielding potential.

Results of the second year, 1958, were both gratifying and disappointing. Although maximum yields of 6,560 pounds (about 117 bushels) an acre were obtained at each of three different stations, several serious diseases, many insect pests, and several difficult soil management and fertility problems were encountered. As these problems constituted barriers to the realization of corn's full potential in Indian agriculture, men with experience in the Foundation's Latin American programs were transferred to India to work toward their solution. Dr. Guy B. Baird, from Colombia, became assistant director of the entire Indian program in November, 1959, and began directing the soil fertility studies. Dr. William R. Young from Mexico and newly appointed Dr. B. L. Renfro tackled the insect and disease problems, respectively, and graduate students from the Indian Agricultural Research Institute in New Delhi began to study some of these problems for their M.S. and Ph.D. thesis research. Indian and American scientists pooled their efforts, and additional specialists were brought over from the United States to help out.

As the program was expanded to cover all of the more important ecological maize-producing zones and hundreds of new crosses were tested each year, training programs were organized to produce the additional specialists that were needed. The system produced results.

The 1961 annual report on the maize improvement program states: "In reviewing the progress made by the Coordinated Maize Breeding Scheme since its inception, one can justifiably say that the year 1961 was a landmark in its five-year history. Four top-performing double-cross hybrids were released for commercial production and distribution to farmers in the northern plains and peninsular India. As the production and distribution of hybrid seed to the farmers gather momentum in the coming years, these hybrids should make a significant contribution toward increased food production in the country."

But the 1961 report continues: "A note of caution should, however, be added here. Potentially high-performing hybrids in themselves are by no means the complete answer. Their cultivation must be carried out under improved and recommended agronomic practices. Although considerable practicable information is available on hybrid maize culture, the optimum conditions suited to Indian climate and soil have still to be determined. It is therefore gratifying to record that plans are being formulated for intensifying research in agronomy and other associated sciences such as entomology and plant pathology within the framework of the maize scheme. Maize breeders can thus look forward to an era of greater progress in collaboration with scientists of related disciplines."

Because the production of hybrid seed is a complicated process and because India had not yet developed much of a seed industry, Dr. Wayne H. Freeman was added to the staff in September, 1961, to help develop the seed production program. The government of India in March, 1963, formed a National Seeds Corporation to guide, finance, and stimulate the production and use of high-quality seeds of maize, sorghum, and other crops. The Foundation has assisted by providing the services of specialists and some of the specialized equipment needed to process and distribute the seed. Several thousand bushels of maize seed were available for trial in 1962, and plans were made for increasing this production to keep pace with demand. For the convenience of small farmers, some of the improved seed is packaged in amounts sufficient to plant one or two acres. Each bag contains a leaflet printed in two languages, which describes briefly the improved cultural practices recommended.

Because of the high cost of producing hybrid seed and the fact that the farmer cannot easily produce his own seed but must purchase it each year from a hybrid-corn producer, the maize breeders are trying simpler and cheaper methods of improving the crop. Widespread trials have been made of synthetics formed by combining outstanding inbred lines (see Chapter 4). Fourteen of these experimental synthetics were tested at 11 stations in 1962. Although their performance was generally inferior to the better double-topcross hybrids, the better synthetics outyielded the best local varieties by from 20 to 60 percent in the different zones. Experience in Mexico and elsewhere indicates that this is a promising approach in the initial stages of corn improvement in underdeveloped countries.

Encouraged by the results obtained to date in the maize program, the government has set a target of getting 25 percent of the total of 11 million acres planted to improved seed by 1965. On the basis of experimental results achieved thus far, this should more than treble production if accompanied by appropriate cultural practices.

Young Indian scientists have now had enough practical experience and in-service training to enable them to take over more and more responsibility for the day-by-day operation of the maize program. Consequently, Sprague has been able to internationalize his efforts by responding to some of the many requests for assistance from other Asian countries. Work is now under way in Thailand, South Vietnam, Indonesia, and the Philippines. The progress in Thailand is especially gratifying. Although corn is a new crop there, annual production has expanded to 700,000 tons during the past 10 years, and corn has become one of the leading exports.

THE SORGHUM-MILLET PROGRAM

The millets, which comprise both sorghums and millets as these terms are used in the United States, occupy over 88 million acres in India—more land than any other food crop. The annual production is about 17 million tons, almost one fourth of the world production, and most of it is used for human food. The total production in India is about four times that of maize and a third that of rice.[2]

Because they require less water than most crops (see Chapter 7), sorghums and millets are grown mostly in the drier regions of India. Sorghum predominates in areas with over 25 inches of rain a year, and millets predominate in the still drier regions. Some millets can even mature a small crop in localities with as little as five inches of rain a year. Many people, accustomed to these cereals, prefer them to wheat or maize. They are consumed in a great variety of ways; certain varieties are eaten when green, others are popped or parched, some are boiled in water like rice, and others are ground and made into pancake-like chapatties, which resemble Mexican tortillas.

Several distinct botanical species are included under the term millet. In general, the larger the size of the grain the more highly the species is appreciated by farmers. Ragi has the smallest grains but it grows on very poor soils with very little rainfall; the more than five million acres that it occupies are mostly in southern India. Forty-two percent of the sorghum crop is found in the State of Bombay,[3] and two thirds of this is grown in the winter dry season.

Experience in the United States has shown that there are vast possibilities for varietal improvement among the sorghum-millet group. Several decades ago various types of grain sorghums were introduced into the United States from Africa, where there are numerous kinds in what appears to be their original home, and the results of selection and breeding have been amazing. Sorghums have virtually revolutionized the agriculture of the American Southwest and are now grown extensively in low-rainfall areas from Texas northward to North Dakota. Because of their relatively low water requirement, not only have they displaced corn in areas that were marginal for that crop but they also are being grown successfully on many lands that previously had been considered as fit only for grazing. The development of dwarf or "combine" types that can be harvested mechanically has facilitated large-scale production, and early-ripening varieties have made it possible to extend the area of production at least 500 miles northward within the past few years. There are similar possibilities for India.

[2] Based on data for 1962–1963 in *FAO Production Yearbook,* Vol. 17, 1963.
[3] Now divided into the states of Gujarat and Maharashtra.

Recognizing the potential value of the diverse genetic materials, Dr. Kenneth O. Rachie, in charge of the sorghum and millet program in India, and his colleague, Dr. Leland R. House, have made collections of sorghums and millets from all over India and much of Africa and have assembled collections from the United States and Mexico. At the beginning of 1962 the collection on hand at the Indian Agricultural Research Institute included 4,516 sorghums, 1,342 pearl millets, and 2,029 small millets. Although these collections are being classified, catalogued, and evaluated as rapidly as possible, it will require several years to complete the job. This extensive collection is, of course, of great potential practical value for India.

The recent introduction of cytoplasmic sterile and genetic dwarf lines of pearl millets, or Pennisetums, from the United States provides germ plasm for expanding breeding programs with this important crop. Since the pearl millets are even more drought-resistant than the sorghums and are a very acceptable food, many agronomists feel that they may eventually have a broader use in India than the sorghums.

Concrete results have already come from the breeding program. Recently two superior sorghum hybrids have been released, one of which has an especially wide range of geographic and ecologic adaptation. Likewise a high-yielding, widely adapted millet hybrid has been released. In tests at various localities from the State of Madras in the south to the Punjab in the north this hybrid yielded from 70 percent to 100 percent more than the local varieties with which it was compared. Interest in the genetic improvement of these crops is increasing.

The Indian government is now placing increasing emphasis on a national program for sorghum and millet improvement, and prospects are bright for more rapid progress in the future than in the past. There are, however, several serious insect and disease problems to overcome. In some localities and seasons, insect pests and plant diseases are a major factor in depressing yields, and considerable work therefore has been done on methods of control. The sweet stalks of the sorghums and millets seem to be very attractive to certain insects. Insecticides are expensive and not very effective during the monsoon season because they are washed off by the heavy rains. Although Young has found that phorate systemic insecticide provides highly satisfactory protection, the economics of its use have not yet been evaluated. The best way of controlling some of the most destructive diseases is by means of resistant varieties, and this fact is being taken into consideration in the breeding program.

The requirements of the sorghums as concerns soil fertility seem to be quite similar to those of maize. Remarkable responses have been obtained from applications of nitrogen fertilizer in particular. In many places around Delhi, for example, sorghums are grown largely for fodder for the dairy cattle and buffaloes that supply the city with milk. Nitrogen fertilizer on some of the fodder varieties has increased yields from five to over 25 tons of green matter per acre, a very profitable return on the investment.

In most respects the sorghum-millet program is similar to the maize program in its method of operation. Conferences are held among the workers to report results and plan future research, and a training program has been established to supply additional workers for the expanding effort.

As is true also of maize, interest in the grain sorghums is increasing in most Far Eastern areas with a long dry season and a shortage of water for irrigation. Where soils are deep and saturated with water at the end of the rainy season, it may become practical to grow a short-season variety following rice on this residual moisture, thus providing additional or emergency feed for animals and food for man.

HELP IN WHEAT PRODUCTION BEGINS

In tonnage produced, wheat ranks third among India's food crops. The production figures for 1963–1964 are: rice, 55 million tons; sorghums and millets, 17 million tons; and wheat, close to 11 million tons.[4] India devotes close to 13.7 million hectares of her cultivated land to wheat, as compared with about 18.3 million in the United States. Yet the production figures are 10.8 million tons for India and about 31 million for the United States, since acre yields are less than half as high in India (790 kg./ha.) as in the United States (1,700 kg./ha.).

Acre yields of wheat in India today are just about what they were in Mexico 20 years ago, about 11.5 bushels, more or less, depending on the season. And the reasons for the low yields are about the same.

[4] *FAO Production Yearbook,* Vol. 18, 1964.

But Mexico has more than trebled her yields, and it is pertinent to ask whether India can make similar progress. Borlaug thinks that yields in India can be doubled within a decade (see Chapter 16), and the Foundation has recently added Dr. Glenn Anderson, an experienced Canadian wheat breeder, to its staff in India to help make Borlaug's prediction come true. Progress should be much more rapid than it was in Mexico because many wheat varieties that were produced in the Mexican and other Latin American programs promise to be very useful in India, and much time can therefore be saved in the breeding phases of the new cooperative wheat improvement program. It appears that materials and methods developed in the Foundation's national and international wheat programs may have high transfer values for India and that the program in India may be of great value in furthering the objectives of the International Wheat Program.

EXPERIMENT STATION DEVELOPMENT AND EQUIPMENT MAINTENANCE

Experience in Mexico, Colombia, and Chile had shown the need for especially trained men with engineering skills to help develop good experiment stations. To supply this need in India the Foundation appointed Jack D. Traywick, an agricultural engineer, in September, 1959.

Regional field experiments are indispensable in crop improvement work in a country as large and diverse as India. There must therefore be a system of experiment stations strategically distributed with respect to weather and soil conditions. The elementary essentials of a good station are suitable land and water, adequate buildings, appropriate tools and machines, and a supply of dependable labor. It is a tremendous undertaking to make comparative tests of thousands of varieties or lines of maize, sorghum, or wheat, or to make extensive fertilizer trials, or to make adequate tests of insecticides or fungicides or herbicides. An experiment station must be so equipped as to facilitate all of the operations needed in making thousands of comparative tests of many kinds.

Extensive experimentation is simply impossible without proper facilities. But all the effort involved is useless unless the accuracy of the results can be insured; results are reliable only when the experimenter can maintain uniform conditions when uniformity is needed and vary them when variation is needed. To determine the relative inherent yielding ability of varieties, for example, requires that they be grown on uniform soil prepared and cultivated in the same way. To compare the effects of different fertilizers requires that the soil in all the plots be the same before the fertilizers are applied. To determine the effect of soil moisture requires facilities for watering some plots and withholding water from others.

Water management is important in India in both the rainy and the dry season. One of the first operations that Foundation staff performed on many of the fields assigned to them for their research was to level the land. Specialized heavy equipment, land levelers, graders, and so forth were purchased for this purpose. If the land is not level in the rainy season, water collects and stands in the depressions, and crops like corn that are very sensitive to such conditions are greatly retarded. When such fields are irrigated during the dry season, the same thing happens; some parts get too much water and others too little. The benefits derived from land leveling were so obvious that many experiment stations requested assistance with their problems, and as new experimental fields have been set up the job has become even more complicated.

Traywick's general responsibility for helping to develop good experiment stations and training Indians in this work also includes responsibility for maintenance of the farm equipment at all stations. Since repair parts of many types are difficult to obtain in India, this function is even more important than usual.

THE EDUCATIONAL PROGRAM

At the time that the cooperative program with the Foundation was agreed upon, Indian leaders were deeply concerned with an even broader problem than maize and sorghum-millet improvement. Almost without exception, the numerous study and advisory teams that had been brought to India by the government, with the assistance of ICA and of the Ford Foundation, had pointed out weaknesses in agricultural education, research, and extension systems. Although there were over 50 agricultural colleges and 17 veterinary colleges, many of them established after independence, most of them were purely teaching centers, without appreciable responsibility for research or extension to serve the farmers of the area. Indeed many of them had but little interest in the problems of the farm, for agriculture had low prestige among educated people. Even the sons of farmers fortunate enough to get a secondary education regarded themselves as above working with their hands on farms. Naturally, most of the professors in the colleges held similar views; consequently, their knowledge of practical agriculture often was very superficial and, even more serious, problems of food production were of little concern to them. Most of the students were city boys who went into colleges of agriculture merely because they could not get into colleges of medicine, engineering, or law. Agriculture therefore seemed to offer the best opportunity for a government job. The disdainful attitude of many educated people toward the practical problems of agriculture still requires a cultural reorientation of many otherwise potentially qualified leaders in the vital problem of food production for India's hungry millions.

It was obvious that India needed many more functioning agricultural scientists than she was educating or than she could afford to send abroad for graduate study. If India was to supply the need herself, it was clear that graduate and undergraduate education would have to be strengthened and reoriented toward the solution of the country's vital practical problems of agricultural production, because the eight colleges of agriculture that were offering graduate work at the time were contributing little of practical value. The strongest agricultural research institution was the Indian Agricultural Research Institute at New Delhi, which had already given a half century of distinguished service to agriculture. It had one of the best agricultural libraries in Asia, much good equipment, and the largest staff of any such institution in India. It seemed logical, therefore, to develop a strong graduate school at IARI.

The government's intention was to make this new graduate school into India's principal center for educating research workers and teachers for all of her agricultural colleges, leaders for the extension service, and competent men for other governmental posts requiring advanced training in agricultural sciences. To help them realize this intention, government officials wanted a man whose qualifications included knowledge of the land-grant college system in the United States, broad administrative experience, and organizational skill. Since the Foundation, as they said, "always picked good people," they asked that a Foundation staff member be given the assignment; and for this reason Ralph Cummings got the job.

The Graduate School at IARI was inaugurated on October 6, 1958, and 150 students were admitted in that year. Because none of the IARI staff had had experience in this type of institution, Cummings was asked to serve as acting dean for the first year. In his report at the end of that period he wrote: "Plans for this school have been carefully worked out and represent a very substantial departure from the established pattern of postgraduate education in most of the Indian universities at present. If successfully implemented, this program will undoubtedly have a profound influence on post-graduate education in India and should make a most valuable contribution to the training of future Indian leaders in the agricultural sciences. Progress during the first year has been very gratifying."

Cummings' services were not the only help that the Foundation provided. During the crucial early period when patterns and standards were being established, it also arranged each year for several experienced American agricultural scientists to serve as visiting professors in fields where outside assistance was particularly needed. At the same time it made funds available for enlarging and modernizing the agricultural library of the Institute to meet the expanded needs, and sent Dorothy Parker, its agricultural library specialist, to New Delhi to assist with the planning of these improvements.

The Graduate School of the IARI has full university status and is beginning to produce the kind of agricultural scientists that India must have to help solve her problems of food production. By the end of 1964 it had granted 322 M.Sc. degrees and 91 Ph.D degrees. The student body totals 400 and includes an increasing number from foreign countries.

The IARI can play an important role in improving India's agriculture, particularly because India is also making valiant attempts to broaden the base of undergraduate education in agriculture through a system of agricultural universities. As early as 1950 the University Education Commission, under the chairmanship of Dr. S. Radhakrishnan, now President of India, had pointed out the need for a new system of rural or agricultural universities. This idea was examined further by the First and Second Joint Indo-American Teams on Agricultural Education and Research and was approved in principle.

The Foundation has encouraged the development of this system of agricultural universities in various ways, principally by providing the services of Cummings as member and then chairman of the national Agricultural University Committee. According to the testimony of all knowledgeable persons, including Indian leaders and many from other countries, the Foundation's encouragement in the form of Dr. Cummings has been indeed a powerful influence in the success of this enterprise because of his wide knowledge of educational systems, his understanding of the Indian people and their problems, his patience, and his tact. He has been extraordinarily effective in helping Indian educators to implement their objectives.

Uttar Pradesh Agricultural University, the first institution of the new type to be established, has made excellent progress since 1959 when its site was just an open prairie. Four colleges are in operation —Agriculture and Animal Husbandry, Veterinary Science, Agricultural Engineering, and Basic Sciences and Humanities—and a fifth —Home Science—is to be added. A 500-acre research and teaching farm is an integral part of the campus, and an extension service has been organized. The first class in agriculture, 99 students, graduated in 1963 and the first in veterinary and animal sciences in 1964. Postgraduate courses leading to the M.Sc. degree in agriculture and animal husbandry have been offered since 1963. An important factor in the university's progress so far has been the assistance of the University of Illinois through a contract with the United States Agency for International Development.

At Ludhiana in the Punjab, another very promising agricultural university is being developed around the existing College of Agriculture with the help of an able team from Ohio State University. Agricultural universities are also in operation or in the planning stage in the states of Orissa, Rajasthan, Andhra Pradesh, Mysore, Madras, Madhya Pradesh, West Bengal, Kerala, Assam, and Gujarat. Most of these states already have one or more colleges of agriculture of the old type, and because each will try to build the new type of university around the best available nucleus, individual problems may vary somewhat. But the aim in all cases is to develop an institution that will serve agriculture as effectively as have the United States land-grant colleges. These new universities with statewide responsibility for agricultural education, research, and extension may well have a profound effect on the development of India over the next century.

New Optimism Replaces Old Pessimism

If when one first approaches the agricultural problems of India he is overwhelmed by their magnitude and the difficulties involved in doing much about them, no such feeling of frustration can be detected among the Foundation's staff in India. They have selected important phases of the overall problem that they have the competence to handle. Like their counterparts in the Foundation's other cooperative programs, they have emphasized the team approach in which each specialist contributes his special knowledge and skills to the progress in attaining major objectives. This way the job does not look so big and progress comes faster. Moreover, the Foundation's scientists in India are filled with enthusiasm and their enthusiasm has become contagious.

They have no doubts about the ability of their young Indian colleagues to deal successfully with India's agricultural problems. They have found that many Indian scientists can and will work in the fields where the principal problems lie, and that many of them want to cooperate and form functional teams. The main task now is to multiply these centers of cooperation and optimism and competence, and the new agricultural universities are designed to provide leaders for more and more such centers.

Chapter 15

The International Corn Program
Assembling and Distributing Superior Germ Plasm

In these days of rapid communication, news travels swiftly from one part of the world to another. Even in Central America, where the countries are strongly nationalistic, jealous of their borders, and not inclined to be especially neighborly, anything that happens in one country is soon known to the others. So when it became evident that the Foundation's cooperative agricultural programs in both Mexico and Colombia were substantially improving food production through agricultural research, the countries in between became more than a little interested. In the early 1950's five of the six Central American republics—El Salvador, Honduras, Nicaragua, Costa Rica, and Panama—formally approached the Foundation, requesting assistance in agricultural research.

Many people suppose that philanthropy, "giving away money" as some express it, must be among the most easily performed of human endeavors. Actually it is one of the most difficult, because no matter how much money is available the amount is still finite and is never enough to meet more than a small fraction of the needs. Each year many a meritorious request must be turned down and many fine opportunities passed by for lack of funds. It would have been wholly impossible for the Foundation, faced with all its other commitments, to respond to the requests of the five Central American republics. But one thing the Foundation could do with a minimum of expenditure, and this Harrar was quick to recognize: it could give support to a cooperative project on the improvement of corn in Central America, extending the work already in progress in Mexico and Colombia. Because corn is a basic food plant and plays a dominant role in the diet of all the Central American countries, the improvement of corn would be an objective they could share. And because corn knows no national boundaries, some of the improved varieties being developed in Mexico and Colombia might prove to be immediately useful to the countries in between.

The Central American Corn Project

Early in 1954 there was inaugurated the Central American Corn Improvement Project. Participating in it were the five republics that had requested the Foundation's help. This new enterprise, though revolutionary in concept—the very idea of Central American countries overcoming antipathies of long standing and cooperating effectively is revolutionary—had an evolutionary history. Like most projects it had precursors. One of these was an international congress of maize breeders, held in Mexico in 1949.

PRECURSORS OF THE CENTRAL AMERICAN PROJECT

"One of the principal objectives of the Foundation's Agricultural Program since its initiation in 1943 has been to develop a spirit of international collaboration among the agricultural scientists of Latin America. . . ." This statement appears in a Foundation resolution appropriating $25,000 toward the costs of the fifth meeting of the Asociación Latinoamericana de Fitotecnia that was held in Argentina in 1961. It was, of course, natural that an organization like The Rockefeller Foundation should want to extend the benefits of its various activities as quickly and widely as possible, and bringing together Latin American leaders in certain of the principal agricultural sciences had been a most important factor in achieving a spirit of common purpose (as we saw in Chapter 1). Because our present concern is with the effect of these meetings on the evolution of the international corn improvement program, we quote again from the resolution of October 21, 1960: "Joint planning of regional research projects for cooperative international execution has been another very important product of these meetings and has helped greatly to provide a favorable basis for the activation of the Foundation's Central American Corn Improvement Project and the subsequent inter-American corn and wheat improvement projects which are now being established."

The 1949 meeting in Mexico, attended by corn breeders from 10 countries of Latin America, was described as a historic event by a pioneer corn breeder from Brazil. He avowed that it was the first meeting of Latin American scientists that he had ever attended in which participants could differ with one another intellectually without provoking verbal violence or becoming personal enemies. (There now are 160 members of the Latin American Corn Association.) And it qualified as a historic event on other grounds: many of those in attendance saw for the first time an extensive and productive corn improvement program in operation, for the meeting was not only devoted to talk but also included study of field experiments and supporting activities. Moreover, this meeting marked the beginning of systematic attempts to channel the flow of genetic materials southward from the Mexican corn program and the beginning of the exchange of similar materials among Latin American corn breeders generally.

Three years after the Mexican meeting, Stakman, after attending the Second Latin American Congress of Plant Geneticists and Plant Pathologists (including entomologists) in Brazil, wrote this in his notes: "There have been formal programs, round tables, and visits to field demonstrations. Practically all have been good and some have been excellent. In corn genetics, for example, workers have passed the stage of imitating programs in the United States. They are making important contributions of their own which United States workers will be compelled to recognize."

Thus, by 1954 there was not only the knowledge that corn could be improved by modern methods of breeding; there was also experience with corn breeders from different countries meeting together, exchanging ideas, benefiting from each other's experience, and working toward a common objective. The time was ripe for beginning the Central American project.

THE PROJECT IN OPERATION

The project had four immediate objectives: (1) to supply each of the cooperating countries with the basic breeding materials for an improvement program; (2) to help alleviate the existing critical shortage of trained personnel by giving young agronomists from these countries practical training in the Mexican and Colombian programs, with the possibility that some of them might later continue their studies in the United States or elsewhere under the

Foundation's scholarship and fellowship program; (3) to purchase certain supplies and pieces of equipment to facilitate research when local funds were not available; and (4) to sponsor annual meetings of the technicians from the cooperating Central American countries and from Mexico and Colombia that would provide opportunities for exchanging ideas and discussing mutual problems and might also serve as a unifying force for the entire project.

From January to November, 1954, the project was directed by Dr. Sterling Wortman, a corn breeder on the Foundation's staff in Mexico. When Wortman resigned to accept a position in Hawaii, he was succeeded by Dr. Donald L. Smith, also of the Mexican program. Ing. Alfredo Carballo Quíroz, with headquarters in San José, Costa Rica, served as coordinator. In January, 1955, the original participating countries—El Salvador, Honduras, Nicaragua, Costa Rica, and Panama—were joined by Guatemala, making Central American participation unanimous.

The first year's response to the cooperative project was encouraging indeed—so much so that it was decided to set up a special center at the new Cotaxtla experiment station near Veracruz, Mexico, to develop improved corns for the humid tropical areas of both Central America and Mexico and to provide breeding materials for each of the local programs.

Uniform yield trials were conducted in each of the countries. These included the more promising materials developed in Mexico and Colombia and, for comparison, a number of the native varieties from each of the participating countries. During the first year the native varieties came to a total of 1,084 entries, but the number was reduced to 193 in 1955.

Short-term training awards were made to five Central American agronomists: one each from Honduras and Guatemala and three from Costa Rica. Four of these young men spent the study period in Colombia, the fifth in Mexico.

At the first annual conference, held in Turrialba, Costa Rica, in October, 1954, some 50 delegates were present, as well as observers from Venezuela, Cuba, and the United States. Formal papers or data were presented by representatives from each of the participating countries. Costa Rica again served as host in December, 1955, when the second conference brought together 39 delegates for discussions concerned especially with the breeding and production of corn for the tropics. Then, at the invitation of the Guatemalan Minister of Agriculture, the 1956 conference was held in his country.

In addition, equipment and certain supplies were furnished on a modest scale to each participating country. These included shellers, graders, seed-treating machines, pollinating bags, and calculators— all essential in any corn improvement program and all somewhat difficult to obtain in countries not accustomed to supplying such items.

The year 1956 continued to record encouraging progress. Two countries each released for commercial production an improved variety and a double-cross hybrid. Whereas three years before there had been five agronomists working part time on corn improvement in Central America, now there were 23 individuals, with varying degrees of specialized training, working full time. A total of 17 Central American agronomists had been given the opportunity to study corn improvement techniques in Mexico and Colombia, and seed for 102 separate experiments had been prepared and sent to the participating countries.

On the whole, the project could be considered a success. True, many problems still remained, but substantial progress had been made. One member of the Foundation's Board of Consultants for Agriculture compared the project to a military operation in which a battle line is anchored at both ends by impregnable positions, in this case the programs in Mexico and Colombia. There was no doubt that a great deal had been achieved with a minimum expenditure of Foundation funds—not the least of the achievements being the effective cooperation that had developed between workers from different countries. Traditional jealousy and suspicion between nationals of neighboring countries had been dissipated, at least so far as corn improvement was concerned. And there was hope that similar cooperation might develop in solving other common problems and that the relatively small Central American countries might learn to do together what none could do effectively alone.

Thus the Central American Corn Improvement Project, which came to be known by its initials, CACIP, paved the way and furnished the nucleus for the Inter-American Food Crop Improvement Program, which was established by the Foundation in 1959 and broadened the work by including wheat and potatoes, as well as corn, throughout the countries of Latin America. Another factor that contributed to the possibility of expanding international cooperation in corn improvement and studies related to it was a highly successful program concerned with the collection and preservation of indigenous strains of corn. This had its beginning with the classification of Mexican races of corn.

Germ Plasm Banks and International Exchange

PRESERVING THE WEALTH AND DIVERSITY OF MEXICAN CORN TYPES

One of the first steps in the Mexican corn improvement program was a systematic collection of Mexican races of corn, begun in 1943. Its original purpose was wholly utilitarian—to provide an inventory of the material available to plant breeders. Varieties were assembled from all parts of the country and in controlled experiments were compared for productiveness, disease resistance, and other characteristics of agricultural importance. (See Chapter 4.)

As the collection grew and the extraordinary diversity of corn in Mexico began to be revealed, the need for a taxonomic classification that would bring some semblance of order out of the bewildering multiplicity of varieties became apparent. Accordingly, botanical, genetical, and cytological studies to supplement the agronomic investigations were undertaken, and, to make the collections as nearly complete as possible, special efforts were made to obtain from remote localities little-known varieties of doubtful agronomic importance. Gradually it became possible to discern relationships between varieties and to group these into more or less well-defined natural races. And since relationships are implicit in any natural system of classification, a definite attempt was made to determine the origins and relationships of the recognized races.

What had begun as a strictly utilitarian venture of limited scope thus evolved into the study of the evolution, in a single geographical region, of America's most important cultivated plant. One result was that the corn breeders in Mexico found themselves the possessors of a far more useful inventory of the breeding material available in that country than they had originally sought. Thus they were able to approach new breeding problems with some degree of confidence in their choice of stocks.

By the fall of 1948 the collection included more than 2,000 entries, and in late December Mangelsdorf was invited to spend six weeks in Mexico working with Wellhausen, Roberts, and Hernández on a monograph classifying and describing the Mexican races of corn. The collection was laid out on all the available space in a new laboratory building at Chapingo, first by regions and then on the basis of resemblances. Grouping of the ears was correlated with data on characteristics of the plants grown in the field. This intensive study led eventually to the recognition of 25 more or less distinct races, divided into four major groups: Ancient Indigenous, Pre-Columbian Exotic, Prehistoric Mestizos, and Modern Incipient.

What had apparently happened in Mexico was this: domestication of native wild corn had produced four different races that had been grown in Mexico from time immemorial and had maintained their identity throughout the centuries up to the present time. These four races, which comprise the group called Ancient Indigenous, were all primitive in one respect: they were popcorns. Although nowhere widely grown, they were maintained by the Indians who recognized them as being a traditional part of their agriculture. These four races are Palomero Toluqueño, Nal-Tel, Chapalote, and Arrocillo Amarillo.

Somewhere in the remote past, perhaps at about the time of Christ or a few centuries earlier, four other races of maize were introduced from farther south. Called Cacahuacintle, Harinoso de Ocho, Olo-tón, and Maíz Dulce, they comprise the group designated as Pre-Columbian Exotic. Hybridization of these four introduced races with the Ancient Indigenous races and with a relative of corn, teosinte, produced an almost explosive diversification in Mexican corn and resulted in the creation of 13 races to which Wellhausen and his colleagues gave the name Prehistoric Mestizos (*mestizo* being the Mexican word for racial hybrid). Finally, the classifiers recognized four races that had come into existence within historical times: Chalqueño, Celaya, Cónico Norteño, and Bolita, being the group called Modern Incipient.

With this job completed, it was no longer necessary to think in terms of 2,000 collections to be tested and maintained. Instead, the research was concentrated on the 25 recognized races. How did they compare with each other as sources of inbred strains? What were the results when different races were combined as hybrids?

The findings in these intensive studies were published in April, 1951, by the Mexican Ministry of Agriculture in a well-illustrated volume of 237 pages, entitled *Razas de Maíz en México*. An English-language edition of the same work, published by the Bussey Institution of Harvard University in 1952, contained in the foreword the following significant statement: "Maize is the basic food plant in most of the Americas and its diversity, the product of thousands of years of evolution under domestication, is one of the great natural resources of this hemisphere. To lose any part of that diversity is not only to restrict the opportunities for further improvement but also to increase the difficulties of coping with future climatic changes or with new diseases or insect pests. The modern corn breeder, therefore, has a responsibility not only to improve the maize in the country in which he works but also to recognize, to describe, and to preserve for future use, the varieties and races which his own improved productions tend to replace and in some cases to extinguish."[1]

OTHER COUNTRIES FOLLOW MEXICO'S EXAMPLE

Both the Spanish and English editions of this monograph were widely distributed and aroused much interest among maize workers throughout the hemisphere. One of them, Dr. Friedrich Brieger of the University of São Paulo Agricultural College, Piracicaba, Brazil, began to explore the possibility of raising funds to finance similar programs of collection and classification in other countries of Latin America, especially in his own. In the course of a trip through the United States, Brieger discussed the problem with Dr. Ralph Cleland of Indiana University, who was then completing a three-year term as chairman of the Division of Biology and Agriculture of the National Academy of Sciences—National Research Council. Convinced by Brieger of the importance of collecting and preserving the races of corn of this hemisphere, Cleland in turn persuaded the Academy—Research Council to name a committee to investigate the problem and make recommendations.

The result was the appointment of a Committee on the Collection and Preservation of Indigenous Strains of Maize. This group, composed of leading corn breeders, geneticists, botanists, and administrators, soon sought and obtained a grant of $86,000 from the Point IV Program (then called the Technical Cooperation Administration).

Three centers, each with cold-storage facilities, were established

---

[1] E. J. Wellhausen, L. M. Roberts, and E. Hernández X. in collaboration with Paul C. Mangelsdorf, *Races of Maize in Mexico* (Cambridge: Bussey Institution of Harvard University, 1952), pp. 5–6.

in Mexico, Colombia, and Brazil, and a fourth—to store "standby" samples from the others—was set up in the United States. The grand total of collections assembled under this program eventually reached 11,353. These represented 32 different countries, from Canada to Chile.

A second grant of $90,000 was obtained from Point IV (by that time the International Cooperation Administration) to classify and describe the varieties. This resulted in the publication of ten treatises on the races of maize of Cuba, Colombia, Central America, Brazil and other eastern South American countries, Bolivia, the West Indies, Chile, Peru, Ecuador, and Venezuela. Together with the original work on the races of Mexico, they represent a virtually complete inventory of the corn of this hemisphere, and the collections in storage represent virtually all the germ plasm available to corn breeders.

It turns out that this program of collecting was undertaken none too soon. Already in parts of Mexico and Colombia the improved varieties and hybrids have replaced the native sorts, some of which are now difficult to find. Another five or ten years and some varieties might have become extinct and their particular combination of genes, the product of centuries of evolution under domestication, forever lost.

CORN FROM GERM PLASM BANKS GOES AROUND THE WORLD

The practical value of the world maize collections has already been demonstrated. Collections have been sent from the centers to plant breeders in Kenya, Ethiopia, Poland, Indonesia, India, and about 35 other countries, and many have been very useful. For example, rust recently became extremely serious in West Africa, reducing yields by as much as 50 percent, and it was found that certain strains collected in the Caribbean area were either resistant or highly tolerant to this disease. Consequently more than 100 strains of maize collected from the Caribbean region were sent to agronomists in West Africa. By proper crossing techniques, their rust resistance can now be transferred to adapted West African varieties.

Varieties from Colombia have done well in the Philippines and in India. Corn breeders in the United States are experimenting with hybrids receiving part of their genes from Latin American varieties. It is now known that the most outstanding races of maize of the hemisphere—the giant-seeded corn of Cuzco, Peru, the giant-eared corn of the Jala Valley of Mexico, and the Corn Belt Dent of the United States, probably the world's most productive corn—are all complex hybrids, the product of repeated hybridization between other races. Recognizing this fact, corn breeders in the United States may now be able to create new hybrids, utilizing those genes that are known to have made contributions to the outstanding races of the hemisphere.

Nor have the collections been used only in practical plant breeding. Geneticists working on theoretical problems have found useful new genes among these varieties. Professor R. A. Brink of the University of Wisconsin, Professor John Laughnan of the University of Illinois, and Dr. M. Gerald Nuffer of the University of Missouri are among those who, in published reports on their research in theoretical genetics, have referred to varieties obtained from Latin America as the source of certain genes involved in their experiments.

Here then is a splendid example of the interaction between science and technology, between "pure" and "applied" science. The practical improvement of corn in Mexico was based on methods developed from theoretical research in genetics. The application of these methods pointed to the need for an inventory of the stocks available to the corn breeder. This, in turn, led to a classification of maize of Mexico and eventually to the collecting and classifying of the corn of all the countries of this hemisphere. Now the collections are proving useful to research in theoretical genetics. The interplay of theory and practice has come full circle.

SCIENTIFIC STUDIES ON A HEMISPHERIC SCALE

The Central American Corn Improvement Project showed that corn breeders could cooperate in developing new improved varieties and hybrids, and the project on the collection and preservation of indigenous races of maize showed that people in many countries could cooperate in studies that had no immediate utilitarian objective but might be of overwhelming importance for the future. Now seemed an auspicious time for further intensive studies designed to obtain a fuller understanding of corn and its genetic potential.

The Foundation enlisted the cooperation of a number of distinguished scientists from the United States to attack problems concerned with corn in Latin America. Dr. Barbara McClintock of the

Carnegie Institution of Washington spent several months in both Colombia and Mexico making cytological studies of the races of maize of Mexico and Central and South America and training Latin American technicians to conduct similar studies. Dr. Albert E. Longley, a cytogeneticist retired from the Agricultural Research Service of the United States Department of Agriculture, participated in these studies. Dr. Oliver E. Nelson, a professor of genetics at Purdue University, engaged in studies on the occurrence of cross-sterility factors in Mexican races of maize. These factors provide the mechanism for preventing hybridization between maize and its relatives and are thought to be characteristics descended directly from the wild maize of Mexico, which is now extinct; their frequency in the various races of maize of Mexico provides some indication of the relative degree of primitiveness of the several races. Dr. H. F. Robinson, a professor of genetics at North Carolina State College, made a statistical study of the known races of maize of Mexico and hybrids between them. Dr. John H. Lonnquist, in charge of corn breeding at the University of Nebraska, visited a number of countries of Latin America giving instruction to corn breeders on recent developments in the theory and practice of corn improvement. Dr. R. E. Comstock, a professor of animal husbandry at the University of Minnesota and a distinguished statistician, gave advice and help in connection with a number of statistical problems, and Dr. G. F. Sprague, in charge of corn investigations in the United States Department of Agriculture, collaborated in various ways.

Official Internationalization on a Global Scale

The Rockefeller Foundation had thus deployed in several ways from the cooperative Mexican program. It had established similar operating programs in Colombia, Chile, and India and had cooperated with other countries in such a way as to construct an international network for the improvement not only of corn but also of wheat and potatoes. As the time approached when Mexico could operate her own program independently, the Foundation gave increasing consideration to the possibility of internationalizing still further its efforts to help the less advanced countries to produce more food. Since 1961 Mexican scientists have operated their own corn and wheat programs, thus releasing Wellhausen and Borlaug for international activities. Because of the long and fruitful cooperation between the Mexican Ministry of Agriculture and the Foundation, however, it seemed desirable to continue their association. Therefore, a newly created International Center for Corn and Wheat Improvement, with headquarters in Mexico, was officially inaugurated on October 25, 1963. On that date, the Mexican Minister of Agriculture, Julián Rodríguez Adame, and J. G. Harrar, president of the Foundation, signed an agreement establishing the Center as a cooperative enterprise, and President Adolfo López Mateos declared it to be in existence.

Directed by Wellhausen, the International Maize Improvement Project had already officially expanded the cooperation established before in Central America to include the principal corn-growing countries of South America: Venezuela, Peru, Bolivia, Chile, Brazil, and Argentina. By 1962–1963, 13 Latin American countries were participating in the program and 67 individuals were involved in one capacity or another. Since the establishment of the International Center in 1963, with Wellhausen in charge, the same type of cooperation has been extended to many countries in the Eastern Hemisphere also. Thus the Foundation's corn programs have expanded from national to international proportions, at first on a regional, then on a hemispheric, and now on a global basis.

The purpose of the present International Center for Corn and Wheat Improvement is to promote the improvement of maize and wheat not only in the countries of this hemisphere but also in those of Africa and Asia, where they are important crops. The location of the Center in Mexico should be mutually beneficial to the two cooperating agencies, which are now expanding their efforts beyond Mexico to the whole world. It is an experiment in cooperation on a grand scale. The experiment is noble in its purpose. If it succeeds, as the programs that preceded it have already succeeded, the millions of dollars that the Foundation has already spent on its national and international corn and wheat improvement activities must be counted one of its most rewarding investments, one yielding rich returns in promoting "the well-being of mankind throughout the world." If it should fail to fulfill expectations—and this possibility must always be recognized with projects containing so large a component of human nature—it may perhaps be concluded that it is easier to improve crops such as corn and wheat than it is to change the ways of man.

Chapter 16

The International Wheat Program
Extending Mexico's Gains Far beyond Her Borders

The International Wheat Program grew out of the Mexican, Colombian, and Chilean programs. Although Mexico in 1943 had no wheats that were entirely satisfactory for her own conditions, she did have the wisdom to import many varieties for breeding purposes and she developed the skills to combine their virtues in new varieties that satisfied her own needs and eventually helped to satisfy those of many other countries, in spite of the fact that wheat is not native to the Western Hemisphere. At the dawn of recorded history there already were several types or varieties in cultivation elsewhere in the world, and the number gradually increased as man carried to new areas mixtures from which he selected lines that were suited to their new homes and discarded those that were not. But the kinds discarded in one area sometimes were selected in another area; hence, regional groups developed, each suited to certain times and regions but not to others. Man thus scattered the numerous characters of wheat among numerous varieties in many different areas of the world. Then, when he learned how to breed wheats scientifically, less than a hundred years ago, plant breeders began to reassemble the scattered varieties and hybridize them in order to combine the best characters from each into new and better varieties. In this story Mexico came to play an important part.

International Aspects of the National Programs

From small beginnings in 1943, Mexico soon became one of the world's important centers for reassembling and recombining wheats. How the results helped Mexico to feed her rapidly increasing population is a significant story, but how the new wheats made their way to other countries and helped to increase and insure their wheat supplies also is an even more significant story. Bread is still the staff of life for millions of the peoples in the world who need more wheat but do not yet know how to get it.

WHERE MEXICAN WHEATS WENT AND WHAT THEY DID

Mexican-bred wheats began to emigrate to other countries as soon as they were fully formed, and some were sent abroad while still in process of formation. Just as Mexico had received wheat varieties and lines from other countries for her breeding program, so she sent similar materials to other countries to enrich their breeding programs. And she also furnished seed of her new varieties to all who wished to try them or to buy them. Wheats from the Mexican program, soon after its inception, were helping to provide more bread for 75 million people, some 30 million in Mexico itself and the rest in several other Latin American countries, especially Guatemala, Colombia, Ecuador, Chile, Bolivia, and Paraguay. And this was long before the International Wheat Program was officially established; it resulted from consistent efforts to make the national programs serve as many people as possible.

The national programs, started in Mexico in 1943, in Colombia in 1950, and in Chile in 1955, naturally had the primary obligation of helping each cooperating country to produce more wheat. Thus, when the first new wheats, Supremo 211 and Kenya 324, were produced by the Office of Special Studies in Mexico, they were designed primarily for various regions of that country.

But these new varieties were soon tested by collaborators in the highlands of Guatemala also, where they proved their worth and showed that climatic conditions, not national boundaries, determined where wheats could thrive. And so, for more than a decade the entire acreage of wheat in Guatemala has been sown to Mexican-bred varieties, with the addition recently of one or two from Colombia. Kentana 48, Lerma 50, Yaktana 54, Lerma Rojo, Huamantla Rojo, Pitic, and Nadadores, all born and baptized in Mexico, have been quite at home in Guatemala and have helped her keep abreast of progress in producing bread without the necessity of duplicating the work and expense of the Mexican program.

TONS OF WHEAT INSTEAD OF TONS OF WORDS IN COLOMBIA

"Tons of wheat instead of tons of words" was the theme of an editorial in *El Tiempo,* a leading Bogotá newspaper, shortly after the first big step had been taken in improving wheat production in Colombia. Lamenting that numerous "do-gooder" missions had come to Colombia, sometimes in tandem and sometimes abreast, producing nothing except tons of useless verbiage, the editorial rejoiced that at last a mission had worked long and hard enough to produce Menkemen wheat, which added thousands of tons to Colombia's annual production. Although the editorial writer may not have known just how Menkemen originated and got its name, he did know that it could yield 25 percent more than the old Colombian varieties that it replaced. And this was indeed noteworthy at the time. But equally noteworthy are the lineage and history of Menkemen itself.

To those who have read Chapter 5 the name Menkemen may suggest that it might have been derived from Mentana, Kenya, Mentana. And that actually is its origin, for it had its genesis in the Mexican program although it attained varietal status in Colombia. In 1950, when Dr. Joseph A. Rupert went from the Mexican program to Colombia as small-grain breeder, he took with him several thousand segregating hybrid lines of wheat, from which he later selected and elaborated the varieties Menkemen and Bonza. The parents of Menkemen were Mentana and Kenya, and, as a cross between the two had been backcrossed to Mentana, the resulting variety was named Menkemen, (Mentana × Kenya) × Mentana. It was a sister variety of the Mexican-named variety Lerma 50, and it started Colombia on the way to better wheats. But it soon was supplanted largely by the still better variety Bonza, which Rupert had also selected from Mexican materials and developed into a variety in Colombia.

Bonza wheat was named in honor of the city Bonza, located in one of Colombia's good wheat-growing areas, and the designation is therefore a simple place name. Had it been designed to symbolize the places from which its parents and grandparents came, the name might have been very complex. Its immediate parents, crossed in Mexico, were Yaqui 48 and Kentana 48. But the parents of Yaqui were Newthatch and Marroquí, and the parents of Kentana were

Kenya and Mentana. And Newthatch and Marroquí also had parents, although those of Marroquí are unknown because this variety had been imported from Morocco without its pedigree attached. Nevertheless, the ancestral trails of Bonza can be traced easily to Mexico, the United States, Canada, Scotland, Italy, Morocco, Russia, India, and Kenya, and less easily to many other countries.

Menkemen had outyielded native varieties by 25 percent, but Bonza outyielded Menkemen by 15 percent, so that Colombia now had a variety (Bonza) that yielded 40 percent more than the varieties that she had been growing. These varieties had a special virtue, resistance to yellow rust. For Dr. Juan Orjuela had shown that this rust, although usually a minor disease in Mexico, was a major one in Colombia because the cool, moist climate in the high savannas, where wheat was grown at elevations of some 8,000 feet, almost always favored its destructive development. Colombia therefore needed varieties with resistance to yellow rust and was a good place in which to breed them.

FROM COLOMBIA DOWN TO CHILE

Naturally, the new Colombian wheats attracted the attention of Colombia's neighbors, especially Ecuador, where wheat is an important crop in the high sierra but does not yet supply the country's needs. The Colombian program soon began to furnish better wheats for Ecuador, just as the Mexican program had furnished them for Guatemala. Thanks to cooperation between Dr. John Gibler of the Colombian program and Ing. Hernán Orellana of the National Wheat Commission of Ecuador, Ecuadorian farmers have been able to profit quickly and directly from all advances made in Colombia. Indeed, Ecuador became an integral part of an international system extending from Mexico to Chile, by way of Guatemala, Colombia, and Peru.

Peru had a wheat breeding program of her own, but also had some men, euphoniously named Villanueva, Postigo, Quijandría, Rondón, and Schuler, who knew a good wheat when they saw it and had the good sense to make the most of it, from wherever it may have come. They tested materials from Mexico and Colombia and from them selected the varieties Sierra 1 and Sierra 2, which were sister lines of the Mexican variety Yaktana 54 and the later Chilean variety Orofén, all derived from segregating materials produced in the Mexico-Colombia programs. Recently, Villanueva stated that the Colombian varieties Bonza and Nariño outyielded all other varieties tested in Peru during the previous three years.

Colombia thus became a springboard from which better wheats moved rapidly southward. But some first went north before going south, for Rupert and his Colombian aides were recombining Mexican and other wheats and sending promising hybrid materials back to Mexico for testing and possible use in the land of their fathers. Among these materials was first-generation hybrid seed resulting from a complex cross between certain Mexican varieties and the South American variety Frontana. From the progeny of this seed Borlaug and his group in Mexico selected the very valuable variety Yaktana 54 and several sister varieties, the products of cooperation between the Mexican program and its offspring in Colombia.

When the Foundation, in 1955, cooperated in the establishment of a third Latin American agricultural improvement center, in Chile, Rupert was made director, and Gibler moved south from Mexico to carry on the wheat work that Rupert had been doing in Colombia.

As Chile was a predominantly bread-eating country that wanted help in wheat production, Rupert arranged to test a large collection of Mexican and Colombian materials and brought Dr. Robert Romig from the Colombian program to help in wheat improvement. Within three years, by 1958, they had produced the superior new varieties Orofén and Rulofén by selecting the best-adapted lines from the wide variety of materials that had been produced in Mexico and Colombia. Thus, Orofén was a full sister of Yaktana 54, bred in Colombia, selected in Mexico, transported to Chile, and reselected to meet conditions there. Rupert and Romig produced hybrids also, designed especially for Chile but freely available to those of her neighbors who wished to try them.

So Chile became the third of the Foundation's cooperative centers for breeding new varieties of wheat and for developing better methods of growing them. There now was a series of breeding and testing stations extending from about 27° north latitude in Mexico to 35° south in Chile, at elevations ranging from a little above sea level near Ciudad Obregón in Mexico to 9,000 feet or higher in Ecuador. Some selections were tested also in Minnesota, in North Dakota, and at Winnipeg, Canada, which is 50° north of the equator. Later, tests were made on a limited scale in Bolivia and Peru. And even these were not the limits of the testing, for some of the most promising materials were included in the Rust Nurseries of the United States Department of Agriculture, which started from small beginnings in the Western Hemisphere in 1942 and now encircle the entire globe. Thus the Rockefeller Foundation national programs became centers of an international system for developing wheats and for showing how they are developed.

THE NATIONAL PROGRAMS AS INTERNATIONAL EDUCATION CENTERS

Although each of the national wheat programs functioned as educational centers, the pioneer Mexican program had the earliest start and maintained its lead. Because of the close cooperation with spring-wheat breeders in the United States and Canada, visitors from those countries were especially numerous, but others came from every wheat-growing country in Latin America and even from such faraway places as Australia, the Union of South Africa, and Kenya. These visits paved the way for closer cooperation among men with the common purpose of helping provide their people with more and better bread through research and education.

Research is "the living source of progress" today just as it was a hundred years ago when Pasteur wrote the words. Retarded countries will always be retarded until they develop men who can do their own research or at least have the wit to utilize the results of researches done elsewhere. Recognizing this simple fact, the Foundation encouraged the use of its national wheat programs as international schools for young men who had the desire and the need for learning.

As practice lagged far behind theory in much of Latin America, students from there were encouraged to come to Mexico, where theory and practice were combined, where field experiments were in progress throughout the year, where there was no appreciable language barrier, and where the customs and mode of life were enough like those back home to minimize problems of personal and professional adjustment. Moreover, as an "emerging country" scientifically solving her problems of food production, Mexico provided unique opportunities for students to learn how to improve wheats in their own countries by helping to improve them in Mexico. They learned to do by doing. During the national phase of the Mexican program, 21 young men from nine Latin American countries spent from six months to a year as interns in the Mexican wheat program, most of them supported by fellowships granted by The Rockefeller Foundation. After completing their internships they returned to their respective countries: Argentina, Guatemala, Colombia, Ecuador, Peru, Bolivia, Paraguay, Chile, and Brazil, where all but two are still engaged in some phase of wheat improvement. Although national in name, the national programs had far-reaching international influence, because the men who operated them had the vision, zeal, and wit to make them internationally useful. They earned their international name by their international deeds.

International in Name as Well as Deed

THE ESTABLISHMENT OF INTERNATIONAL PROGRAMS

The original objective of The Rockefeller Foundation in Mexico was to work itself out of a job. It did, but it took on a new and bigger job, first of hemispheric and then of global scope. The Foundation helped Mexico to realize its national aspiration to conquer hunger, and Mexico is now helping the Foundation to realize its aspiration to conquer hunger internationally. The Office of Special Studies passed into history December 31, 1960, respected but not lamented, and on January 1, 1961, the newly created National Institute of Agricultural Research began operations. Although Dr. Ignacio Narváez had been in charge of the wheat project since February, 1960, Borlaug had continued as friendly collaborator; complete dissociation would have been a separation of heart and body. But Borlaug had long sought ways of expanding his sphere of usefulness, and he had no difficulty in finding what he sought.

In order to contribute more effectively to the improvement of basic foods in the Western Hemisphere, The Rockefeller Foundation in 1959 established the Inter-American Food Crop Improvement Program. Under this program were the International Maize Improvement Project, with Dr. Edwin J. Wellhausen as director; the International Wheat Improvement Project, with Borlaug as director; and the Inter-American Potato Improvement Project, with Dr. John S. Niederhauser as director. On October 25, 1963, a new International Center for Corn and Wheat Improvement was officially inaugurated when Julián Rodríguez Adame, Mexican Minister of Agriculture, and J. George Harrar, president of The Rockefeller Foundation, in a ceremony presided over by Adolfo López Mateos,

President of Mexico, signed an agreement establishing the Center as a cooperative enterprise. Since 1960, therefore, Borlaug has operated wheat improvement programs that are international in name as well as fame.

Borlaug had begun to concentrate on international wheat improvement in 1959, when he and others visited and evaluated the programs in Mexico, Colombia, Ecuador, Peru, Chile, and Argentina and arranged for similar studies in Brazil, Uruguay, Paraguay, Bolivia, and Guatemala. Then he went even farther afield.

In 1960 Borlaug and José Vallega, then in the Ministry of Agriculture of Argentina and now an officer of the Food and Agriculture Organization of the United Nations, served as temporary consultants to evaluate the FAO's wheat and barley project in the Near and Middle East. It was natural that these two realistically imaginative men should visualize wheat fields for the East like those they had seen in Mexico. The question was how best to realize the vision, and there seemed to be no better way than by experimentation and education, old in principle but always new as concerns effective tactics. Borlaug and Vallega knew that fruitful experimentation could be done only by competent experimenters, and they therefore concocted concrete plans for training men from the Near and Middle East to do the experimenting. Their plans became a part of the Foundation's International Wheat Improvement Program, which quickly yielded useful results.

The Foundation already had gone far in systematizing worldwide efforts for wheat improvement. The results have projected possibilities of future progress that were scarcely dreamed of a few decades ago. Visions seen but dimly in 1943 are far more clearly seen in 1963, for probabilities already have become realities in many places, and possibilities have become probabilities in many others.

The ambition of the International Wheat Program is to convert possibilities into realities everywhere, by operating on three coordinated fronts: (1) ecological experimentation; (2) basic researches;

(3) educational activities. This is still a "package deal," but with broader scope geographically and greater depth scientifically than heretofore.

Ecological experimentation. The objective of these studies is to find out the range of soil and climatic conditions under which wheat varieties can thrive. The method is to grow the varieties in uniform nurseries in selected geographical locations. The results have been surprising.

That every plant or animal is as it is at a given time because of the interaction of its hereditary factors, genes, and the factors of the environment in which it lived, is one of the most elementary and useful principles of genetics. Most plant and animal characters vary more or less, and breeders must learn the limits of the variation. Thus, earliness is a character needed in a good variety of wheat. But will an early-ripening variety ripen early only somewhere or will it ripen early wherever it is grown? The earliest spring wheats of the United States and Canada, for example, ripened too late and yielded too little when tested in Mexico in the early days of its wheat improvement program. They needed the longer days of the northern summers; Mexican days were too short and the nights too long. Much time could have been saved in the breeding program if some of these excellent wheats had been able to develop their excellence in Mexico as well as where they came from. And thus it is with many other characters; hence many varieties can flourish only in certain areas or seasons that suit their special needs. Varieties that are less particular about where they grow can have a wider sphere of usefulness than the temperamental ones. The wider the range of adaptability of a good variety, the greater the good it can do in the largest number of countries, and this is why tests are now being made in so many of them.

During the past three years varietal tests were made by 61 collaborators at one or more places in each of 25 countries in different parts of the world. Two standard cooperative nurseries were organized: (1) the Inter-American Spring Wheat Yield Nursery, grown in Argentina, Brazil, Bolivia, Chile, Colombia, Ecuador, Guatemala, Mexico, and Peru, with collaborators also in Australia, Kenya, Canada, and the United States; (2) the Near East-American Spring Wheat Yield Nursery, grown in Iran, Iraq, India, Jordan, Lebanon, Libya, Mexico, Pakistan, Saudi Arabia, Syria, Turkey, and Egypt.

Seed for both nurseries was sent from Mexico to collaborators in the 25 countries and the data were compiled in Mexico by Borlaug, Dr. Jacobo Ortega, and Ing. Ricardo Rodríguez.[1]

Borlaug wrote in his report for 1963–1964: "Both the magnitude and the impact of the international project have grown during the past year. This impact is measurable in several ways, namely: (1) the increasing number of requests from many different countries of the world for small experimental samples of wheat seed of both advanced and early generation segregating materials, as the outstanding adaptation of these materials becomes more widely known; (2) increasing numbers of purchases by other countries of commercial quantities (ranging from 1 to more than 2,000 tons) of seed of the newer Mexican and Colombian varieties; (3) requests by many countries for consultation and guidance in wheat research and production problems; and (4) increasing numbers of requests for permission to send young scientists to spend training periods in Mexico." The growing demand for Mexican and Colombian varieties is not surprising because their overall performance has been outstanding.

In the Inter-American nurseries of the 1962–1963 season, comprising 25 varieties grown at 11 stations, located at latitudes of 0° to 50°, the five highest yielders were four Mexican varieties and one Colombian. Three popular regional varieties grown for comparison, Canadian Selkirk, Argentinian Klein Rendidor, and U.S. Thatcher, ranked 22, 24, and 25, respectively, in average yield at all stations. Although they are excellent wheats in the areas for which they were developed and are now being grown, their average yield in the nurseries was about 23 bushels an acre, whereas Mexican Pénjamo 62, number one in rank, yielded 40 bushels.

In the 18 Near East nurseries, the Mexican variety Pitic 62 yielded close to 35 bushels an acre, about 10 bushels more than the average of the 25 varieties tested and 20 bushels more than average national yields in that area, which ranged from 10 bushels in Syria, about 12 in Pakistan and India, to 15 bushels in Turkey. Moreover, the Mexican varieties Pitic 62, Pénjamo 62, and Nainari 60 together took first prize for yield at 14 of the 18 stations, Pitic taking nine firsts, Pénjamo three, and Nainari two. Averaging the yields of each of the 25 varieties at all 18 stations, the five highest yielders were Mexican-bred wheats. Several varieties from Colombia, Australia, and Egypt

[1] The two nurseries were combined into one during 1964.

also displayed special virtues that can be useful in breeding programs for Africa and the Near and Middle East.

The 18 Near East nurseries on which these data are based were grown at one or more locations in each of 12 countries: Mexico, Cyprus, Libya, Egypt, Sudan, Lebanon, Syria, Iran, Iraq, Jordan, Saudi Arabia, and West Pakistan. The locations were between 35° and 17° north latitude and at elevations from about 500 feet below sea level in Jordan to 5,000 feet above in Mexico. Some nurseries were grown on good soil and some on poor; some were irrigated and some were not. Temperature, length of day, and incidence of pests and pathogens differed considerably also; hence all varieties had to run several kinds of gauntlets under many combinations of conditions, good and bad. Obviously, those varieties that consistently yielded best had the best combinations of characters for success under a wide range of conditions.

Evidently, wheats can be produced with wide adaptability to diverse climates and various soils. Thus, the Mexican varieties Pitic 62, Pénjamo 62, Nainari 60, Lerma Rojo, Lerma Rojo 64A, and Sonora 64 and the Colombian varieties Bonza and Nariño 59 thrive equally well where days are long and where they are short. Certain other excellent spring wheats, on the other hand, (like the Canadian Selkirk and the U.S. varieties Thatcher, Justin, and Crim, all developed where summer days are long) can thrive only when grown 35° or more from the equator. Certain of the climatically adaptable varieties appear to be adapted also to a wide variety of soils; like some people, they can gain weight with little food and are therefore a potential boon to retarded countries that have poor soils and poor present prospects for getting enough fertilizers to enrich them.

These international nurseries already have yielded practical results by providing better wheats from distant sources hitherto unknown to several of the retarded countries that received them. And that is progress. But they also are furnishing facts for formulating general principles on which future progress can be based.

The horizons of knowledge regarding the potential performance of wheat in this wide world of ours are rapidly expanding. Among the vast federation of wheat varieties there are some that can thrive wherever wheat is grown; to find out why will require basic researches that can tax the abilities of many guilds of highly competent scientists. The results of such researches will be satisfying intellectually and may become useful in practical procedures. In the meantime, however, it is gratifying to know that empirical experimentation already has shown how to speed the fight against hunger by producing wheats with universal values. The attempts of The Rockefeller Foundation "to make its efforts systematic and worldwide" already have borne abundant fruit and promise soon to yield much more, if basic researches do not defer too much to the exigencies of immediate practical demands.

Basic researches for superwheats. That wheat has the capacity for still greater productivity is evident, but only fundamental researches can tell what its maximum capacity may be. If the best characters from each of the thousands of varieties of bread wheat can be combined into a single variety, how much can the variety yield and how high can be the quality of bread made from it? The objective of researches now in progress is to answer the question by breeding into the best varieties now available those characters that they lack to be perfect wheats.

Roughly speaking, the relative excellence of a wheat variety is the algebraic sum of its good and its bad characters. Assuming 10 characters, A, B, C . . . , each with a maximum value of 10 for goodness and a minimum of -10 for badness, a plant breeder might represent a wheat as follows: A, 9; B, 9; C, 7; D, 5; E, 9; F, 10; G, 7; H, -7; I, 9; J, 10 = 68. This may be the best variety now available, but character D evidently should be strengthened and the deficiency in H must be supplied. Assuming, however, that D is quality as measured by ability of the flour to produce a spongy loaf of bread, this character may be important in well-fed countries but not in those that are hungry. Similarly, if H represents reaction to yellow rust, H, -7 indicates a high degree of susceptibility, which is unimportant where or when yellow rust does not occur but is very important where it does. As the general aim of the basic researches is to produce wheats that will be as near perfect as possible wherever they are grown, resistance to yellow rust must be added to this hypothetical wheat. In reality some of the Mexican varieties with the highest average score do need more resistance, which can be supplied by crossing them with some of the more resistant Colombian varieties. Likewise, if G represents resistance to stem rust, then the aim is to raise the 7 to 10. Practically, attempts are being made to raise it by the means that we have described in Chapter 5.

It has been assumed that 10 represents the best now available for each given character. But can the best be made even better? The standard of perfection has been rising. For example, a yield of 40 bushels an acre was considered high in Mexico a few years ago, but now it is only fair, since yields twice this high are not uncommon. New records are continually being set for most characters that affect yield and quality, and no one knows to what limits the records can be pushed. But Borlaug and his collaborators are trying to find out.

According to his report for 1963–1964, "many intercrosses have been made during the past season between the best dwarf *T. durum*, dwarf *T. polonicum*, and dwarf *T. turgidum* derivatives." As Borlaug explained it orally: "Crosses between dwarf durums and dwarf turgidums have the AB genome; when these are crossed with rye to get the R genome, the F_1 is sterile But if you treat the tip of the young embryo with colchicine, the number of chromosomes is doubled, so that you get genomes AA, BB, and RR, and have produced fertile amphidiploid triticales." This statement may not be crystal clear to most of us, but it is clear to Borlaug and several investigators from the University of Manitoba, Winnipeg, Canada, who are cooperating in attempts to produce superwheats and have already produced some amazing things.

A number of high-yielding, short-stem, stiff-straw Mexican bread-wheat varieties were produced by crossing Japanese dwarf wheats with bread wheats (see Chapter 5). Borlaug and his group also produced some good dwarf durums, which yield up to 100 bushels an acre, by crossing some of these semidwarf bread wheats with a high-quality durum and then backcrossing to the durum. They then went farther and crossed dwarf durums with similarly produced dwarf turgidum (poulard) types, whose heads tend to branch and produce many kernels. Among the segregates are some with large, sorghum-like heads that contain upwards of 200 kernels instead of the usual 40 or 50. But the kernels tend to be small, possibly because of crowding on the rachis, the central axis of the head, and so they may need a longer rachis to relieve the crowding. The problem is to supply it, and Borlaug and others are on the way to supplying it from rye.

Rye has a good long rachis, but rye is *Secale* and wheat is *Triticum*, two different genera. When the big-headed durum × turgidum segregates were crossed with rye, the first-generation plants were sterile because they had only one set of chromosomes from rye and needed two. Fertility was therefore induced by treating the embryos of seeds with colchicine, a chemical that tends to stimulate the formation of two sets of chromosomes instead of one. And thus a fertile hybrid species "triticale" (*Triticum* × *Secale*) has been formed. And this is what the talk about genomes and amphidiploid triticales was all about.

Once the rachis is lengthened to accommodate the many kernels in these triticales, will the kernels themselves be bigger? If not, what then? There are two principal sources of genes for big kernels, *Triticum polonicum*, Polish wheats, and some Colombian varieties that produce big, plump kernels of high bushel weight. If necessary, therefore, the big-headed triticales will be crossed with varieties of these two groups to put bigger kernels onto the bigger and longer heads. But how good will the kernels be, for quality is needed as well as quantity?

Strength of gluten in the flour is important in making a good loaf of bread. Because some wheat varieties, including the Mexican Yaqui 54 and Sonora 64, have a strong-gluten character that is inherited simply, it should be easy to transmit it to the large-headed triticales that are now in process of creation. And ways have been devised for testing for this quality early in the breeding program.

During the past three years Borlaug and Mexican cereal technology experts Ing. Federico Chacón, Chem. Biol. Evangelina Villegas, and Ing. Arnoldo Amaya adapted and developed methods for determining quality of potentially new varieties as early as the second generation, instead of waiting until the hybrid populations are in the fifth or sixth generation of their existence. From each plant that is selected for good characters in the second generation they take a few kernels and make them into a little ball of dough whose properties they determine by a modified Micro-Pelshenke Test. Thus they discard about 75 percent of second-generation plants among the thousands that would otherwise have been grown for several generations more. They have saved thousands of hours of labor and large sums of money by this early elimination of lines that do not meet the standard of quality. Grain from the progeny of all plants that are saved must again pass tests, including a mixogram test, in order to remain in the breeding program. Finally, grain from the survivors of the Micro-Pelshenke and mixogram tests must pass the final standard milling and baking tests. But the percentage of poor prospects that get this far has been greatly reduced, and the percentage of good ones that have been saved has been substantially increased.

Thus, through ecological experimentation and basic researches, more and more good wheats are being produced for more and more needy countries, and it even appears that a superwheat may be on the way. Moreover, more and more young men are learning how to breed better wheats and how to grow them better. For education too is on an upward path.

Education: A practical school for wheat apostles. The most urgent need of many countries in their fight against hunger is men with practical experience in improving wheat and apostolic zeal for doing it. To help meet the need, a "Practical School for Wheat Apostles" was developed. Its beginnings were in the early years of the Mexican program, but it soon served international needs also and is now a part of the International Wheat Program. (How the school helped train and educate young Mexicans has been told in Chapter 5; how it helped a score or more from additional Latin American countries has been told earlier in this chapter; how it became even more widely international in scope will be told as soon as possible.)

One of the concrete results of the Borlaug-Vallega trip in the East in 1960 was the establishment of a special cooperative educational program between The Rockefeller Foundation, the Food and Agriculture Organization of the United Nations, and several Mexican agricultural agencies.

Since 1960 four groups of young men, principally from the Near and Middle East, have come to Mexico on fellowships to study wheat improvement for eight months, February to mid-September; 30 men have come under this arrangement, from 13 different countries. Prior to 1960 there had been 21, making a total of 51 from countries other than Mexico. Thus, by 1964, there were more than 50 non-Mexican alumni of the School for Wheat Apostles. They came from Argentina, Guatemala, Colombia, Ecuador, Peru, Bolivia, Paraguay, Chile, and Brazil in the Western Hemisphere, and from Afghanistan, Cyprus, Egypt, Ethiopia, Iran, Iraq, Jordan, Libya, Pakistan, Syria, Saudi Arabia, Turkey, and the Philippines in the Eastern half of the world —22 countries in all.

How did these alumni study, what did they learn, and what are they doing with what they learned?

Learning by active participation in actual operations has always been a cardinal feature of Borlaug's system of education. It still is, for all students and teachers work together in the breeding nurseries at the CIANO experiment station, in the Yaqui Valley, near Ciudad Obregón, Sonora, and for shorter times at other stations. Recently, however, some formal instruction has been added. The director and staff of the Irrigation District of the Yaqui Valley, National Ministry of Water Resources, give an intensive one-week course in irrigation, water use, and drainage in their relation to waterlogging, salinity, and other problems that plague many irrigated areas. The Postgraduate College of the National School at Chapingo, near Mexico City, gives intensive six-week courses in genetics and plant breeding, cytology, soil science, plant pathology, and statistics. With few exceptions, the professors of these courses once were interns in the Mexican program. Numerous conferences and special seminars give the students a chance to express themselves and refine their concepts. And, finally, visits to farms and storage plants, mills and bakeries, and various educational and research institutions broaden their concepts about the long series of events from the production of more and better wheat to the production of more and better bread.

What did the alumni learn before they became alumni? They learned that acre yields of wheat in the Yaqui Valley are now among the highest in the world and that acre yields in all of Mexico are upwards of three times what they were in 1943. They learned that this increase in wheat production alone yielded to Mexico about 800 percent annually on the entire expenditure for wheat research in the cooperative Mexican-Rockefeller Foundation program from 1943 to 1962 (see Chapter 5). Small wonder that most of them developed apostolic zeal for learning, so that they might go back home and help their own countries reap similar profits from wise investment in education and research.

These men studied in a school where the ideal was social service and accomplishment the badge of merit. The ideal was to help provide more bread for hungry people, and the method for attaining it was intelligent dedication to the cause. These men did not become mere visionaries, because idealism was tempered well with realism. They had to work, hard and effectively; otherwise they could not have survived the exacting requirements of their teachers, who set a pace that only the best could follow. But all were learners together, as is always true in the best of schools.

What are the alumni of the School for Wheat Apostles doing with what they learned? They have gone back to the countries from which they came, with ability and zeal to alleviate hunger by providing more bread and with hope for opportunity to do it. Some are realizing their hope; others have returned to turbulent or oppressive political climates that could have frustrated the most courageous. They went back home from a school where supercilious complacency, selfishness, self-aggrandizement, political manipulation, unnecessary bureaucratic restrictions, and whatever else might obstruct progress in the fight against hunger were stigmatized as gross misdemeanors—not against scientists but against the hungry people who sorely need the services of the scientists to help them get more bread. Unless this concept is absorbed and applied by those who manage the affairs of retarded countries, their countries always will be retarded.

The training of wheat specialists is only the first step in making them productive; continuing self-education and opportunity to use it must follow. So Borlaug is enlisting the alumni as colleagues in the ecological experimentation whenever feasible. Many are true apostles of wheat, and continuing efforts are being made to help them revolutionize wheat production in their own countries as wheat production has been revolutionized in Mexico.

A VISION OF THE FUTURE

"What Mexico did, your country can also do, except that yours should do it in half the time." This is the doctrine that Borlaug preaches to his apostles. And he means it. He is convinced that India,[2] Pakistan, and certain other countries can easily double their wheat production on present acreage in from seven to 10 years if they go right at it and go at it right. But will they? The hope is that they will, but more than hope is needed. Those countries that first learn to develop and mobilize their scientific and educational resources effectively will be the first to alleviate the hunger of their people. They may need help, but they must also learn to help themselves.

The Mexican wheat program blazed the trail; acre yields of wheat are now about three and a half times as high as 20 years ago. And

[2] The Foundation has recently employed Dr. Glenn Anderson, an experienced Canadian wheat breeder, to help in India (see Chapter 14).

the International Wheat Program is now directly or indirectly helping 750 million people in 25 different countries that produce a billion
bushels of wheat a year to increase their production as Mexico has
increased hers. Because average yields are a scant 12 bushels an
acre in the most populous of these countries (India and Pakistan,
for example), Borlaug's opinion that yields can be doubled within a
decade seems conservative enough. If they actually are doubled,
there could be almost three bushels of wheat instead of 1.4 for each
of the 750 million people who comprise almost a fourth of the people
of the world and about half of the neediest. If these countries can
do what Mexico did, they could easily provide four bushels of wheat
a year for every man, woman, and child instead of the present 1.4,
provided the rate of population increase could be reduced. And
surely that would be commendable progress toward the conquest of
hunger.

By making its efforts systematic and worldwide The Rockefeller
Foundation has already accomplished much and has surprised many
skeptics by the accomplishments. If the efforts are continued and all
collaborating countries will do their part, the results may be so
surprising as to amaze even the most starry-eyed optimists.

Extending the Mexican pattern (Chapter 13). The Tulio Ospina Experiment Station at Medellín, Colombia, where cooperative corn improvement work was begun in 1950.

Better varieties soon were on the way and generated enthusiasm among both farmers and government officials, as did new wheats produced near Bogotá.

The Tibaitatá Experiment Station near Bogotá, dedicated in 1954, provides ample facilities for research on both crops and animals. It has recently become a National Center for research, postgraduate education, and extension.

The Foundation also has helped develop modern experiment stations in Ecuador and Chile. Above, the Santa Catalina station, near Quito. Below, the La Platina station near Santiago, Chile, where better methods and materials are developed and students from the National and the Catholic Universities are given opportunities for experimentation and thesis research.

India: modifying a pattern to suit special conditions (Chapter 14). Chapatties, the daily bread of India, are hand-made from wheat, corn, or sorghum.

India wanted help in corn improvement and got it. Left, two ears of double-cross hybrids developed from crosses between the two types on the right, a United States dent and an Indian flint.

Sorghum is one of India's most important food crops, but acre yields are generally low.

But better varieties, bred in India, promise better yields. In the center is a high-yielding hybrid, flanked by its parents.

Millets also are important, because they can be grown in areas that are too dry even for sorghums. Numerous types, including finger millets shown here, have been collected for use in varietal improvement programs.

The cooperative education program has been fruitful. Dr. Ralph W. Cummings, director of the Foundation's program in India, addresses students of the Graduate School of the Indian Agricultural Research Institute. A key figure in the development of the School since its beginning in 1958, Cummings also has helped Indian educators establish a system of rural universities.

The Foundation officially internationalizes its efforts (Chapters 15–17). The first Latin American conference of maize breeders, held in Mexico in 1949, generated a spirit of cooperation that was essential to success in the Foundation's Central American Corn Improvement Project and other international programs.

Cooperative tests, such as this one in Costa Rica in 1954, have helped produce more and better corn in many countries.

The products of international corn programs have brought happiness to many people in needy countries.

A feature of the international wheat program is a "Practical School for Wheat Apostles" in Mexico, in which young scientists from 22 countries have studied. Above, a cosmopolitan group of students, or trainees, study the rust reactions of wheats with Borlaug and other wheat specialists.

They also learn to use instruments like this for quality determinations.

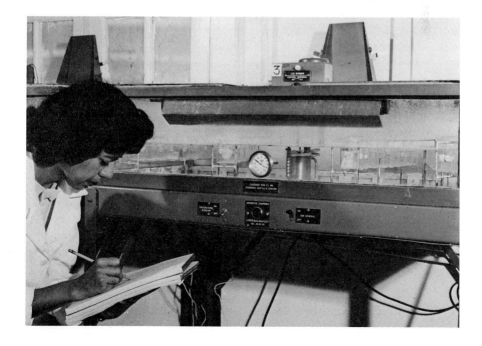

They get acquainted with improved wheats and learn how to make even better ones.

A superwheat may be on the way. Four heads of wheat, each containing three to five times as many kernels as the heads of their parents, which are above them.

Upon rice depends the life and economy of most countries in the Far East, but acre yields are distressingly low in most of them. With the aim of helping to increase yields in all countries, the Ford and Rockefeller Foundations cooperated in the establishment of the International Rice Research Institute (IRRI), at Los Baños in the Philippines.

Preparing soil for planting at IRRI.

Transplanting rice seedlings one at a time, as is common practice in the Far East. Traditionally this is women's work.

Because hand-harvesting also is common practice, most farmers pay a tremendous price in labor for the rice that they produce.

Despite all this labor, yields are low in most countries, partly because the varieties grown tend to lodge (right); they are higher in Japan and Taiwan where nonlodging varieties are grown (left).

As short, stiff-straw varieties with other desirable characters are basic to increased yields, breeders at IRRI soon made numerous crosses to produce them, while "trainees" from various countries learned how the crossing was done.

On the right is one of the most promising hybrids. Its parents were Peta, a vigorous but tall Philippine variety that is subject to lodging, and Dgwg, a short, stiff-straw variety from Taiwan that is resistant to lodging. The hybrid combines good characters from both parents.

Stem borers cause heavy losses in many areas, and spraying with insecticides to control them is laborious, expensive, and only partially effective. But entomologists at IRRI have obtained spectacular results by adding systemic insecticides to the water in the paddy fields. Below, right, nontreated plot; left, treated.

Board of Trustees of IRRI, 1962. Left to right, front row: Sinco, Philippines; Damle, India; Harrar, Rockefeller Foundation; Gozon, Philippines; Garcia, Philippines. Back row: Shen, Taiwan; Kihara, Japan; Chakrabandhu, Thailand; Chandler, director of IRRI; Hill, Ford Foundation.

Many distinguished people have visited the Institute. President Adolfo López Mateos of Mexico, where The Rockefeller Foundation's agricultural activities began, is shown here (dark suit) with Director Chandler.

IRRI stands as a symbol of dedication to a cause and is a living example of effective cooperation among men from many countries.

Chapter 17

The International Rice Research Institute

A New Pattern of Joint Operations by the
Ford and Rockefeller Foundations

The Rockefeller Foundation, chartered "to promote the well-being of mankind throughout the world," could not long resist having a look at the Far East after its initial successes in Latin America. Not only did this region contain half the world's population; it was also the home of most of its hungry people. Rice had been the Far East's staple food crop for centuries; the life and economy of most countries was built around it, and in some places it was almost worshiped. Yet, except in Japan and Taiwan, yields were distressingly low and relatively little research was being done toward their increase.

Surveys made by the Food and Agriculture Organization of the United Nations had indicated that the improvement of rice diets probably ranked first among the food problems of the world. Even more emphatic were the words of Sir Harold Tempany, a lifetime student of tropical agriculture: "The increase of rice production is one of the major agricultural problems: upon its solution, world peace and security are largely dependent."[1]

In 1952, therefore, The Rockefeller Foundation sent three representatives—Warren Weaver, J. George Harrar, and Paul C. Mangelsdorf—to the Far East to make preliminary studies as to how the Foundation might be of assistance. The following year Weaver and Harrar made a second visit and discussed the agricultural problems of the various countries with government officials and leaders in agricultural education and research.

It was soon evident that the major agricultural need of the area was to produce more rice at lower cost. Just as obvious, however,

[1] D. H. Grist, *Rice* (London: Longmans, 1963), p. v.

was the fact that a successful attack on the huge problems involved would require large sums of money over a long period of time. With limited funds and worldwide commitments in many fields, the Foundation could not lightly undertake a project of this magnitude, and accordingly Richard Bradfield of Cornell University and Robert F. Chandler, Jr., of the Foundation's staff, were assigned to the Far East in 1955–1956 to make a thorough study of the situation.

Officers of the Ford Foundation, which had been operating for some time in India, Burma, and Indonesia, were convinced by experience there that research designed to improve rice production was indispensable to the region, and they later expressed willingness to collaborate with The Rockefeller Foundation in such research.[2]

The outcome of these and other studies and consultations was a decision to establish an International Rice Research Institute at the College of Agriculture of the University of the Philippines, at Los Baños. The Philippine government donated the necessary land, the Ford Foundation agreed to supply funds for capital construction, and The Rockefeller Foundation assumed responsibility for operating expenses and for providing key scientists to organize and direct the scientific program under the control of an international board of trustees. The new Institute, now widely known by its initials, IRRI, opened its doors early in 1962.

Rice in the Culture and Economy of the Far East

THE UNIQUE PREDOMINANCE OF RICE AND HOW IT CAME ABOUT

Few people in the West appreciate the enormous importance of rice on a worldwide basis. Per capita consumption in the United States is only about six pounds a year, but in many places in the Far East

---

[2] The International Rice Research Institute has certain elements of uniqueness in efforts toward the conquest of hunger. It is a joint product of the initiative of the Ford and Rockefeller Foundations, has been supported financially by them, is dedicated exclusively to the improvement of a single food crop, and is truly international in operations as well as in objectives. Because our book purports to portray the campaigns of The Rockefeller Foundation against hunger, we must not arrogate the privilege of detailing the contributions of the Ford Foundation as well. In any case the gratitude expressed by thousands of people in the Far East for that Foundation's wise liberality far outweighs the value of any words that we could write. Nevertheless we, too, do pay tribute, in thought if not in words.

one person may eat this much in a week; the average per capita consumption is about 300 pounds a year, or almost a pound a day. Sixty percent of the world's people get 80 percent of their food calories from rice.

Rice has been cultivated in the Far East since the dawn of history, and the countries of the area currently produce over 90 percent of the world crop, employing the services of from 40 to 70 percent of their labor forces in so doing. For the vast majority of the people, rice is the prestige food. In Japan, for example, sweet potatoes are produced abundantly, but the people eat them only when they cannot afford rice.

How has rice acquired this unique position in the agriculture of the Far East and in the affections of her people through the centuries? It seems likely that the monsoon climate characteristic of most tropical areas of the region had a great deal to do with it.

Permanent agriculture generally originated in river valleys and deltas where soils were deeper and had greater reserves of fertility than elsewhere. Although such soils are usually heavier in texture and more difficult to drain, management problems ordinarily remain simple if rainfall is adequate and uniform, without harmful excesses or deficiencies during the growing season.

In monsoon Asia, however, excesses and deficiencies form the pattern; annual rainfall totals between 60 and 150 inches and most of this occurs during a six- to seven-month rainy season, with little if any occurring during the rest of the year. Presumably the pioneering farmer originally lacked the skills as well as other resources for coping with either of these extreme conditions, and so he learned to live with them. Because he could not bring in water to irrigate his land during the dry season, he confined his farming largely to the rainy season, as is still the case in most of the region. Crops are normally planted at the beginning of the rainy season, after the soil, parched by four to six months of heat and drought, has been moistened enough to permit plowing, sowing, and the germination of seeds. As the heavy rains continue day after day, often 10 to 25 inches a month, the soil is saturated much of the time and seldom becomes dry enough to permit cultivation for controlling weeds. Although some crops are planted on ridges to provide aeration of at least a part of their root system, it is difficult to grow crops requiring a well-aerated soil in such an environment. But rice is unique in being able to thrive under just such conditions; accordingly, the early farmers naturally turned more and more to rice.

From being a liability, wet land now became an asset. The rice farmer learned that he could cultivate his soil while wet and change its structure—"puddle" it—and still grow good crops of rice. Instead of trying to drain his heavy soil, he put a contour, bund, or dike around his small fields to entrap the water. With the soil thoroughly saturated, plowing was easier for man and beast; the water buffalo or oxen and the farmer himself learned to like working in the mud. It was also easier to level such land with primitive tools, because the mud would almost flow from the higher to the lower spots by gravity. Weed control too became easier, for the rice farmer could cultivate immediately after or even during a heavy rain; he did not have to wait a week for the soil to dry out, as do most row-crop farmers. Harvesting was a problem, but if the farmer cut his rice with a hand sickle or some other kind of hand tool, often one head at a time, it did not matter if the soil was wet. His "harvester" would not bog down in the mud!

Viewed in these terms, the "paddy" or flooded-field culture of rice seems logical for these regions with heavy soils and heavy, almost daily rains. At any rate, it eventually developed throughout the Far East. As populations increased and the level land in the valleys and on the deltas had been occupied, terraced paddies were established on the valley slopes. These involved so much work and constant care that it probably was neither a logical nor an economic development, but people had become so dependent on rice that it seemed to be their best recourse. Even steep mountain slopes were terraced as long as three or four thousand years ago, and some terraces are still being constructed. One cannot but admire the laborious construction of narrow, level fields and the ingenious impounding of water for rice on the mountainsides. No wonder the cult of rice became so deeply rooted in the lives of the people. For forty centuries each generation of rice farmers learned something new and handed it down to its sons, thus compiling one of the largest and most deeply entrenched stores of traditional knowledge about agricultural practices accumulated any place in the world. In no other region has a single crop plant been grown so long and continuously on the same land and its yields maintained at such a high level when the farmers' sole reliance was the simple resources available on their own farms. Given the difficult climate, it is doubtful whether any crop other than rice could have done as well in supporting one of the world's densest populations.

But however admirable this culture, one must deplore the fact that the level of subsistence is so low among these people, that famine so often threatens them, that their burden of labor in producing rice is so heavy, and that the amount of rice they get for their labor is so often scarcely enough to keep body and soul together.

TOO MUCH WORK FOR TOO LITTLE RICE

Reliable information regarding the labor costs of growing rice in the Far East is difficult to come by; in many sections, labor is so cheap that it scarcely figures in calculating costs of production. Some studies indicate that between 600 and 1,000 man-hours of labor are required to grow and harvest a single acre. This is a high price to pay for any cereal, even the "honorable rice." In fact, if costs are measured in terms of human labor, the poor rice farmers of the Far East probably pay more for their "cheap cereal calories" than any other group on earth.

Practically all the rice in the region is transplanted by hand. The seed is planted in beds, and two or three weeks later the young seedlings are laboriously transplanted by hand in the fields. The operation usually requires many extra field laborers, many of them women, and often it is a social occasion accompanied by music. Soon after transplanting, the rice must be weeded. Although the water in the fields inhibits the growth of many kinds of weeds, some kinds thrive in water just as rice does, and many ingenious schemes have been evolved for eliminating them. The early weeding is often done by men down on their knees in the mud, using their fingers as cultivating tools. In other cases a small rotary cultivator is pushed between the rows to bury the weeds in the mud. The rice must be cultivated at least three or four times, to control weeds. To simplify this procedure, the rice seedlings are often planted in rows about a foot apart, with plants about a foot apart in the row. This checkerboard pattern makes it possible to cultivate in two directions. Where controlled irrigation is possible, water is usually maintained at a depth of from one to six inches from the time of transplanting until the rice begins to ripen. It is then drained off and the soil allowed to dry in preparation for the harvest.

Harvesting too is an exceedingly laborious operation. In some localities of Malaya and Indonesia, for example, the rice is cut one head at a time with an instrument containing a small blade about the size of a safety razor blade. Because there is a tradition—probably invented and perpetuated by men—that rice is best when harvested by women's hands, the men let the women do the work. After the heads are cut off, they are tied into neat bundles and carried on bamboo poles to a storage shed where they are dried and then threshed. On the smaller farms the grain is stored as brown rice, which is hulled and prepared for the table as needed.

In the more highly industrialized countries, these processes are mechanized and the rice is also polished before being placed on the market. Unfortunately, although this final step improves the appearance and keeping qualities of the rice, it also reduces the nutritive value. People who subsist largely on polished rice often suffer from beriberi, a vitamin-deficiency disease. Beriberi formerly afflicted hundreds of thousands of people within this area and it still exists in places, but the cause is now understood and suitable remedies can be provided once the disease is diagnosed.

The excessive labor requirement is one of the most serious weaknesses of the traditional paddy rice system. Because from 40 to 70 percent of the labor force is required to produce so little rice, wages are very low and labor cannot be spared to produce other foods, goods, and services that the country needs. Even in Japan, where average yields are among the highest in the world and where there is a liberal government subsidy, the small rice grower's income is much less than that of the industrial laborer. Because rice farms in the East often require 600 to 1,000 man-hours an acre, one man can farm only one to three acres and earn a net income of only $100 to $200 a year if yields are good. In contrast, the California rice grower, who has mechanized his operations, uses only eight to 10 man-hours of labor an acre and can therefore farm 100 to 300 acres, enough to support a good standard of living if yields and prices are good. It probably will be difficult or impossible to duplicate this system of operation in the highly populated Far East, with its small land holdings, heavy soils, and monsoon climate, but progress must be made in that direction. The people of the Far East want not only more rice, but cheaper rice, and more besides rice than their present system provides.

Important as it is to reduce the man-hours of labor needed to produce a bushel of rice in the Far East, it is of even greater importance to make each acre of land produce more bushels. For this broad-gauge reason, the system of rice production that has worked so well for so many millions for so long must be changed. Apparently yields obtained by traditional systems have reached their ceiling, and all the land available for rice in many countries is in use. Yet millions of people do not get all the rice they need, and millions more are clamoring for food each year; population is increasing faster than the rice supply in most of the region. What can be done?

RESEARCH MUST RESCUE HUNGRY MILLIONS

Science is urgently needed to help increase rice production in the Far East. Recent advances in the agricultural sciences, advances that have had such a dramatic effect upon the supply and cost of food in the United States and other Western countries, have thus far had little impact on Far East rice production except in Japan and Taiwan. The high yields in these two countries are fruits of the marriage of the ancient art with the modern science of rice growing. Farther south in the more tropical areas, however, a great deal of research and education still lies ahead, for the problems there are different in both kind and degree.

One important difference concerns the kinds of rice grown. In Japan and Taiwan and also in Korea, the short-grain japonica type, which is slightly sticky when cooked, is preferred. But the long-grain indica type, which is drier when cooked, predominates throughout monsoon Asia—in India, Burma, Thailand, Indonesia, Cambodia, Laos, Vietnam, and the Philippines. These two types of rice can be crossed, but with difficulty. In general, the japonica type yields more than the indica, probably because it has been studied more scientifically and as a result superior strains have been developed by selection and breeding.

Relatively, the japonica types have short straw, are more resistant to lodging, and respond more favorably to fertilizers, especially nitrogen. The indica types are taller, have weaker straw, and are less responsive to nitrogen, apparently because abundant nitrogen tends to make them grow so tall that they are likely to lodge even before the grain is fully formed and thus they suffer decreased yields. As a consequence, little if any fertilizer is used on much of the indica rice, and yields in the tropical countries often fail to exceed even 1,000 pounds an acre. In contrast, japonica types in Japan and Taiwan yield about 4,500 pounds an acre on the average.

There is no quick and easy way of revolutionizing rice production in the tropical areas. The problems are both biologic and sociologic. Because the monsoon climate imposes certain restrictions and because most varieties of the indica type can tolerate only a limited amount of fertilizer without lodging, it will be necessary to produce superior varieties of the desired type. To do so will take time. Moreover, certain diseases and insect pests are destructive and have defied complete control even in the advanced countries. Although it has been demonstrated experimentally in India, East Pakistan, and elsewhere that yields can be increased—sometimes doubled—by known methods, many years are still required to persuade millions of small, tradition-bound, uneducated, peasant-type farmers to adopt new materials and methods, even when they are available.

Even in Japan, it has taken three quarters of a century of concentrated scientific effort to reach the present stage of efficiency in production per unit area of land; and Japan is a highly literate country that has adapted quickly to the scientific and technologic revolution of the West. Even so, her efficiency of production still is low as measured by the amount of labor required to produce her high acre yields; most Japanese rice fields are too small to justify the capital investment in machines by which rice growers in the United States and Australia have reduced labor costs to a minimum. Yet Japan has succeeded in making her rice lands extraordinarily productive.

Can the tropical countries of the Far East raise their acre yields to the levels achieved in Japan and Taiwan? Those two countries, through their strong rice research programs, have pointed the way for the others. Significantly, Japan still spends almost 90 percent of her agricultural research funds on various aspects of the rice problem. But the results obtained in Japan and Taiwan with japonica types cannot be utilized directly in the improvement of indica types for the tropical areas, and the countries that grow indica types have invested far too little in research—not enough to reap even a small fraction of the potential that could benefit their people. They need much more research, most of them are not ready to do it themselves, and so the Rockefeller and Ford Foundations set out to do it for them and, insofar as possible, with them.

IRRI Meeting the Challenge

The research program of the International Rice Research Institute began almost before its doors were opened. Dr. Chandler, formally appointed director of IRRI in April, 1960, had been on assignment in the Philippines since 1959, making further studies of problems in the rice belt and developing plans for the new Institute. Chandler was splendidly qualified for his new position. A soil scientist by training, he had had extensive academic experience in teaching, research, and, in addition, administration, first as dean of the College of Agriculture and then as president of the University of New Hampshire. After serving as temporary head of soil work in the Mexican program 1946–1947, he had rejoined the Foundation's staff in 1954 and had been given special responsibilities for the Foundation's agricultural program in the Far East. By 1959, therefore, he was well acquainted with the region and its problems and knew personally many of its agricultural leaders. It is a tribute to Chandler's enthusiasm and tireless energy that the Institute's program began so promptly and that its fine set of buildings were constructed and in operation in less than two years.

"More rice per acre" is the common goal of the racially, linguistically, and scientifically diverse staff at IRRI. This common purpose is the connective tissue that binds them into a cohesive and effective entity. And because implementation of their purpose will require better rice, the staff has already drawn preliminary specifications for the type of rice plant needed to help produce more rice on every acre.

This ideal rice plant must mature in a short growing season; its time of flowering must not be greatly changed by length of day; it must have a short, stiff straw so that it will not lodge when heavily fertilized; it must be resistant to rice blast (the most serious disease of rice in the area) and to the stem borer (the most serious insect pest); it must have a wide range of adaptability throughout the Far East; it must be more nutritious, with a high protein content and a better balance of amino acids in the proteins; and last but not least, it must have a table quality that will satisfy the palates of all the varied millions of rice eaters.

How can such a rice be produced? Earlier experience with corn and wheat (see Chapters 15 and 16) has convincingly demonstrated the importance of collecting varieties of these crops from all over the world in order to have them readily available to any scientist who may need them. One never knows where he will find a variety or strain of a species with the unique genes needed to combine with others to give the qualities desired in a specific situation. Such a collection or gene bank of rices was initiated even before the Institute was officially opened, and it has already become the largest in the world. The more than 10,000 entries are being classified at the rate of about 2,000 a year. This huge stockpile will be drawn upon to supply the genes needed to breed better rices for the future, not only at IRRI but also at other rice-breeding stations.

The first experimental crops of rice were harvested in 1962. What a thrilling sight—rices from all over the world growing side by side —short and tall, white and red, short-grain and long-grain, upland and wet-land. What a wealth of types have evolved in different environments!

One or more of the rices in this vast collection probably has one or more of the characters specified for IRRI's ideal rice plant. These desired characters must be located and studied and then combined by making appropriate crosses between the types or varieties that possess them. It will be a long, painstaking job, and it will involve much tedious work; but if past experience is any guide (that with hybrid corn for example), the job will also be richly rewarding and one of the best investments possible to promote the welfare of that half of the world's people who live in the Far East.

That there are genes for productivity in the rice collection is evident from the fact that yields of over 5,000 pounds per acre were obtained with the first summer, or rainy season, crop and that certain varieties yielded 8,000 pounds per acre in the first dry season trials. It is gratifying that potentialities for greatly increasing the yields of indica rices in the tropical areas have already been clearly demonstrated.

In his terse report for 1964, Chandler describes some of the progress made to date: "A primary objective of the Institute is to conduct basic and applied research on the rice plant, directed toward improving its productivity and quality. A rice breeding program, parts of it now in the F_4 generation, shows promise of developing within the next two years high-yielding, nitrogen-responding varieties that are short, stiff-strawed, early maturing, non-photoperiod sensitive, and resistant to the rice blast disease. These varieties are expected to have wide adaptability on well-managed soils throughout the rice-growing regions of the tropics and, if generally used, could increase greatly the total production of rice.

"Remarkable control of the rice stem borers is being obtained with the gamma isomer of benzene hexachloride applied to the irrigation water as a systemic insecticide. This chemical has low mammalian toxicity, and two applications seem sufficient in a single growing season.

"Studies in plant physiology have definitely shown that the early lodging and low yields that occur in the cloudy monsoon season are associated with the deficiency of carbohydrates within the rice plant. This deficiency appears to result from the low light intensity caused by clouds and by the mutual shading of the plants. Nitrogen responsiveness seems to be positively correlated with light intensity.

"Institute scientists are steadily gaining information on spacing, crop rotations, and fertilizer requirements of the rice plant. They are studying chemical weed control, water losses, drought tolerance, photoperiodism, the carbohydrate and nitrogen metabolism of the rice plant itself, and the cooking, eating, and nutritional value of the grain. Extensive studies of the chemical and microbiological aspects of flooded soils are under way. Plant pathologists screened more than 6,000 varieties for resistance to the rice blast disease, helped establish blast nurseries in more than 15 countries, expanded work on viruses, and initiated studies of bacterial diseases.

"The statistician is studying sample size, sample number, and plot size and shape for efficient data collection, and the agricultural economist is studying the cost of new technologies and other economic problems associated with rice production and marketing. The agricultural engineer is developing more efficient tillage and threshing machinery, and the communication specialist is working on procedures for and studies of the effective dissemination of the research results to national agencies and through them to rice producers."

Thus this truly international institute is already well on the way to assembling and recombining the best genes that can be found in the numerous rice varieties of the world, and new and better varieties already are appearing on the horizon. Experimentation and research on soil management, cultural practices, nutrition, and physiology are revealing new possibilities for increasing the yield and quality of rice. Plant pathologists are helping to build the basis for control of certain diseases by means of resistant varieties, and entomologists are learning much about the control of destructive insects by the use of modern insecticides applied in new and better ways. And this is progress. Research and experimentation are casting new light on the vast potential of the "honorable rice."

Moreover, students are beginning to see the new light and use it to light their own torches of learning, for additional generous grants from the Ford Foundation have assured support for ten years of the Institute's international activities, including a research program for resident scholars and fellows, sponsorship of scientific symposia, and travel and cooperative research by members of the staff in other countries.

During 1964 a total of 65 scholars and fellows were in residence at IRRI. Many of them are candidates for a master's degree in the College of Agriculture of the University of the Philippines under a cooperative arrangement whereby the research fellows take classwork at the College and do thesis research at the Institute; members of the professional staff at IRRI have professorial rank in the College.

Through its sponsorship of international conferences IRRI is helping to focus the attention of rice scientists from many countries on specific problems related to the rice plant. The five symposia held thus far have dealt with rice genetics, the rice blast disease, engineering aspects of rice production, the mineral nutrition of the rice plant, and the major insect pests of rice.

In addition, members of the staff travel widely throughout the rice-growing areas of the Far East to get acquainted with research workers in the various countries, learn more about the problems encountered in each, and, in several instances, to make plans for cooperative research. Chief among the research projects is a standard rice blast testing program and the development of machinery for rice cultivation.

The Institute is also becoming a mecca for visitors from all over the world. Hardly a day passes but someone comes to see the facilities and to find out about the program. Thus the Institute is functioning actively and productively in research and in education. But even more, perhaps, it is a living example of the feasibility and value of effective cooperation.

Cooperation Can Vanquish Hunger and Contention

The International Rice Research Institute is a noble example of international cooperation in which institutional, national, and personal interests and ambitions are subordinated to the ideal of alleviating the hunger of millions of human beings.

The fact that two large foundations, Ford and Rockefeller, have joined forces and funds to support and operate the Institute is noteworthy and praiseworthy. The Ford Foundation has furnished both the capital necessary for constructing and equipping the physical plant, making a generous grant that eventually totaled over seven million dollars, and additional grants for other purposes. The Rockefeller Foundation has supplied the funds necessary to operate the Institute, the salaries of its staff, the supplies needed, travel funds, and numerous items not otherwise provided.

From the outset the proposal to locate the new Institute in the Philippines was enthusiastically received there. The Honorable Juan Rodriguez, Secretary of Agriculture, gave the proposal his whole-hearted support and rendered valuable service along with his colleagues in the government. As a result, the Congress of the Philippines granted a charter to the new institution that gave it the autonomy and the privileges needed to enable it to function with a maximum of freedom. The president of the University of the Philippines, V. G. Sinco, and the dean of the College of Agriculture, L. B. Uichanco, pledged the support of their respective institutions and provided sites for the buildings and the experimental fields. Thus the Institute was established by interinstitutional and international cooperation.

So too the governing body is international in composition. The charter vested control of the Institute in a board of trustees made up of a representative of each of the sponsoring foundations, Ford and Rockefeller, the Secretary of Agriculture and Natural Resources of the Philippines, the president of the University of the Philippines, the chairman of the National Science Development Board of the Philippines, three members selected from other countries in the area, and the director of the Institute. The staff too has been international from the beginning. Chandler, the director, and Dr. Sterling Wortman, the first associate director, were Americans, but both had had considerable foreign experience and were internationally minded. The architect who designed the much-admired buildings was a Filipino, A. J. Luz; and those in charge of their upkeep and maintenance are Filipinos.

The scientific staff has been cosmopolitan from the beginning. The various departments are manned by people from many countries, as shown by the following list: agronomy, Moomaw, Hawaii; plant breeding and genetics, Beachell and Jennings, United States, and Chang, Taiwan; soils, Ponnamperuma, Ceylon; plant physiology, Tanaka, Japan, and Vergara, Philippines; plant pathology, Ou, Taiwan; entomology, Pathak, India; chemistry and biochemistry, Akazawa, Japan, and Juliano, Philippines; microbiology, MacRae, Australia; statistics, Oñate, Philippines; agricultural economics, Ruttan, United States; agricultural engineering, Johnson, United States; communications, Byrnes, United States. Thus there are senior staff members from eight countries who are working harmoniously and effectively.

As in all educational and research institutions, a vital organ of the Institute is the library, in which are to be stored the results of previous research and experience on all aspects of rice production throughout the world. Arrangements have been made for translations into English of all of the more important papers published in the Japanese language. The goal of the librarian, Lina D. Manalo, is to make the collection at IRRI the most complete in the world, and toward this objective she is making splendid progress.

All who have visited the Institute consider the physical plant to be one of the finest of its type in the world. Scientists consider it a privilege to work there. Thanks to the generosity of the Ford Foundation, the equipment is the best that can be obtained, and virtually any problem involving rice can be investigated. The Institute is a monument to the vision and wisdom of those who conceived and established it. To those who operate it remains the task of making it a living instrument for the alleviation of hunger and suffering among the millions of humble human beings who need its help. And the international staff are on the way to doing exactly that.[3]

---

[3] The above was written in 1964. Among the hundreds of crosses made in 1962 by IRRI plant breeders was Peta × Dgwg. Peta was a tall, vigorous, vegetative Philippine variety that usually lodges badly during the rainy season when adequately fertilized. The other parent, Dgwg, is a short, stiff-strawed indica from Taiwan. The resulting cross had the short, stiff straw of Dgwg and much of the vigor of Peta. Sixth-generation selections from this cross planted in yield trials for the first time in the dry season of 1965 showed unusual promise. Some of the limited amount of seed available was planted in regional tests in the Philippines and Thailand; the rest was multiplied at IRRI in the fall of 1965. Results appeared so promising that all available seed was multiplied as rapidly as possible. About 70 tons of seed was harvested in May to July, 1966. By this time more reports of preliminary regional yield trials from the spring dry season plantings were coming in. In practically every yield test from the Philippines to Pakistan, IR8–288–3 was either at the top or near the top, with yields usually ranging from six to 10 tons per hectare. In countries where average yields range from one to two tons, these results opened many eyes to possibilities previously undreamed of. IRRI was flooded with demands for seed. The 70 tons available is being distributed as equitably as possible, most in the Philippines but enough for numerous trials in most of the other countries throughout the tropical rice belt of Asia.

This new rice is far from perfect, but it is demonstrating that with good varieties grown with good cultural practices, including adequate fertilization, and water, insect, disease, and weed control, yields of rice comparable to the best that have been produced anywhere can be produced throughout the monsoon rice belt of Asia. The promise of the Institute is already being fulfilled only four years after it was opened! The investment which the Ford and Rockefeller Foundations have made in it seems destined to yield unprecedented dividends.

Chapter 18

Lessons Learned and Future Prospects

The Rockefeller Foundation is now nearing the quarter-century mark in its agricultural improvement activities. It has operated directly or indirectly in a number of countries in all of the major retarded areas of the world, has wrestled with many kinds of problems, has enjoyed many successes, and has experienced some disappointments. It has contributed much and it has learned much.

The three of us have been associated continually with the Foundation's agricultural programs from their beginnings to the present time, sometimes as a group and sometimes as individuals. Although each one has at various times participated temporarily in the operations of one or more programs, all have functioned principally in an advisory capacity. Given wide opportunity to study the various programs at first hand, we have never been permanent participants in any of them and therefore are in a position to be objective about all of them. Objectivity, of course, is not a special virtue; it is expected of all scientists. So also is good judgment, which, in order to be good, must be based on adequate information.

Intimate association with the Foundation's agricultural activities and close observation of certain other aid programs have emboldened us to write this chapter—"Lessons Learned and Future Prospects." We know that we are not omniscient, and we know that we are critical. But our criticism is designed to be measured against a standard of perfection: millions of hungry people so urgently need the best possible performance in aid programs that even the best is scarcely good enough. We hope therefore that our criticisms may be considered objectively, judged charitably, and interpreted constructively.

Some Countries Have and Some Have Not

The countries of the world can be divided into the "haves" and the "have-nots": those that have utilized science and technology to improve their agriculture, and those that have not. During the interval between the two most recent world wars, these terms were used to distinguish countries on the basis of their physical resources; here they are used to distinguish those countries that have developed their intellectual and physical resources from those that have not, or, in other words, to distinguish those that are relatively affluent and those that are poor.

During the past two decades the world family of nations has developed deep concern about its poorer members and has tried in various ways to help relieve their poverty. That there are wide differences in levels of subsistence and standards of living among countries is obvious, and it has become customary to designate those with a high standard as "advanced" and those with a low standard as "developing" or "emerging" countries. The implications of the words "developing" and "emerging" are clear, but they are not necessarily pertinent to some countries with low standards of living. For this reason, the word "retarded" has sometimes been used in this book, not in an invidious sense, but to indicate a relative situation at present, without implying what the future will be. Hopefully, the future will be better in all countries, but hope is no guarantee. The future may be even worse than the present unless sufficient wisdom is put into the efforts to make it better.

Education often is quite as important as natural resources in determining levels of subsistence and standards of living. It is axiomatic that the material development of any country depends on its physical and human resources and the intelligence with which they are used. The optimum utilization of resources obviously depends on a high degree of scientific and social sophistication, attainable only by education. Science can show society what to do technologically, but society must enable science and technology to function and must contrive to distribute their contributions fairly among its members. Advanced countries have learned this lesson; retarded ones have learned it either imperfectly or not at all.

It is significant but not surprising that science has made the greatest progress in those countries that have provided the best schooling for their youth. Advanced countries have tried to educate every child to the limit of his capacities, aptitudes, and will to study. These countries have made elementary education free, compulsory, and universal, and they have provided further education for those with the necessary ability and industry. Secondary education is provided by the state, both for those who want to prepare for college and those who want training for a trade. Although there may also be private secondary schools in these countries, the important fact is that if they want to, all qualified students can get a free education in state-supported schools.

Thus, advanced countries have tried to keep poverty from becoming a barrier to education. The theory: education is a social necessity, and parents and the state have a joint obligation to provide it. The practical result is that the advanced countries have developed literate populations in which upwards of 95 percent can read, write, and cipher well enough to meet ordinary needs and in which talented youth are discovered and encouraged to develop their talents in schools of higher learning. Higher education is available at reasonable cost in colleges and universities, supported principally by tax moneys, supplemented to some extent by student fees. Although there also are many privately supported institutions in some countries, the governments have long tried to enable all worthy students to obtain a university education at a cost that they can afford.

Universities have become progressive and creative in the most advanced countries. Instead of merely teaching what is known, they have explored the unknown; they have amplified their curricula and expanded their objectives. They have added more of the natural and social sciences, have come to grips with problems of life and living, have promoted productive scholarship, and have increasingly combined research and teaching. They still try to preserve and perpetuate past values, but they also try to develop individual and institutional creativity in the arts and in the sciences. They still dedicate themselves to the service of intellectual enlightenment and spiritual refinement, but they have also assumed the additional obligation of serving society in more direct and concrete ways.

"Town and gown" and its implications are obsolete in most advanced countries, for gown has become part of town. Universities do not remain aloof from practical affairs; they study them and contribute to their improvement. They help to develop not only the human resources through education but also the physical resources through research and experimentation.

Conditions in retarded countries can be defined most concisely by saying that they are just the opposite of those in advanced countries. In retarded countries the high percentage of illiteracy is tragic evidence that they have not educated their children. The average percentage in a sample of 10 countries where The Rockefeller Foundation is cooperatively engaged is 54 percent, ranging from 16.2 percent in Chile to 88.5 percent in Nigeria. The individual percentages are 16, 30, 35, 38, 44, 62, 71, 76, 81, 88 (omitting decimals),[1] and, because the percentages are highest in some of the most populous countries, these figures do not tell the whole story. The total population of the 10 countries under consideration is close to 700 million. About 500 million of them can neither read nor write.

Worse still from the standpoint of the conquest of hunger is the fact that illiteracy usually is highest among rural populations. Thus, although the percentage for Chile is 16.2, it is more than twice that high—36 percent—among the rural population. Moreover, the criteria for literacy are low in many countries; people are classed as literate even if their reading and writing ability is so elementary as to have little practical value.

"The very foundation of the republic is the proper education of its youth," said Cicero two thousand years ago. Universal education certainly is prerequisite to the permanent success of a democracy in the complex modern world. And it is prerequisite also to the development and maintenance of adequate dietary and health standards in the crowded modern world.

Progress in food production has been phenomenal in educated countries during the past century, but it has lagged and always will lag in any country that fails to educate her youth. It is only the educated countries that have contributed significantly to the scientific progress that is essential to the optimum utilization of their natural resources; indeed, the prosperity of many of them has been built principally on the scientific intelligence, the inventive ingenuity, and the highly developed skills of their people. Many a country with meager natural resources (like Switzerland, Holland, and Denmark) has developed a good standard of living by wisely

[1] UNESCO, *Statistical Yearbook*, 1963.

developing its human resources, and many another with abundant natural resources has become impoverished because it failed to educate its people.

The need for education and training increases as populations increase and press more heavily on means of subsistence. Countries with three acres or more of agricultural land per capita (like Canada, the United States, and Australia) do not yet have an urgent need to make every acre produce its maximum; those with considerably less than an acre (like India, China, and Japan) must make every acre produce as much as possible to help feed their soaring numbers. Because the amounts of land and other natural resources are limited in each country, population too must eventually be limited to the carrying capacity of its country.

Unfortunately, the rate of population increase is highest in many of the countries that can least afford it. Some already are so dangerously overpopulated that many of their people are always hungry and often are on the verge of starvation. Because the percentage of illiteracy is deplorably high and the efficiency of agricultural production is deplorably low in such countries, the ultimate remedy for their overpopulation must be an education that develops, first, the intelligence to raise the efficiency of production and, second, the wisdom to restrict the population to the means of subsistence. But the achievement of this educational standard will take time; population brakes operate slowly and progress toward wisdom is at best an evolutionary process.[2]

The pressing need for better education to help make a better world is now widely recognized. So also is the acute need for immediate remedial measures to alleviate the plight of hungry peoples. That many countries desperately need help while learning how to help themselves is obvious. The critical question: How can available help be most effective?

We have discovered no magic formula for success in aid programs. We visualize no miracles and few easy solutions. But we do think that persistent use of science and common sense is the best guaran-

[2] As one example, Mexico has tried valiantly for almost half a century to eradicate illiteracy by a system of free and compulsory elementary education. From a pre-Revolution high of around 75 percent the percentage had been reduced to 43.2 by 1950 and to 34.6 by 1960, a rate of a little less than one percent a year during the past decade. (Percentages for 1950 and 1960 taken from UNESCO, *Statistical Yearbook*, 1963.)

tee of progress. And so we proceed to write what we think is sensible.

What is really needed is a humanistic realism as a guide toward true wisdom in helping those who most deserve the help. Some guidelines have already been drawn. Conspicuous among the organizations that drew them is The Rockefeller Foundation, and preceding chapters have indicated how they were drawn for the several programs and why they led to success. It may be useful now to draw the lines together to see more clearly the pattern that they have made.

Ingredients of Success in Rockefeller Foundation Programs

The Foundation's operating programs were extraordinarily successful—even though not perfect—because they were conceived with realistic idealism and prosecuted with resourceful persistence under exceptionally able and stable leadership. Admittedly, the Foundation was in a favorable position, both in making plans and in putting them into operation. Unhampered at home by political and bureaucratic caprice, it could make long-term commitments and get competent long-term men to carry them out. And that is exactly what it did; it took especially good advantage of its special advantages and thereby did an especially good job in its campaigns toward the conquest of hunger.

The general aims of the Foundation's national programs were these: (1) to improve agricultural materials and methods as directly and quickly as possible by experimentation and research; (2) to help develop national scientists and institutions toward maximum efficiency in agricultural research and education; (3) to help disseminate all benefits accruing from experimentation and research as quickly and widely as possible, both nationally and internationally; (4) to help each country toward independence in the various phases of agricultural improvement. These were ambitious aims whose attainment would require sustained effort by able and ambitious men, and the Foundation had noteworthy success in enlisting and retaining the services of such men.

Men can make or break any program. Certainly it was a group of outstanding men who made the Foundation's programs work. More than once and in more than one place we have met Harrar, Wellhausen, Borlaug, McKelvey, Roberts, and Dorothy Parker, the

Persistent Pioneers. Under Harrar's superb leadership, it was this group who set a pattern for operations and paved the way to geographical and conceptual expansion. All were good scientists with the desire and ability to humanize their scientific activities. They established ideals of attainment and set standards of performance that have persisted because they themselves persistently propagated them. They were creators, not imitators; and their creativity was encouraged, not stifled.

The long tenure of men in the Foundation's programs was a potent factor in their productivity. Men were selected because of their scientific ability and presumptive capacity for professional and personal adjustment to conditions in foreign countries. Considering unforeseen problems of family health and happiness and the competition from United States institutions for successful men, the record of tenure is surprisingly good. Consequently, there always were enough experienced men in established programs to help staff the new ones, thus helping to provide continuity and coordination of effort.

The officers of the Foundation wisely provided a high degree of freedom to the men in the field. President Fosdick set a pattern for liberality of view in plans and operations. Naturally, major undertakings were determined by the major officers and Board of Trustees, but field tactics were entrusted largely to the discretion of the operating scientists. As we said in Chapter 2, the administrative responsibility for the initial agricultural activities was assigned to what was then the Division of Natural Sciences. Although Warren Weaver, in charge of the Division, and his associates, Frank B. Hanson and Harry M. Miller, Jr., were not agriculturists, they were scientists who well understood the conditions under which scientists are most productive. Administrative regulations were necessary but were not permitted to become an unnecessary evil. The general concept of administration as a help and not a hindrance to worthy causes has been a strong factor for success.

The liberal policy set for Harrar, and by him for his associates, was an important reason why the scope of the program was quickly broadened. Chapters 15, 16, and 7 tell how the national corn, wheat, and potato programs were international in effect even before they became so in name. Although this exportation of values from the national programs was evolutionary, it was skillfully guided by imaginative scientists operating in an atmosphere that quickened initiative instead of smothering it. The seeds of the present international programs were sown in the early years of the Mexican program.

Most biological problems in agriculture are international rather than national in scope, simply because they are peculiar to agroclimatic zones that may extend across the boundaries of many countries. Recognizing this elementary fact, the Foundation strove to extend the benefits reaped in its national programs to other countries in the same agroclimatic zones. Notable examples are the Central American cooperative corn improvement program, which was an organic extension of the Mexican program, and the analogous extensions of the Mexican and Colombian wheat programs. Thus the national programs were not merely a series of separate entities; they became parts of a functional international system. The Foundation's programs constituted a living organism.

Aid Programs Should Be Living Organisms

MEN ARE THE VITAL ORGANS

The principles of organic growth and development are applicable to aid programs as well as to biological organisms. Higher organisms have anatomical structure, but the structure is only a skeleton unless it has some vital organs. The most vital organs of institutional structures are the men that they comprise. Designing the structure is easy, but giving it life and making it work is harder. Every productive and progressive institution must be constructed of human beings who themselves can be progressively more productive. Growth in size alone is not enough, and overgrowth can have its own inherent dangers. Mere magnitude may give the semblance of productive power, but the optimum productivity of any organization depends on the full development of the potential powers of the men who do its work.

The improvement of agriculture in any retarded country is a scientific and technologic problem; the improvement of the living nation is an educational and sociological problem. That top-grade men are needed to help solve the problems is obvious; that there are too few of them to man all programs adequately has become painfully apparent. That any foreign scientist can make a contribution in a retarded country merely by virtue of his being a foreign scientist is a naive, fallacious concept. To make a lasting contribution, far more than scientific ability is necessary, so we proceed to tell what we think is needed.

In aid programs, a man should have both breadth and depth, the qualities of scientist, philosopher, teacher, diplomat, farmer, and day laborer; and he should be imbued with true missionary spirit. What a man! Yet, this is what we "Three Ancients" wrote and what we mean. But was there ever such a man? Like beans or wheats, most men are the algebraic sum of all their qualities—deficiencies and defects as well as virtues. The law of compensation may operate, but the law of the minimum also applies; excellence in one quality may compensate for moderate deficiency in another, but the usefulness of every man is limited by the minimum degree to which he possesses any one quality that is essential to success.

The better the scientist, the better his deeds, provided he uses his science to do good deeds. The minimum requirement is that he be good enough to make useful contributions within a reasonable time; some men do and some do not. Sad but true are the words of the Minister of Agriculture in a country where a group of American scientists were "sharing their know-how": "They have done nothing useful for us, absolutely nothing. The hours they spent in shaking our hands and slapping our backs and talking about sharing their know-how were fortunately not too many; but the hours they spent in sampling the drinks, in seeing the sights, in collecting souvenirs, and in clicking their cameras would run into the millions."

And from too many alleged apostles of science in foreign fields came this kind of comment: "I've been here almost two years and am ready to go home. I don't know whether I've done much good, but I'm not sorry I came. I've enjoyed myself, seen a lot of temples and ruins, collected lots of souvenirs, and have at least a thousand colored slides with which I can entertain the folks back home." Such scientists might better have spent their time in solitary philosophic contemplation—but evidently they lacked the philosophic quality.

"You are philosophizing when you reflect critically on what you are doing in your world" said philosopher Josiah Royce. And we should like to add "what you are doing in your world *and to it.*"

The back slappers and camera clickers were doing things in their world that were harmless enough in themselves, but philosophic sense, or even simple common sense, should have told them that they were bringing a worthy cause into disrepute. What is needed in aid programs is a kind of pragmatic philosophy that comes down to earth and truly earns its way by illuminating life and helping solve human problems, as John Dewey suggested in similar but better words. Every foreign aid scientist should periodically ask himself: "What am I doing and why? Can I do better and how? What have I done to help attain the final goals of the program?" The answers could be self-revealing and should broaden one's perspective regarding all program activities.

These activities can and must include teaching. "I am too busy with my experimental work to do any teaching; I leave the teaching to the teachers" is an often-heard remark. But who should be a better teacher than the investigator who is continually learning something new himself? Every experimenter should be a teacher, and every experiment can be a teaching aid; the best teaching often is done by those who do not profess to teach. Of course, some men must concentrate on teaching and others on research, but everyone in a foreign mission should want to teach—informally, incidentally, by demonstration, by example—even though formal teaching is not his primary job.

It may seem incongruous to discuss the quality of a diplomat after making numerous statements that have no diplomatic quality at all but only the quality of truth. Yet true diplomacy too must be based on truth—on sincerity, intellectual integrity, and capacity for understanding. John Fiske long ago said in effect that half the cruelty in the world is due to the stupid incapacity of men to put themselves in the other man's place. And there would be much truth in a statement that half the failures in foreign aid programs are due to the failure of the aides to put themselves in the place of the aided.

"Do unto others as you would have others do unto you" is the best diplomacy in foreign aid programs. "We came to work and learn together with you" should replace "We came to teach you," not only in word but also in spirit. Many and subtle are the ways in which a man reveals his feelings, and many humble human beings perceive them quickly. "That man be big; other man play big, but he be small small." Many times "Houseboy Charley" said this about people with a mission to brighten the darkness of Africa. Although his English was pidgin, his verdict was usually right; he sensed the difference between men of ability and character, "big men," and the big pretenders who actually were "small small men." Genuineness and sympathy are ingredients of the best diplomacy.

The qualities of farmer and day laborer—why? Because the improvement of agriculture depends on better farming, everyone in aid programs should know what good farming is and what it takes to make it better. Although some apostles of better farming may not know exactly how to farm, they should at least know how their activities can help the cause of better farming. "What have I ever done and what am I doing now to help these farms to produce more food or to ease the farmers' burdens?" is a question that every mission man should ask himself when he is out in a farming area. Fair answers should be humbling to most of us and a stimulus to greater efforts by all of us.

Farming may be mechanized but it cannot be dehumanized, because there must always be some labor on the farm, even if it is only labor skilled in managing machines. The burden of human labor is now too great in many retarded countries that are not yet ready for extensive mechanization. Can we not design better tools to lighten labor while we wait until machines can do the work? Those who have farmed or done day labor can best give the answer. To teach others how best to work, the teacher himself must know how to work.

A man should have the missionary spirit if he engages in mission work. What is this spirit, and how many men in foreign missions have it? And how many of those who direct mission organizations have only the mechanistic spirit and no missionary spirit at all? Let each one commune with his own spirit and give an honest answer! Our answer: less than 10 percent of those whom we have known.

Lack of missionary spirit is not a taint in all men, but it is in all those engaged in mission work. A true missionary must have zeal for helping others; he must have faith in what he is doing and courage enough to do it. For if the way were always easy and the end assured, there would be little need for missionaries. To change men's way of thinking and their ways of doing things is seldom an easy task. The most important factor for failure or success is the missionary himself; he must be sympathetic, resourceful, and persistent, because facilities may be meager and discouragements may come thick and fast. A missionary must be a dedicated man.

Thus we have constructed our ideal man. But where can we find him? That there are too few good men to man all good programs is obvious to any objective observer. So some organizations get the best they can and send them out as foreign missionaries. The good men seldom stay long enough to do much good; the poor ones stay too long and often do more harm than good. Are we trying to do too much good without enough good men to do it? Sometimes it were better to do nothing at all than to waste money in bungling a job.

But once a job is undertaken, the missionaries who do it must do the best they can; and seldom can they do their best, whatever their best may be, without good plans and organization.

PLANS SHOULD BE SENSIBLE AND FLEXIBLE

A sensible program aims at the ideal but does what is feasible. Idealists who do not temper their idealism with realism are likely to become visionaries; realists who do not leaven their realism with idealism are likely to become myopic or even cynical. And neither the visionaries nor the cynics are very useful in setting and attaining the goals of foreign missions. The immediate goal of most aid programs is to produce more food for retarded and hungry countries as directly and as quickly as possible. The ultimate goal is to help transform retarded countries into independently progressive ones. Plans must be made accordingly.

No exotic seers are needed to see the needs of hungry peoples. Methods for increasing food production are no longer unexplored mysteries that require repetitive seances and special gobbledygook for their solution. The primary needs of most food-deficient countries are easily determined by anyone with scientific knowledge of food production, and it requires no gargantuan intellect to tell how to go about the job of increasing it. Whatever the approach of pedantic planners might be, the scientific approach can be simple, sensible, and direct.

Hunger will not be alleviated by spinning gossamers in ivory towers. We must get down to earth and make the earth produce more by whatever methods work best where the hunger exists. As an example, acre yields of corn are low in many retarded countries, but poor varieties are the principal reason in some, poor soil in others, and pests and diseases in still others. Naturally, concentration of effort must vary with special problems. People and their institutions differ also, and tactics must vary accordingly. Good plans must be flexible enough to fit special needs.

Plans should provide for team balance in operations because there are many interactions, good and bad, between the various phases of food production. The basic need in the most populous of the emerging countries is to raise the acre yields of food and feed crops on the land now under cultivation, because there is little additional land to cultivate. To increase the yields requires better varieties, better soil cultivation and fertilization, and better control of pests and diseases. Obvious but often ignored is the fact that harm can be done by concentrating on one of these phases while neglecting the others. As an example, a few years ago one aid agency was pressing an Eastern country immediately to adopt a high-yielding hybrid corn from the United States. Fortunately, another agency cautioned against wholesale adoption without further tests and thus helped to avert a calamity, for a third of the plants in the first big increase field were ruined by a pest-disease complex that was of no importance back home but devastating in the hybrid's new environment.

Other examples can be taken from Chapters 5 and 17, which all fertilizer fanatics should read. Mexican wheats needed nitrogen, but it was not safe to give them all they needed until strong-straw varieties were produced to replace the weak-straw ones that could not stand up on fertilizer-enriched soils. Similarly, it was pointed out in Chapter 17 that yields of the short, strong-stem japonica rice varieties of Japan and Taiwan can be substantially increased by giving them abundant nitrogen, whereas it can be used only sparingly on the tall, weak-stem indica varieties without danger of reducing yields because of lodging. Fertilizers cannot do their full share in increasing rice production in the Far East until varieties are produced that can use them. And aid agencies cannot do their full share anywhere until they learn that a team is no team unless it pulls together and in the same direction.

Aim high but keep feet on the ground is good policy in planning. But more is needed for success, for projects as well as people usually have to earn their way by doing useful things; good works, not words, are the most persuasive advocates for liberal support of their endeavors. And it is hard to do good works without good organization and administration.

ADMINISTRATION CAN BLIGHT OR STIMULATE

Administration is essential but defeats its purpose when it is so mechanized as to become dehumanized. "The Commander of the Army seems to think it is profound strategy to keep his generals in ignorance of what he is trying to do." So spoke a division commander during a critical campaign of the American Civil War, and the principle is just as pertinent to some campaigns in wars against hunger. How can an organization function efficiently unless the men who make it function understand what its functions really are? Too often we have heard statements such as this: "We don't know whether we are doing what is expected of us because we don't know what our organization expects to do."

Arrogance of omniscience in operating remote controls has put the blight of failure on many a foreign mission. Many an organization never musters all of its potential wisdom because its members do not know its aims and are not encouraged to contribute ideas for their attainment. If anyone thinks that these are shots against a bogeyman, let him talk to a sample of conscientious men with experience in foreign missions.

"Lord, Lord, give me light and air; I have just come from a dark, damp cellar," remarked one good missionary-scientist as he came from an interview with the Top Brass in the Office. "How can I always be so successfully wrong when I'm with King Tut Tut in his Throne Room?" asked another. "How can everything always be bad unless it emanates from self-crowned Caesar?" asked still another. Unhappily, these questions were not merely facetious; some men at the top have talent for helping the men below to waste energy in spitting and sputtering. Of course, some men in the ranks may have a similar talent, but they rarely have opportunity to do as much harm as the men higher up. Foreign missions should be headed by leaders of men, not by mere makers of rules.

Men in foreign missions must have freedom to operate freely. Genius may flourish in a garret but not in a straitjacket. Constraint is the curse of too many organizations. Of course, freedom is for those who know how to use it, but of what good are men's talents if the men are not free to use them? Do we preach the doctrine of freedom to all the world and deny it to those who are trying to help make a better world? Sometimes we do, and many are the ways by which we do it. Good causes should not be condemned because of their imperfections, but it is no service to a cause to ignore its imperfection. Self-criticism can be the first step toward self-improvement, and many a program could be improved by wiser leadership.

FACILITIES—FOR WORK, NOT OSTENTATION

A good missionary needs no cathedral to do useful mission work. A scientist needs facilities, but they need not be excessively lavish. In the early stages of maize or wheat or rice improvement the greatest need is for brains and land and labor. Machines can help, but tools can do the work if necessary; elaborate machinery and expensive apparatus are not indispensable for breeding crops, for fertilizer tests, or for tests of disease and pest control. They are feeble in spirit indeed who immobilize themselves because they do not have ideal facilities or claim lack of facilities as an excuse for failure. A productive man should be given the facilities really needed to increase his productivity; nevertheless, the measure of progress is not the facilities themselves but what they produce. Dozens of times have men proudly shown us beautiful laboratories with impressive instruments that never had been put to practical use or any other kind. Emerging countries also have creators of images, but to substitute image for substance is naive or worse. Heard very recently was this exchange after a visit "to see the facilities": "What a wonderful installation!" "Yes, indeed, but one wonders what has ever come out of it except a lot of wondering visitors." The truth was—nothing!

REALISM, PERSPECTIVE, PERSISTENCE

Realism, perspective, and persistence are essential to success. Lack of realism about the nature of a job too often results only in a wasteful and futile pyramiding of short-term experts, usually to help revise the planning of previous experts but seldom to do any work. It seems to be a chain reaction, in which each successive expert recommends another expert and useful results are always just beyond the expert who is next to come. How refreshing was this conversation: "I see that the grain disease problem has been solved. Who did it?" "We did." "No outside help?" "No, we had a string of visiting experts, and each one just wanted to lengthen the string. We were supposed to be experts ourselves, so we decided we'd be expert enough to solve some of our own problems; and we did."

Perspective is needed, because so often it is sadly lacking. To spend millions of dollars in artificially changing a naturally beautiful landscape in an area where people were hungry for food seemed like poor perspective, at least to the hungry natives and to simple scientific souls. And to spend time and money in elaborate planning for a plant quarantine system in a spot where no one could operate any kind of system was certainly putting the cart ahead of the donkey. And to furnish an expensive facility for inducing mutations in food crops in a spot where no one knew even how to use it certainly looked like poor perspective to those concerned with hunger rather than with the prestige value of the installation. These things happened in the past, of course; there has been improvement, but there still is a long way to go. To teach others perspective, we ourselves must have it.

Persistence and continuity of effort are essential to permanent success in any program. It is difficult to accomplish much with temporary and shifting personnel and with distracting diffusion of effort. Often there is a strong temptation to yield to the whims and pressures of officials or special interest groups in the region where the mission group is working, but yielding usually results only in tinkering.

National tinkering is one of the banes of many retarded countries. What permanent impacts were made on a small emerging country by a dozen short-time missions from several different organizations, for unrelated purposes, and within the short space of three years? And what was the permanent value of the 40 men or more from the same organization, each of whom stayed from six weeks to a year to do separate jobs, big or little, at different times, and often quite unrelated to each other? According to some of the men themselves, their efforts amounted only to tinkering. Should we then be accessories to the baneful effects of tinkering when concentrated and coordinated effort is needed? It might be better to do nothing at all if all we can do is to tinker.

There are no easy solutions to complex problems. Whatever is done should be well done if it is worth doing at all. Perhaps the most important and most difficult lesson that retarded countries have to learn is that only intelligent, concentrated, coordinated, and persistent work can solve their problems. And that is the way aid missions must work if they are to set an example. Cooperation is essential within each mission and between the missions and the countries in which they operate. The primary obligation for insuring cooperation rests with the members of the mission, for supposedly they are the teachers and the nationals are the learners.

Cooperation would be easy if all men in a program were reasonable and were always in a reasonable mood. But they are not. Jurisdictional disputes, personal vendettas, and secret resistance are all too common. "He will not oppose us, but he will filibuster us to death" is a common verdict against some nationals who are friends on the surface but apathetic or antagonistic beneath. "He ought not to feel that way" or "I think it will be all right if we use the right approach" are bland statements that do little to solve the problem. But what will solve it?

"When persuasion fails, it is time to use compulsion." Hunger and ignorance and disease are so tragic that anyone who obstructs or delays their alleviation commits a gross misdemeanor against those who suffer. Failure of one key man in a program to cooperate with others can thwart the entire program, because nonfeasance or malfeasance of the one can reduce the effectiveness of all the others. A man who plays a lone hand may be useful where cooperation is not essential, but he is intolerable in a cooperative program and should be eliminated from the mission unless he has only a limited technologic task to perform.

Institutions too must cooperate. But many countries are so highly and capriciously institutionalized that it is difficult to learn what all of the institutions and their functions are, and still more difficult to get them to working cooperatively. Sometimes foreign missions are almost as guilty in this respect as the countries they are trying to improve.

But effective cooperation cannot really be compelled, nor can it be exorcised at pleasure. The ideal solution would be to convince everyone that the cause of fighting hunger and ignorance is so worthy that it is utterly unworthy to hinder the cause. Unless this can be done, the highest efficiency cannot be attained in getting results nor in getting them to the farmer.

Channeling Research Results to Farmers

Every leader of a foreign mission should study the elements of fluid dynamics, as exemplified in irrigation systems. The object of an irrigation system is to get water to land that needs it. And the object of a foreign mission is to help get information and materials to people who need them. An irrigation system must have an adequate supply of good water and a good system of canals and channels through which it can flow to the land. What good is the water if it is only impounded and never reaches the farms that need it? If the canals and channels are not connected or are clogged if connected, how can the water get to the farms? Certainly that would be a silly system and really no fluid system at all.

But are we not sometimes just as silly in our so-called systems for conducting benefits to farmers, which often are not systems at all but only a number of separate agencies and institutions without any effective connections between them? Why produce better corn or chickpeas if the seed never gets to the farm? And why produce new knowledge or devise new methods if they never get to the farmer? Too many potential values are impounded and never start for the farm; and too many that do get started are obstructed somewhere on the way.

Proliferation of uncoordinated agencies defeats its purpose, unless the principal purpose is to produce more political plums. If a research agency produces a superior variety of corn, another agency multiplies the seed, another distributes it to the farmer, another tells him when to plant it, another how to fertilize and cultivate it, another how to kill weeds, another how to prevent diseases, another how to poison insects and another not to use poison, and yet another tells him not to plant the new variety after he has already planted it, it is small wonder that in confusion the farmer curses the experts. Bottlenecks in the series of events and agencies that stand between the better corn and the farmer are bad enough, but conflicting advice from mutually aloof or feuding agencies is even worse. It would be poor engineering to force a lot of irrigation water through a series of pinholes, but it would be worse to make it flow against itself. We do not mean to be facetious; all too often this is tragic fact.

Compartmentalization is one of the seven or more curses in retarded countries. The separation between research, education, and extension is so sharp and wide in many countries that the gaps are seldom bridged, and, if anyone ever does bridge them, his bridges are likely to be burned behind him. "This is the narrowest road and the widest road in the country" was a favorite remark about a road between an agricultural college and an experiment station in a very interesting country. And then the explanation: "It is the narrowest because it is scarcely wide enough for one vehicle, and yet it is so wide that no one ever crosses from one side to the other." Fortunately, this little joke, which once was not a joke at all, is rapidly becoming outmoded. Contiguity of agencies can help but does not assure their cooperation; dedication to a common cause should be the tie that binds for all those who really care about producing more food and educating more people to produce their own.

Education—Sources and Uses

Whatever they may call themselves, developing countries will never develop very far without a sound education. Any country that can afford ostentatious luxuries but cannot afford to educate its children should decree a "National Day of Shame." What is wrong with nations that profess religion and culture when the illiteracy of most of their people is a glaring negation of what they profess? Turgid oratory about social justice, declaimed by demagogues who themselves are completely undemocratic, we hear all the time. But does not social justice start with the education of children and does not wisdom tell us to give all children a chance for education? How much talent is wasted or lies dormant because it is never discovered or developed? It is not our business to deal here with the problems of universal education, but we do reassert that any country that does not discover and develop its human resources has very poor prospects for progress.

The greatest service of foreign missions to hungry countries is to help select and educate young men who can and want to serve their country as hunger fighters. Most missions do not themselves engage in formal education; they start with young professionals or sub-professionals and operate something akin to an internship system, like the Mexican system described in Chapter 11.

To modernize their agriculture, emerging countries need modern men. As science is making modern agriculture continually more progressive, science and education must be progressive in every country that aspires to be independently progressive, for what is modern today may be obsolete tomorrow. Men are needed who know not only what progress is but also how to make it.

As a country advances in agricultural development it needs successively more and better men: for experimentation, research, education, extension, administration, and private and public services. The problem is how best to select and educate them for useful purpose. Many aid organizations have done well by means of internships, scholarships, travel grants, grants in aid, conferences, and other devices that help individuals or organizations. Whatever the device, however, its final success must depend on what it contributes to the education, motivation, and utilization of the individual selected.

Emerging countries need leaders, but it is futile to try to make leaders of those who have no capacity for leadership. "Every man to his own last" is as important in education as it is in a trade, and it is as important in the utilization of men as it is in their selection and education. With a good catcher on the bench, would we use another man behind the plate if he couldn't catch the ball? Or would we make a man manager of the team if he had never learned to play any position at all? Or make him an umpire if he couldn't even see the ball? It has been done, but always with unhappy results. And baseball is a game. We are concerned with the very serious business of alleviating hunger.

Most foreign missions participate in "training leaders" by sending prospective ones on fellowships to advanced countries to obtain academic degrees. Unfortunately, many of them come back home too proud to do anything useful for anyone except themselves. Few ask, "What can I do for my country?" Too many ask, "What can my country do for me?" Are we too careless in our selection or too narrow in our education? Or both? Too often we are guilty in both.

The utilization of scientifically educated men is as important as their education. And because scientific productivity depends on the

ability and attitudes of the scientist and on his opportunities for
work, their motivation generally is as important as their erudition.

Many a subsidized student goes back to his own country from an
American or some other university with a degree, a superiority
complex, and a supercilious attitude toward his own countrymen
and their problems. Science has become a sacred cow, and he fears
to demean it by putting it to useful purposes. And many fear also
that they themselves may lose caste by doing something of practical
value. Even if they do deign to do something that may possibly be
useful, they are unwilling to work as pioneers; they want all the
facilities and emoluments that scientists in advanced countries have
earned by long and useful social service. Too many of them never
think of earning their own way; they want their way paid for them,
whatever their ways may be. Too bad and too true!

And too bad it is also that many good men come back with zeal
for doing good, only to struggle against political prejudices or sense-
less administrative restrictions in the suffocating atmosphere of an
oppressive bureaucracy. Unless some countries develop a merit
system and a decent salary scale, their scientists will be dead capital
much of the time; and without reasonable freedom and facilities for
important work, they are likely to be dead capital all of the time.

Administrators and scientists must jointly make science function
—and in useful ways. Not long ago two countries wanted help in
food production. Two plant breeders trained in the United States
were there to help: one was breeding for quality in garlic and the
other in dill. With due respect to salami and pickles, it does seem
that these breeders might better have been trying to produce more
meat and cucumbers before trying to perfume them better with
garlic and with dill.

Lest there be misunderstanding of our meaning, we who are writing appreciate the value of so-called pure research designed to
satisfy intellectual curiosity or to expand man's understanding of
the universe. But some countries cannot yet afford much pure research without depriving their hungry people of the services of more
mundane scientific activities designed to help relieve the hunger.
It is fact that millions in some countries hunger for food; it is fact
also that a few may really hunger for knowledge. And, unfortunately, some who profess to hunger for knowledge "don't give a
continental for those of their countrymen who hunger for food," as

a sociologist put it after listening to a group of the intellectually elite pontificate about the scientific needs of their "emerging countries."

It is well to remember that an efficient agriculture can contribute much more than an abundant and cheap food supply. Often it can produce a surplus for export, thus earning badly needed foreign exchange. By enabling each farmer to produce more, it can release many people no longer needed on farms for other needed services as teachers, engineers, doctors, civil servants, and industrial workers. Because those remaining on farms produce more, their earnings will be greater and they can buy things that they could not afford before. A chain reaction of economic development can thus be triggered and the standards of living of the people can be raised. That, after all, is the major and ultimate objective of aid programs. More and cheaper food is an indispensable step toward this broader goal.

Critical but Optimistic

We have been critical but are not pessimistic; we are optimists still. Our information has come from many sources, and our criticisms are not aimed at special targets. We take our position on a standard of perfection, for the best is hardly good enough. There has been some improvement in aid programs; although it is neither so great nor so rapid as is desirable, there is at least a progressive trend. Progress in future can be more rapid if we profit from the lessons of the past. But we must study them and learn them, because smugness and self-satisfaction can be fatal to what we are trying to do. The fight against ignorance and hunger is a tremendous undertaking and it will take tremendous efforts to win it.

Index